THE
MEDIEVALISM
OF
LAWRENCE
OF
ARABIA

THE
MEDIEVALISM
OF
LAWRENCE
OF
ARABIA

M. D. ALLEN

THE PENNSYLVANIA STATE UNIVERSITY PRESS

UNIVERSITY PARK, PENNSYLVANIA

Library of Congress Cataloging-in-Publication Data

Allen, M. D. (Malcolm Dennis), 1951–
The medievalism of Lawrence of Arabia / M. D. Allen.
p.   cm.
Includes bibliographical references.
ISBN 0-271-00673-0 (alk. paper)
1. Lawrence, T. E. (Thomas Edward), 1888–1935—Knowledge—
Middle Ages.   2. Medievalism.   I. Title.
D568.4.L45A64   1991
940.415092—dc20   88–43433

It is the policy of The Pennsylvania State University Press to use
acid-free paper for the first printing of all clothbound books.
Publications on uncoated stock satisfy the minimum requirements
of American National Standard for Information Sciences—Permanence
of Paper for Printed Library Materials, ANSI Z39.48–1984.

For my parents

CONTENTS

Abbreviations   ix

Acknowledgments   xi

Introduction   1

1. Origins of a Medievalist   7

2. The Nonliterary Background to Lawrence's Medievalism   12

3. Lawrence and the Medieval Revival   34

4. Lawrence's Early Medieval Reading   51

5. The Impact of W. S. Blunt   73

6. Chivalry and the Nomadic Code   93

7. Lawrence's Literary Medievalism   104

8. *Seven Pillars* and Neomedieval Romance   125

9. Lawrence and Ruskinian Medievalism   141

10. Further Questionings of the Chivalric Ethos   151

11. Lawrence the Ascetic   169

Conclusion   193

Appendix: "Orientalism" and the Undiscovered Subtexts in *Seven Pillars of Wisdom*   203

Selected Bibliography   209

Index   217

ABBREVIATIONS

BHF   A. W. Lawrence, ed. *T. E. Lawrence by His Friends*. London: Cape, 1937.

HL   M. R. Lawrence, ed. *The Home Letters of T. E. Lawrence and His Brothers*. Oxford: Blackwell, 1954.

Letters   David Garnett, ed. *The Letters of T. E. Lawrence of Arabia*. London: Cape, 1938.

RGLH   T. E. Lawrence. *T. E. Lawrence to His Biographers Robert Graves and Liddell Hart*. 2d ed., 1938. Reprint. London: Cassell, 1963.

ACKNOWLEDGMENTS

Over the years of work on Lawrence I have acquired a number of debts of gratitude, which it is now a pleasure to acknowledge, although in some cases I shall never be able to repay them. Stanley Weintraub, Evan Pugh Professor of Arts and Humanities at Penn State, has been a patient and unfailingly helpful adviser, both before and after the formal end of my studies. I am also especially grateful to Gerard J. Brault and Caroline D. Eckhardt, who freely lent their knowledge and time. Mohammad Asfour and Salah Al-Hamarneh of the University of Jordan have been generous with advice, on both general topics and those specifically Arab. The late Warren O. Ault, the late J. A. W. Bennett, Brigadier T. W. Hackworth, Cecil R. Humphery-Smith, and Tony Waters have answered my letters in precise and helpful detail, and I thank them all. At the same time I must make it clear that any eccentricities of interpretation or plain errors of fact in the book are the responsibility of the author.

I am grateful to the London Library Trust for financial help given from 1978 to 1983; without this assistance, access to academic books would often have been difficult indeed. The Principal and Fellows of Jesus College, Oxford, have kindly allowed me to quote from J. G. Edwards's 1935 article on Lawrence in the *Jesus College Magazine*; and I thank Major Charles Blackmore for permission to quote from his private report "Expedition Jordanian Ride."

Acknowledgment is due the *Seven Pillars of Wisdom* Trust for permission to quote from the Oxford *Seven Pillars* and the letters to Mrs. Charlotte F. Shaw (British Library Add. MSS 45903 and 45904). Unless otherwise specified, quotations from *Seven Pillars* are from the readily accessible 1976 Cape reprint of the 1926 text. (See "Publisher's Note," *Seven Pillars*, [1976], xiv.)

Finally, I would like to thank my wife, who has hardly known me without Lawrence in the background, for encouragement, advice, and help.

INTRODUCTION

THE first full-length study of *Seven Pillars of Wisdom* to be published appeared in 1973. Its author, Jeffrey Meyers, lamented the neglect of T. E. Lawrence as a writer.

> Like *The Decline and Fall of the Roman Empire* and the *Life of Johnson, Seven Pillars of Wisdom* is more often praised than read. It is not taught or studied today, does not appear significantly in either the histories of modern literature, or in more specialized works like Bergonzi's *Heroes' Twilight: A Study of the Literature of the Great War*, which dismisses the best book about the war with a mere paragraph. Of the great number of books and articles on Lawrence only three or four essays treat *Seven Pillars* as a work of art. A prominent journal of modern literature wrote to me recently that they did not consider Lawrence as a literary figure. For most people the book has been superseded by the film. (Meyers, *Wounded Spirit*, 11)

The situation has changed somewhat in the last fifteen years. The day when *Seven Pillars* is universally regarded as (again in Meyers's words) "essentially and primarily a literary work of genius, beauty and insight" (11) has not yet arrived. Indeed, it probably never will arrive. The book is lengthy, highly wrought, and intensely self-conscious; it puzzlingly straddles several genres, and was produced by a man who was (surely?) a soldier or a fraud, not a writer. Initially difficult for all, the book remains permanently indigestible for some. Nevertheless, progress has been made, and Lawrence is now taken seriously as an artist. Stanley Weintraub and Rodelle Weintraub have published a book-length examination of what they term the "Literary Impulse" in Lawrence's life; Stephen E. Tabachnick's *T. E. Lawrence* deals with Lawrence as a writer; Thomas J. O'Donnell sets Lawrence in a specifically literary tradition. Of a recent collection of fourteen new essays on Lawrence, six dealt with the writer.[1]

If we are steadily moving toward a more just (because more knowledge-able) appreciation of the artist, we have advanced yet further in our estimate of the man. Gone are the uncritical, hero-worshiping days of the twenties, thirties, and forties, and the view of Lawrence as a Great White Sheik instituted by the American mythopoeist Lowell Thomas. Gone are the days when a biographer could write that Lawrence might have made himself emperor of the Arabs, but instead "came away and left [them] to employ the freedom that he had given them, a freedom unencumbered by his rule, which, however just and wise, would always have been an alien rule."[2] But gone too are the days of the later, equally extravagant, reaction, led off by Richard Aldington's vicious and hate-filled *Lawrence of Arabia: A Biographi-cal Enquiry*. As Tabachnick has written, "We no longer see Lawrence as *either* the chivalrous knight of the desert, unselfishly helping an alien nationality gain its independence with no second thoughts, *or* as the unscrupulous adventurer who wishes only to satisfy his own twisted personal needs and the interests of British imperialism" (*T. E. Lawrence Puzzle*, 28).

This book examines one thread that runs through Lawrence's life from his schooldays almost to the very end. It is a thread without which the fabric of Lawrence's life would lack a vivid and essential color, without which the pattern could scarcely be discerned. An examination of Lawrence's medieval-ism helps explain how he could be seen (sometimes by himself) as a "chivalrous knight of the desert"; it also illuminates the "adventurer" with "twisted personal needs." A careful look at Lawrence's interest in the medi-eval world—its art, especially literature, and its beliefs and attitudes to life—throws light on both the writer and the man.

It has long been known that Lawrence had an interest in the medieval world, and that the interest was intense. A collection of reminiscences (*BHF*) published soon after his death revealed, for example, that the young Lawrence had rubbed brasses assiduously and had studied the military

1. Stanley Weintraub and Rodelle Weintraub, *Lawrence of Arabia: The Literary Impulse;* Stephen E. Tabachnick, *T. E. Lawrence;* Thomas J. O'Donnell, *The Confessions of T. E. Lawrence: The Romantic Hero's Presentation of Self;* Stephen E. Tabachnick, ed., *The T. E. Lawrence Puzzle.* My essay "Lawrence's Medievalism" is one of the six.
2. Robert Graves, quoted in Tidrick, 216.

architecture of the Middle Ages, upon which he had written a thesis that earned him a First (a B.A. degree with highest honors). Statements of his identification with knightly ideals and the literature that is their expression are scattered throughout his letters and the memoirs of those who knew him. Robert Graves says that Lawrence is better understood when the influence of the troubadours upon him and his devotion to the ideals of chivalry are considered (*Poetic Craft*, 191–92); and a contemporary at Jesus College, Oxford remembered his feeling that Lawrence had "been there" after he had talked at some length about "the epic poetry of several languages" (Edwards, 345). But Lawrence's attempt to live, in some ways, as though the last four hundred years had not taken place, and the manner in which *Seven Pillars* manifests this medievalism, has attracted almost no serious critical attention. The fourth chapter (41–47) of John E. Mack's biography *Prince of Our Disorder* is a brief but stimulating suggestion of possibilities for further work and exploration along these lines.

I begin this study with introductory biographical material. In the course of the biography—to borrow Lawrence's own words, used in a similar situation—"Violently controversial points are settled by a plain assertion, for simplicity and peace" (*Crusader Castles*, 11). Chapters 2, 3, and 4, look at the background to Lawrence's medievalism. Chapter 2 deals with the antiquarian pursuits he indulged in as a boy and young man. He began by collecting medieval artifacts accidentally unearthed by Oxford workmen in the course of rebuilding; he soon went on to acquire a thorough knowledge of brasses and their rubbing, of heraldry (heraldic terminology, artfully transformed, is later to appear in *Seven Pillars*), of medieval weaponry, and of medieval architecture, especially the castles he visited in England, Wales, France, and the Middle East. The B.A. thesis later published as *Crusader Castles* (the need to gather material for which was the ostensible cause of Lawrence's first trip to the Middle East, his punishing walk of 1909) is seen to incorporate revealing prejudices. These prejudices, at this early and hopeful stage of Lawrence's career, consolidate his view of the world without doing violence to his (or our) intelligence. Chapters 3 and 4 look at Lawrence's ferocious and formative reading, in the literature of the nineteenth-century medieval revival and in that of the Middle Ages proper. Identification with the knightly heroes of Tennyson or Malory enabled Lawrence to escape from the demands of town and time into what he imagined as the brightly colored chivalric world of his ancestors. (He had discovered at an early age that he was the illegitimate son of a baronet.) I attempt to determine Lawrence's level of scholarship in medieval literature. More important, I examine the world-view that such literature expresses and the attitudes to life it inculcates. The young reader of the *Chanson de Roland*, of the *Morte d'Arthur*, of Froissart, eventually became involved in a notably anachronistic war, in which the sword could figure literally as well as metaphorically.

The heart of this book is Chapter 5. To read of and admire the heroes of the Middle Ages in Western Europe is well enough, but to be told by the man whose disciple one has become that chivalry has an Arab origin, and that Arab chivalric heroes rank among the most entrancing was, to Lawrence, far better. One of the greatest influences on *Seven Pillars* was W. S. and Lady Anne Blunt's version of a collection of early medieval Arabic poetry, *The Moallakat*. This translation provides a justification for and suggests the content of Lawrence's heroic dreams about a people who in the first quarter of this century still managed to practice, up to a point, the valorous life their old verse celebrates.

Chapters 5 through 10 have as their subject *Seven Pillars* (and the lesser writings to a lesser extent). The medieval and neomedieval subtexts of *Seven Pillars* are traced, and we see how and why they underlie Lawrence's own, twentieth-century, epic account. Lawrence freely admits, "As a great reader of books, my own language has been made up by choosing from the black heap of words those which much-loved men have stooped to, and charged with rich meaning, and made our living possession. Everywhere there are such phrases and ideas, not picked out by footnotes and untidy quotation marks, since great lords of thought must be happy to see us tradesmen setting up our booths under their castle-walls and dealing in their struck coinage."[3] A comparison of such subtexts (and note that Lawrence explains and justifies one of his most important literary methods in an explicitly medieval metaphor) with their transmuted versions in *Seven Pillars* shows our twentieth-century author claiming a congruency of idealistic endeavor, of belief and of practice, over eight or more hundred years. Lawrence does not claim idly that his book is "a chronicle in the spirit of the old men who

3. T. E. Lawrence, *Seven Pillars of Wisdom* (1922), 12.

marched with Bohemond or Coeur de Lion."[4] (He might also have said "in the spirit of the old men who marched with Roland and Oliver," or even "with Sir Lancelot and Sir Tristram.") That the identification is not represented as perfect—Lawrence includes unacknowledged quotations from works that mock chivalry, as well as works that exalt it—is testimony to the honesty with which he records his experiences among the chivalrous, but imperfectly chivalrous, Bedouin. It is not only evidence of his readiness to examine the validity of the ethos that had, over the years, become almost sacred to him; it is also a sign that Lawrence was inevitably of his century, and was intelligent enough to know it. Medievalism, in Lawrence's case, could animate a life, suggest the form of its ambitions and actions, and invest an extraordinary book with an antique spirit. But it could do none of these things with complete authority. There is a gap between the aspirations of the student of 1909, in the East for the first time, and the achievements, impressive though they are, of the Lawrence of 1926. Finished now with his war in an archaic theatre, finished with his diplomacy on behalf of the people and family who had seemed to embody his chivalric fantasies, finished at length even with his medievalizing account of acts that took place by "the old Crusader fort of Monreale . . . very noble against the night sky,"[5] the man and writer becomes a tragic figure. It is the gap between expectation and the reality of 1916–18 in Arabia that helped produce *Seven Pillars of Wisdom*. The work signally fails to present a consistent view of the possibilities of chivalric action in the twentieth century, yet is probably the only epic treatment of war that our century has given us.

Finally, in Chapter 11 Lawrence's recently discovered flagellation disorder is linked to his reading of the lives of saints and his lifelong detestation of the physical.

Lawrence's life describes a parabola of aspiration, partial achievement, and defeated disillusion, each stage of which can illuminatingly be viewed in terms of his immersion in the medieval past. Paul Fussell, writing of the Great War on the Western Front, has hoped "to probe into the origins of what some future 'medievalist' may call The Matter of Flanders and Picardy" (x). In *Seven Pillars of Wisdom* we have a medievalist's version of the last of

4. *Seven Pillars of Wisdom* (1922), 12.
5. *Seven Pillars of Wisdom* (1976), 374, 393.

the old-style wars, in comparison with which Flanders and Picardy are abundantly of our own age. Lawrence's greatest achievement is an account of The Matter of Araby, and it is now time to look in more detail at how it came to be produced.

· I ·

ORIGINS
OF A
MEDIEVALIST

THE first sentence of *Seven Pillars of Wisdom* (1922)[1]—"Some of the evil of my tale may have been inherent in our circumstances"—could serve as an introduction to Lawrence's life as a whole, not merely to the two years in the desert. Vigorously intelligent, variously capable, impressionable, and high-mindedly ambitious, Lawrence imbibed the neochivalric enthusiasms of his class and time, making himself vulnerable to the shattering effect of the discovery of a largely nonchivalric world beyond Oxford's walls. Thomas Edward Lawrence was the second of five sons born (on 16 August 1888), out of wedlock, to Thomas Robert Tighe Chapman, an Anglo-Irish landowner, and Sarah Madden, the governess and companion to his legitimate daughters. Sarah Madden had left the Chapman establishment in County Westmeath, Ireland, and been set up in nearby Dublin, where she lived as Thomas Chapman's mistress until the affair became public. Chapman was to spend the rest of his life in exile from Ireland, "married" effectively but not legally, to Sarah (his legal wife refusing a divorce) until his death in the influenza epidemic of 1919.

The Lawrences, as they called themselves, settled in Oxford in 1896 when Thomas Edward was eight, attracted partly by the educational opportunities offered to impecunious but gifted boys and partly by the presence of an Evangelical clergyman, Canon Alfred Christopher, whose teachings allayed

---

1. Excluding the so-called "Introductory Chapter," which was omitted from the 1926 edition on Bernard Shaw's advice, but later reinserted.

the couple's sense of guilt—particularly strong in the case of the mother. It was Lawrence's knowledge of his illegitimacy (acquired we do not know when, but early) that helped sour his attitude toward women. He could rarely, if ever, induce himself to accept the courtly reverence toward them that went with the era's renewed interest in an idealized Middle Age. Uninterested in his youth and disgusted in maturity, Lawrence generally avoided women, for whom deeds of honor were purportedly often performed, homosexualizing and politicizing the sexual urge. Sarah Madden, in the words of her second son, had been "brought up as a child of sin in the Isle of Skye, by a Bible-thinking Presbyterian, then she became a nursemaid, then 'guilty' (in her own judgement) of taking my father from his wife."[2] The mother wanted her sons to redeem her sins by the moral excellence and achievements of their own lives. T. E. Lawrence and his brothers lived somewhat isolated lives in a house in North Oxford, their parents discouraging all but a few friends and neighbors. The sons were urged to rely largely on each other for company and friendship. T. E. attended the City of Oxford High School and then went on to Jesus College, where he studied history, being especially interested in the medieval period. "Remember," he later wrote to the biographer Basil Liddell Hart, "that my 'period' was the Middle Ages, always" (*RGLH*, pt. 2, 48).

Lawrence's long summer vacations were spent in cycling holidays in France, where he studied military architecture. It is particularly during this impressionable stage of later childhood and adolescence that Lawrence read the medieval literature the influence of which is the subject of this book. "Spent nearly three years reading Provençal poetry, and Mediaeval French chansons de geste," he wrote to another biographer, Robert Graves, claiming that he devoted so much time to this extracurricular reading that he was not prepared for final examinations (*RGLH*, 1:48). The simplified world of the *Chanson de Roland* and *Huon de Bordeaux*, experienced in the atmosphere created by close-knit and lively minded parents and brothers, reinforced Lawrence's native idealism. Living in a family that saw itself as different and superior, with what would have been his normal social and professional advancement hindered by his illegitimacy, the gifted young man took his

2. British Library Add. MS 45903. Letter of 14 April 1927 to Charlotte F. Shaw.

sustenance from a world that did not entirely correspond to the one in which he found himself living.

The summer of his second year at Jesus College—that of 1908—Lawrence spent in Syria, examining the castles of the Crusaders. The resulting thesis, written as an optional extra to final examinations, helped earn Lawrence his First Class Pass. He returned to the Middle East after graduation, liking the simplicity of life there, and spent most of the years before the outbreak of war working as an archaeologist, in Carchemish, in Syria, an ancient Hittite town. At Carchemish he developed a close friendship with Dahoum, the water-boy or donkey-boy. During the holidays the two would sail down the Syrian coast or sightsee together. Lawrence later looked back on the Carchemish period as the happiest of his life.

Lawrence spent the first two years of World War I behind a desk in Cairo, where he worked as an intelligence officer. In the course of the next two years, he attached himself to Faisal, whom he considered the most capable of the Sherif of Mecca's sons, and helped organize Arab guerrilla raids against the Turks, on the right flank of the steadily advancing British Army. That much, at least, can be agreed on. George Bernard Shaw describes the background to the Arab rebellion and claims an important role in it for Lawrence.

> In the War of 1914–18, all those of the belligerent powers which were holding alien peoples in subjection for their own good or otherwise, had to face the risk of such peoples seeing in the War their opportunity to rise and strike for independence. The Germans banked on a rising in Ireland. What is more to the present point, they considered the possibility of a nationalist rising in Algeria against the French. If they could have brought that about, the consequences might have been serious. . . . The thing could have been done had there been a man of genius on the German side to do it.
>
> The proof of this is that England, having a man of genius at her disposal, succeeded in effecting the parallel operation of stirring up a nationalist rebellion against the Turkish Empire in Arabia. (*BHF*, 241)

Lawrence's admirers, who have been obliged to retreat, but whose most important positions have not been successfully assailed, say that Lawrence rapidly became the most important of the forces molding the rebellion. He worked through his personal ascendancy over Faisal, and his ability to understand simultaneously the needs and capacities of both British and Arabs and to act as liaison between them. He impressed the Arab warriors with extraordinary feats of physical endurance and hardiness, and profited by his clear perception that the best Arab strategy was to dominate the desert, hit the unwieldy and expensive army of the enemy or the railway upon which it relied, and then disappear back into the wastes, where the Turks could not follow.

Aqaba, the important port at the north of the Red Sea, was taken after a demanding detour through the desert of El Houl and an attack from the rear. The fall of Aqaba and its immediate consequences—official recognition and interest, more money and supplies—represent perhaps the most triumphant and unclouded moment of the campaign. Greater victories did follow, Damascus itself being liberated in September 1918, but Lawrence's pleasure in his role was increasingly marred by the strains and responsibilities of command. He was deeply disturbed by the constant need to hide his knowledge of French colonial ambitions in Syria, which clashed with the promises of self-determination made to the Arabs. He was disturbed too by the massacres and cruelties he witnessed, and by the death of friends. The war was physically exhausting: Lawrence found himself subjected to extremes of heat and cold, to disease, wounds, hunger, thirst, and fatigue. But the single most shattering and degrading experience proved to be the torture and homosexual rape he endured when he briefly fell into enemy hands at the rail junction of Deraa.

Lawrence hastened back to London after the capture of Damascus, and began his efforts to frustrate French policy in Syria and to give the Arabs what amounted to dominion status within the British Empire. He appeared in Arab robes at the Versailles Peace Conference, thus causing the first ripples of intrigued interest that were later, to his guilt and delight, to become waves. Four years' work, first at the conference and later as an adviser to the Colonial Office under Churchill, was necessary before Lawrence was satisfied that his Hashemite friends had been treated honorably: Faisal was installed on the throne of Iraq, and Abdulla, his brother, became Emir of Transjordan.

Feeling that he had done what he could, Lawrence resigned from the Colonial Office in 1922 and enlisted in the ranks of the R.A.F. under an assumed name. His reasons for doing so may always remain obscure. He turned his back on his previous life of striving and high-minded effort to take up one of obedience and self-obliteration.

Of the remaining thirteen years of his life, relatively little need be said. He had schemed to get into the armed service of his choice at the rank of his choice—the lowest—and was later obliged to scheme equally hard to be readmitted after newspaper publicity provided an excuse for his ejection. His harmless presence in one of the remoter R.A.F. camps in India elicited Soviet accusations of spying: Lawrence was speedily brought back to England. During the pre-India stretches of time when Aircraftman T. E. Shaw (he eventually took this name legally) was left in peace, he finished writing *Seven Pillars of Wisdom* and had the volume privately printed. A shortened version, *Revolt in the Desert*, was published to recoup the financial losses of his expensively produced full version. He wrote *The Mint*, an account of his early days in the R.A.F., but the work did not appear until twenty years after Lawrence's death. Much of his later work for the R.A.F. was concerned with the development and testing of air-sea rescue boats. Lawrence died in 1935 after a motorcycle accident, only a few months after the end of his last enlistment.

I·I

THE
NONLITERARY BACKGROUND
TO
LAWRENCE'S MEDIEVALISM

THE fear of public exposure of their irregular union led Mr. and Mrs. Lawrence to live quietly in Oxford. They lived strictly and decently not only in the hope of avoiding unfavorable comment but also because of the concern they felt for their children. It may well have been true, as the most famous of his sons later wrote, that Mr. Lawrence "never touched a book, or wrote a cheque" (Hart, 14), but his five children had the advantage of living in a lively and intellectual family. Great importance was placed on the boys' formal education and extracurricular activities (partly, of course, because the boys' future advancement would depend entirely on their own efforts). T. E. Lawrence was to write home in such great technical detail about the castles he had visited (largely to the exclusion of more personal matters) not because of cold-bloodedness or emotional dislocation, but because he knew his parents would be interested in and mostly understand what he was writing about, as the beginning of his enthusiastic description of Château Gaillard in August 1907 ("I have talked so much about this to you . . . ") makes clear (*HL*, 55).

We are told that Lawrence "got interested in archaeology in seeing some old tiles in a pit some workmen were excavating on his way to school, asked them to keep all of them for him, and he took them to the Ashmolean."[1] Or, perhaps the first awakening of interest in the past occurred when he watched his father (whose sense of caste prevented him from taking salaried employ-

---

1. Mrs. Lawrence reported this 17 February 1936. Thomas Jones, 174.

ment) at his various hobbies, which "included photography, the architecture of mediaeval castles and cathedrals, and bicycling, of which he was one of the earliest enthusiasts" (Mack, 8). But it is certain that any smoldering interest in the Middle Ages would have been fanned into flame by the reminders of the past to be found in many of Oxford's streets. Turn-of-the-century Oxford may have lost a little of its former glory, but was still, as Henderson tells us, "in its outward aspect a mediaeval city, 'a vision of grey-roofed houses and a long winding street and the sound of many bells,' as William Morris [had] described it" (Henderson, 11). Morris's disciple Lawrence found himself in a more modern environment; even so, had he been offered the opportunity, he could hardly have chosen a place that would have better stimulated interest in the past.

There are several testimonies to the thoroughness with which he knew the Oxford of his own day and its antecedents. C. F. C. Beeson writes: "Our acquaintance ripened under his desire to share with others an already masterly appreciation of the treasures of Oxford. . . . The enduring bond of our friendship was archaeological research, undertaken by Lawrence with a passionate absorption beside which my urge was more akin to the curiosity of a magpie in a Baghdad bazaar" (*BHF*, 52). And T. W. Chaundy comments,

> He was then best known, almost to notoriety, for his archaeological rummagings . . . in and about Oxford. Every excavation and rebuilding in the city was penetrated, and fragments of glass and stoneware zealously recovered: a cellar in the old wall bounding the school was identified as a one-time place of confinement for 'hussies'; and we became familiar with mediaeval names of the Oxford streets; Fish Street, Canditch, Horsemonger Street, one of which the soldier burnt down through over-roasting a pig. (*BHF*, 41)

The celebrated exploration of subterranean Trill Mill stream, by a canoe that was fitted with a candle at the bow and an acetylene cycle-lamp at the stern, was inspired by a reading of the seventeenth-century Oxford historian and antiquarian Anthony à Wood. Lawrence had established the identity of the stream "at the mouth of a sewer at Hythe Bridge and desired to know if the other outlet was at Folly Bridge"[2]

Like Morris before him, Lawrence was delighted by the opportunity Oxford offered for study of Gothic buildings, especially those of the Late Gothic Perpendicular style: Merton College and the Cloisters of New College are noted examples. He gave the workmen responsible for the excavation and rebuilding of 1906 in the Cornmarket, the High Street, and Balliol and Jesus Colleges a few pence for each specimen that they "carefully dug out and preserved" (*BHF*, 56).

Lawrence became familiar with the excellent museums of Oxford, the Ashmolean and the University; he frequented the Bodleian and Radcliffe libraries. He studied medieval pottery; he made a collection of brass rubbings: "Cut out and pasted on the walls of his bedroom were life-sized figures of knights and priests with Sir John d'Abernon and Roger de Trumpington, a Crusader, in pride of place" (*BHF*, 52–53). Monumental brasses— flat pieces of metal, usually latten (a yellow, mixed metal, closely resembling brass) on which are engraved the figures of the commemorated deceased, possibly accompanied by his heraldic arms, inscriptions or canopies—first appeared in England during the second half of the thirteenth century. The two cited above are among the very few of this period that have survived. Indeed, d'Abernon is the very oldest (it dates from 1277 and is to be found at Stoke d'Abernon in Surrey; the Trumpington, to be found in Trumpington in Cambridgeshire, dates from 1289).

Lawrence assiduously rubbed the brasses of Oxford, city and university, of Oxfordshire, and of southern and eastern England as a whole. By the time he was fifteen, he was knowledgeable in the subject and had a good collection (*BHF*, 52). Warren O. Ault, an American historian who was at Jesus College in the same years as Lawrence, still possessed in 1978 two brass rubbings of the several they did together (each always made a copy of every brass). One of them, made in 1908, is that of Thomas Cranley, archbishop of Dublin from 1397 to 1417.[3] This brass, which is described in the Ashmolean's pamphlet

---

2. *BHF*, 47. Lawrence had probably been reading Anthony à Wood and J. Peshall's *Antient and Present State of the City of Oxford* or the later, and better, edition by A. Clark, *Survey of the Antiquities of the City of Oxford*.

3. Letter to the author from Warren O. Ault, 10 October 1978.

Notes on Brass-Rubbing as "especially notable," shows the former warden of New College, where the brass is still to be found, in pontifical vestments with miter and pastoral staff.[4] Lawrence's own rubbing is among those held by the Ashmolean Museum. H. T. Kirby was told by Mrs. Lawrence that "a few of her son's best efforts were presented to the Ashmolean Museum, Oxford, as they were found to be of superior quality to some of the examples housed in the collections there." Kirby examines two specimens of Lawrence's rubbings— Thomas de Braunstone (1401, Wisbech, Cambridgeshire) and William, Viscount Beaumont and Lord Bardolf (1507, Wivenhoe, Essex)—and comments on the "clear evidence of patient care" they show (Kirby, 18–19). He observes too that the museum's MS catalogue, prepared by the Oxford Architectural and Historical Society, was "largely amended and corrected by Lawrence himself, and the characteristic handwriting appears on many of its pages."[5] Obviously, this argues for a great deal of erudition on Lawrence's part.

A thorough knowledge of monumental brasses demands a knowledge of armor and heraldry, among other subjects. It is impossible to understand a brass properly if one cannot date it roughly by any armor borne by the engraved figure. As *Notes on Brass-Rubbing* tells us, "the heraldry of a brass can, to the discerning, be almost as informative about those commemorated as the inscriptions" (32).

Charles J. ffoulkes lectured on armor at Oxford University in 1909–10 and met Lawrence regularly then. "We used to discuss the whys and wherefores of style, construction and design of military equipment, on which [Lawrence] had heretical but always practical views." Ffoulkes asked Lawrence to look in Syria for a man who still made chain mail, "for the technique of this mystery craft has always intrigued students of arms and armour"; he suggested that Lawrence photograph the man at work and try to buy his tools (*BHF*, 65). One of the books in Lawrence's library at his death was ffoulkes's *Armour and Weapons*, inscribed "With kind regards from the author, Charles

---

4. Ashmolean Museum, *Notes on Brass-Rubbing*, The front- and back-cover illustrations of the seventh edition are reproductions of two of Lawrence's rubbings: namely, that of Thomas, Lord Berkeley (1417), Wotton-under-Edge, Gloucestershire (front); and William, Viscount Beaumont and Lord Bardolf (1507), Wivenhoe, Essex (back).

5. Kirby, 18. This catalogue is no longer in existence. It was the property of the Oxford Architectural and Historical Society, and was probably destroyed by an officer of that society unaware of the catalogue's value (or perhaps stolen by someone who *was* aware of its value).

ffoulkes, Nov. 1909" (*BHF*, 486). *Armour and Weapons* is a handbook describing the development of armor from 1066, with a brief chapter at the end about weapons. The different pieces are named and described, diagrams show what they looked like and how they would be worn, and explanatory references are made to medieval inventories and literature. One may imagine that Lawrence, who was currently reading the literature of the period, would be particularly pleased at this last feature. One of the most accessible of ffoulkes's literary explanations is that of Chaucer's lines (75–76 of the Prologue to the *Canterbury Tales*) about the knight's attire: "Of fustyan her wered a gepoun / Alle bysmotered with his haburgeoun." These lines "would refer to the rust-stains that penetrated through the interstices of the mail," says ffoulkes (*Armour and Weapons*, 61).

Lawrence and C. F. C. Beeson, a school friend, made their own heraldic rolls of arms, "painted in their proper tinctures." As Beeson points out, "a herald's jargon . . . eventually enriched the vocabulary of *Seven Pillars*" (*BHF*, 53). It also enriched at least two of the young Lawrence's letters: "All the country is of one colour, a murrey brown, but very subtly beautiful," he wrote of northern Syria (*HL*, 238–39). "Murrey" is the heraldic name for the color (it is a "stain" in heraldic terminology) "purply-red (Mulberry colour)" (Brooke-Little, 27). The *OED* says that the word is now invariably historical or archaic and gives no example of its use after 1847.[6] The second example occurs in a letter to his brother W. G. Lawrence. In discussing Indian carpets, T. E. uses the word "ramping" ("their wall hangings are usually stamped with yellow figures of tigers ramping" [*HL*, 290]), which is almost certainly suggested by "rampant," a common heraldic term that describes an animal (often a lion) "erect with one hind paw on the ground, the other three paws being raised, the head facing forward and shown in profile and the tail erect (Brooke-Little, 290).

Beeson says that heraldry offered an "alluring field" and it is not difficult to see why. It combines the appeal of a logically consistent system with the romance of chivalric endeavor; originally only the knightly class was armigerous. One herald, in rejecting Thomas Gray's lines in "Elegy Written in a

---

6. One does occasionally see the word in modern nonheraldic contexts; e.g., Thomas Hardy writes of Sue Bridehead in *Jude the Obscure* (1895) that "She wore a murrey-coloured gown with a little lace collar" (III.i).

Country Churchyard" about "the boast of heraldry" ("The boast of heraldry, the pomp of power, / And all that beauty, all that wealth e'er gave, / Awaits alike the inevitable hour. / The paths of glory lead but to the grave") claims that "true heraldry does not boast—it aspires. For some, indeed, it possesses a spiritual value" (Brooke-Little, 3). Lawrence's identification with chivalric values will be discussed more fully later.

Oxford offered then, as it does now, various clubs and societies to cater to the interests of university members. It is difficult to be sure about what groups Lawrence joined. He and Beeson certainly heard Flinders Petrie, the distinguished archaeologist (whose excavations in Egypt Lawrence was later to join) address the Ashmolean Society (*BHF*, 26); we know that at least once ("a rare occasion" [Edwards, 345]) Lawrence attended the "College Literary Society" and that the *Chanson de Roland* was under discussion. If the Oxford University Brass Rubbing Society, founded in 1893, admitted nonmembers of the university, he would probably have joined the organization, which in 1901 became the Oxford University Antiquarian Society "for the study of monumental brasses and kindred subjects" (Dixon, 1). Lawrence, formally a member of the university from 1907, is not mentioned in the archives of these societies; it is true, though, that the archives for the period in question are slim.

Of course, not everything of interest was in Oxford. In London, the Tower Armouries and the Wallace Collection, with their representative examples of European and Oriental arms and armor, became familiar. But before relating in greater detail Lawrence's travels outside Oxfordshire, and later outside England, let us attempt some explanation of this strong interest in a past world. Lawrence felt a great disaffection with the time he had been born into, and once praised Algernon Blackwood's *The Centaur* (1911) as "more reasoned and definite as an attack on the modern world than anything I've ever read—bar Morris" (*HL*, 184). Let us consider briefly the now-forgotten work. Blackwood's admirer must have been smitten by *The Centaur* from the beginning of chapter II: the egotistic young man (his description of the book dates from 1912) must have thought, with a jolt of pleasure, that the book was about him.

> O'Malley himself is an individuality that invites consideration from the ruck of commonplace men. Of mingled Irish, Scotch, and English

blood, the first predominated, and the Celtic element in him was
strong. A man of vigorous health, careless of gain, a wanderer, and by
his own choice something of an outcast, he led to the end the
existence of a rolling stone. He lived from hand to mouth, never quite
growing up. It seemed, indeed, that he never could grow up in the
accepted sense of the term. (Blackwood, 4)

Lawrence at that time may not have recognized the applicability to himself of
the last comment, but we are reminded that George Bernard Shaw wrote of
him that "at forty he still had the grinning laugh and artless speech of a
schoolboy; and powerful and capable as his mind was, I am not sure that it
ever reached full maturity" (*BHF*, 247). The second paragraph of this same
chapter must be approached with more caution, but it too has its relevance
to the personality of our subject: "An ardent lover of wild out-door life, he
knew at times a high, passionate searching for things of the spirit, when the
outer world fell away like dross and he seemed to pass into a state resembling
ecstasy. Never in cities or among his fellow-men, struggling and herded, did
these times come to him, but when he was abroad with the winds and stars
in desolate places" (5). Here, the last words remind us of certain phrases in
the first chapter of *Seven Pillars. The Centaur* tells how O'Malley, after a
meeting with "a Cosmic Being—a direct expression of cosmic life . . . [a]
little bit, a fragment, of the soul of the World, and in that sense a survival . . .
of her youth" (66), recognized in himself a radical dissatisfaction with the
world of "Stock Exchanges, twopenny-tubes, Belgravia dinner-parties, private
views, 'small and earlies,' musical comedy" (183), and the obsession with
material possessions and mechanical progress that is the basis of such a
society. He eventually escapes through death into a greater earth-conscious-
ness. Lawrence appreciated Blackwood's contempt for modern civilization,
but he did not escape from it into a vaguely Grecian paradise where the
conscious life of Earth can be felt and shared. If Lawrence too was beginning
to feel a desire for "very desolate and lonely places, unsmothered and
unstained by men as they exist today" it was not because he wished to
experience there "Earth's stupendous, central vitality" (Blackwood, 175).
Lawrence too wanted to avoid stock exchanges and everything they represent,
but he eventually hoped to do so by sharing, in untarnished areas of the
earth, the life of a people whom he had always suspected of adhering to

preindustrial, that is, to chivalric, values. Lawrence took refuge not in mysticism but in medievalism.

In turning toward the Middle Ages, Lawrence is not unique. Such an interest is apparent not only in the works of the Romantics but also in the paintings, poetry, and other productions of the Pre-Raphaelites, who were particularly influential in the three decades preceding Lawrence's birth (1888) and the decade or so following it. The Pre-Raphaelites are so called because they criticized Raphael's *Transfiguration* and the Classical doctrines of Sir Joshua Reynolds, while praising the purity and simplicity they saw in medieval (pre-Raphael) painting. Ruskin (whose *Stones of Venice* Lawrence read with great interest) claimed that the ugly was not a suitable subject for treatment in art, and this doctrine seemed to exclude much of the contemporary world of increasingly industrial England.

Lawrence's medievalism, then, was in tune with the artistic preoccupations of the age. It occupied his considerable physical and intellectual energies as he gradually extended his horizons by means of trips farther and farther afield in search of evidence and artifacts. His first published piece (an article entitled "An Antiquarian and a Geologist in Hants," which appeared in the school magazine in March 1904 [quoted in part in Mack, 22]) and his first surviving letter (to his mother from Colchester, written in August 1905, when he was seventeen), were both the fruit of these trips. The holidays, even the earlier ones, were often spent in bicycle tours. As early as 1903 Lawrence and his father spent the summer bicycling; the first letter from Colchester gives an idea of the tone and content of the schoolboy and undergraduate letters home.

FLEECE HOTEL
COLCHESTER
August 13, 1905

DEAR MOTHER

It seems rather a long time since I wrote to you, and so, as its [*sic*] Sunday, we have decided that it is my turn to write to you. This morning Father and I went to St. Botolph's, the modern church near the old Priory Ruins. We have Picture P. Cards of the present state of the ruins so you will be able to compare the two views. The Ruins

are all made of Roman tiles;—thousands of them,—and even the
arcading is made of tiles. The actual large Norman Arch in the centre
is, however, faced with stone. Behind this entrance there are a
number of Norman Piers all made of rubble and bricks; they were
once faced with plaster. The modern church (Built in 1836) is a very
good specimen of modern Norman; in fact Father and I had only two
holes to pick in it, and it harmonises excellently with the old being
made of a greyish brick. Colchester is all over Roman remains; all the
churches are full of Roman tiles and brick work, from Saxon Holy
Trinity to Italian Renaissance St. Peter's: the castle is brick from top to
bottom; and large portions of the old walls still remain all round the
town. The West Gate (Roman) still exists entire. It is rather like a
tunnel and is about 11 feet high but only 5 feet wide. Its masonry is
rubble and every two feet up are four courses of Roman tile. The
stone work is about 13 ft. high. The mortar is as soft as cheese. Next
the gate was a guard room; nearly perfect; all except its roof, which
had been of wood. The stone vaulting of the gate & guard room
passage was perfect.

If possible I shall get post cards of the gate. It was far in a way [sic]
the most interesting thing I have seen this trip. We came here from
Ipswich over a rather hilly road 18 miles long. Still we took two
hours over it; and walked about six hills; a proceeding Father does
not like. We are feeding splendidly.

Father is much better and has not coughed since Lynn. I have had
to give up Bures. We came by the other road because of the wind;
still I hope to get Pebmarsh tomorrow; and I got one yesterday
so I'm not altogether mournful. I have sent off all my rubbings to
Miss Powell; hope she'll like them. I expect you have Will with you
now. Will you please tell him not to let you do more work than is
necessary to keep you in condition? Also tickle Arnie when he gets
up and when he goes to bed all from me. Tell him there are dozens
of butterflies of all sorts about here, some Red Admirals; and a lot of
other queer ones. Ask Beadle [his brother Will] to come up here as
he has never seen a Death's Head or some such insect. Norwich
Museum he would have enjoyed. There was the largest collection of
raptorial birds in existence 409 out of 470 species: I wonder if he'll

shriek with horror when he hears that I did not look at them but went off and examined the Norman W.C.s. In the hall was a thrilling stuffed group a boa constrictor strangling a tiger. We hope to return to Oxford Wednesday. Kindly take heaps of love from me for yourself; and when you've had enough, divide the remainder into three portions, and give them to the three worms you have with you. I wonder how the doctor is enjoying Jerry [a dog]. Don't forget the Canon's birthday next Sunday. We have one post card from Will, 1 from yourself and one letter from you. Loud snores to all. Love to yourself.

NED[7]

This precise and scholarly reporting of the dimensions, materials, and quality of the buildings or ruins visited is typical. Domestic trivia, although present, take second place to recent discoveries and frequent hypotheses. The Bures and the Pebmarsh are both monumental brasses, the former, of Sir Robert de Bures, 1302, in Acton, Suffolk, being "the finest military brass in existence" (Clayton, 13); the latter, of Sir William Fitzralph, c. 1323, in Pebmarsh, Essex, being of interest as an illustration of the change from banded mail (small metal discs sewn onto leather so as to overlap in rows) to plate armor.

It was in 1906 that Lawrence made his first extended acquaintance with France since childhood. The month of August was spent in the north, in Dinard as Lawrence's parents had kept in contact with friends and neighbors of their stay there. "Towards the end of 1905, most of the accessible British examples [of Gothic architecture, and military buildings] had been exhausted; a winter's reading in the Radcliffe and Ashmolean libraries prepared the way for an investigation of the ruins and restorations of France. . . . The Côtes du Nord and Finisterre were covered closely in search of cathedrals and the less known fortifications (*BHF*, 54).

Fifteen letters survive from this tour. They record in some detail Lawrence's impressions of individuals he met in his travels to various points in France, including Lehon, Guingamp, Château du Guildo, and St. Servan. They

---

7. *HL*, 3–4. Three diagrams and a sentence referring to one of them have been omitted.

show a young man (Lawrence was then eighteen) who had thoroughly immersed himself in his period, was knowledgeable in several branches of its learning, and apparently directed all his physical energies to gaining, through personal examination, more knowledge of the period, especially its buildings. On the way down to the ferry, Lawrence made a brief excursion to Netley, the thirteenth-century abbey, calling it "certainly the finest ruin I have ever seen, and much the most picturesque. I do not think that the Chapter House and guest room can be equalled" (*HL*, 5). The moon during the crossing reminded him of Tennyson, and even the furniture of the family with whom he was staying elicited a comparison suggested by visits to medieval sites: "I never saw the equal of a buffet in the dining-room, while a buhl table in the drawing room beats any at Warwick Castle" (*HL*, 6).

Lawrence showed, often casually, his knowledge of heraldry and armor, and had great faith in his ability to work out from mute evidence the intentions of medieval architects. In fact the letter of 16 August 1906 has strong overtones of pedantic self-importance. Quotation of part of the letter may give the tone of the whole:

16 August, 1906

My dear Will,

Your letter has put me in a fever heat of expectation: but—what is it you are going to dig up? Your letter bristles with inconsistencies. You think it is a Roman or Celtic camp (the two things are absolutely opposed to each other) and then you proceed to say that it is a mound on some rising ground. If it includes a mound, say 40 feet high, it is a Saxon or Danish fortification, with probably an interment or two on the top; if the mound is 10 feet high or less, and is about 30 feet in diameter, then it is a barrow, as you say in the former part of your description, which has a lamentable lack of exact figures. (*HL*, 21)

The following is from a letter written from Dinan. Lawrence is describing a monumental effigy:

The sleeves (no man's jupon ever had sleeves), were fairly full and descended to the wrist; underneath it was seen the edge of the vambrace. She wore genoullières [*sic*], with square plates beneath them, jambs and sollerets, of three large and heavy laminated plates. She also had rowel spurs, and her feet rested on an eagle expansed bearing a shield (billets or) on the front, held in its beak. The eagle was very faithfully and clearly drawn, and the claws drawn very true to nature. At the sides of the effigy were six other shields, bearing the billets or; the arms of her husband the count of Beaumanoir. The eagle expansed is the badge of the Duguesclin family. . . . [H]er hair, confined by a narrow fillet alone, flowed in two curls while the rest was cut short and parted regularly down the centre. The effigy of her husband has a beard, and wears jupon gorget pauldrons, brassarts, coutes and a large sword. His feet of six lames were resting on a lion. He bore a shield with nine billets or. Two almost identical figures of Lords of Lehon (14th cent.) were interesting as having slipped off their gauntles & coifs de mailles, just as Septvans [*sic*] whom they greatly resembled. One of them had his feet covered with scale armour. They wore surcoats, and demi-jambs. (*HL*, 11–12)

This is fairly representative of Lawrence in full flight. The passage is remarkable for the powers of observation it bears witness to; note particularly the precise description of the confinement and arrangement of the hair (and its felicitous phrasing). It also shows a considerable knowledge, all the more impressive in an eighteen-year-old. The little errors in no way compromise the impression of extensive learning. The errors are mostly eccentricities of spelling or punctuation: "genoullières" is usually spelt "genouillères"; the particle of Lawrence's "Duguesclin" is usually a separate word; "Septvans" has the "p" in it for a reason soon to be discussed.[8]

Lawrence uses with confidence a dozen or so technical terms concerned with armor, detailing the clothing of Tiphaine Du Guesclin, "daughter of the famous Constable," from the jupon ("which came into fashion about 1360, and was a short sleeveless and closefitting tunic, usually of leather" [Brooke-Little, 23–24]) to the sollerets ("jointed plates of armour protecting the feet

---

8. Spelling was never Lawrence's strong point anyway. See *Letters*, 668 n.3.

[Brooke-Little, 336]"). Heraldic terms, too, are used easily; the shields bear *billets or* and Lawrence knows the heraldic use of "badge." "Expansed," however, is a little puzzling: the normal term would be "displayed." Perhaps Lawrence was thinking of "expanded," which, when referring to an eagle, "implies, perhaps, that the wings are more displayed than usual."[9] We can infer from the letter that Lawrence noted the lifelikeness of the eagle supporting Tiphaine's feet ("very faithfully and clearly drawn . . . the claws . . . very true to nature") because of its contrast with the stylized depictions with which he would be familiar. (This was especially true in heraldry. The king of the beasts and the king of the birds, both popular charges because of their connotations of strength and valor, were presented in one of a number of conventional forms and postures.) Lawrence would have known about the monumental brass of Sir Robert de Setvans (1306), to be found at Chartham in Kent; it was often reproduced in heraldic manuals of the day, as indeed it still is, because of its provenance in the prime of brass engraving; and because the knight bears a memorable example of canting arms, that is, arms that make a punning allusion to the name of the bearer. Sir Robert's surcoat and *ailettes*[10] show seven winnowing fans—*sept vans*—and his shield, three similar fans. (Note Lawrence's etymological spelling.)

The 1906 tour seems to have been a happy one. Lawrence, at the peak of physical fitness, cycled vigorously, made notes about what constitutes the absolute minimum of luggage, tried to eat in accordance with his wishes and principles, and read Ruskin's *Stones of Venice*. He pursued his interests with a unique thoroughness: "I think I must be practically the discoverer of the little carvings, since they are not in a place to which the ordinary antiquary would attain." "Just imagine the delight of going round a four-inch ledge in semi-darkness, and trying to write notes on sculptures, only half-seen" (*HL*, 39, 41). Loving and detailed letters were sent back to Oxford. Tonquédec, "a wonderful Château," the "Tour Solidor" at St. Servan, Montfort Priory, and the castle at Fougères were all described: the Château de la Hunaudaye received especially thorough treatment. Again, technical terms are repeatedly

9. Gough and Parker, 214. I thank Professor Gerard J. Brault of the Department of French, The Pennsylvania State University, for this reference.

10. *Ailettes* "were small shields fastened at right angles to the shoulders, to lessen the force of a sweeping blow" (Clayton, 13).

used ("enceinte," "newel," "capitals," "Perpendicular"). Lawrence's capacity for imaginatively reconstructing his period in practical specifics is in evidence: "By the side of the large gate is a little postern about 2 feet wide, also with drawbridge: this saved moving the enormous pont-levis that the large door must have had, since the little one was large enough for ordinary purposes" (HL, 38). On the other hand, he apparently believes the popular fallacy that a cross-legged effigy indicates that the deceased was a Crusader (HL, 26). It is now generally agreed that many of the men whose figures have crossed legs never saw the Holy Land, and that their creators, rather, were influenced by the taste of the time, which sought variety and movement:

> During the thirteenth and early fourteenth century the effigy type of the cross-legged knight reaches a peak of vigorous action. Hands may be crossed or folded in prayer, but most common between 1270 and 1290 is the alert pose of the right hand crossing the body to grasp the hilt of a sword to unsheath it. . . . The whole figure with legs crossed and knees bent may be turned over on its side "dancing with springy vigour."[11]

In the last letter of the tour he reports the purchase of three glass medallions, hoped to be fourteenth century, and laments the absence of good ecclesiastical Gothic architecture, which he ascribes to the devastations of civil wars.

Other tours followed, in the summers of 1907 and 1908. April 1907 was spent examining Welsh castles: Crow Castle, Carnarvon, Harlech, Chepstow, Caerphilly, and Monmouth were among those visited. The high point was "magnificent" Caerphilly: "The Hornwork is most interesting, and the outworks could not be excelled, either for preservation or attractiveness" (HL, 52). Not for the first time, Lawrence's reading in literature offers a different perspective on his historical, architectural researches: he remembers that Yniol's castle in Tennyson's "Geraint and Enid" is based on Caerphilly. He mentions "Poor Henry VI," who was born in Monmouth, where the townspeople no longer know where the castle is to be found. I shall deal briefly with the French tours of the next two summers and then examine in more

---

11. Brieger, 204–5. I thank Professor Gerard J. Brault for this reference.

detail the first considered writing that Lawrence produced, largely as product of these and other travels, namely *Crusader Castles*.

Some of the highlights of the French tours were the castle of Richard I, Château Gaillard, the Mont-St-Michel, Carcassonne, and Chartres. The letters give a strong impression of Lawrence's delight in each place, at finally having seen places he had known only from study, but this very emotion militates against a reasoned assessment of the attributes and quality of each. The letter home from Evreux reporting the stop at Château Gaillard is largely an excuse for hero-worship of Richard, its builder, "a far greater man than we usually consider him: he must have been a great strategist and a great engineer, as well as a great man-at-arms" (*HL*, 55). The crusading and chivalrous Richard occupied a central part in Lawrence's imagination.[12] A letter to Beeson written five days later discusses Richard's final wound and where exactly the arrow came from. "The dream of years" was fulfilled when a night was spent at the Mont-St-Michel (*HL*, 57). Carcassonne he found a diachronic model of the "first-class fortress," calling it "absolutely indescribable . . . of all dates: much Roman work: much Visigothic, a splendid Saracenic tower, some Carolingian work, and mediaeval of all sorts to the end of the 14th century" (*HL*, 67). He called Chartres Cathedral "the noblest building . . . that I have ever seen, or expect to see" (*HL*, 80).

The letter about Chartres Cathedral has been treated rather as a set piece. Mrs. Lawrence was delighted with it, supposing that it implied her son's eternal salvation. After Lawrence's death, Mack tells us that Lord Carlow chose it to print privately in an "elaborate edition" (51). David Garnett described it as "the most beautiful and emotional of his early letters" (*Letters*, 86). Approximately 650 words in the letter from Laigle (28 August 1908) are devoted to the cathedral. Lawrence begins the letter rather unconvincingly: "I expected that Chartres would have been like most French Cathedrals spoilt by restoration, so I slipped out before breakfast to 'do it.' " This adds force by contrast to the admiration that follows, even though it is difficult to believe Lawrence ignorant of such a great, perhaps the greatest, example of the Gothic style. Superlatives follow, which their author later admits to be inadequate but unavoidable. Then:

12. *HL*, 166. A passing reference in a letter of 1911 will show that Lawrence was familiar with writings about the château (see *HL*, 166). See also T. E. Lawrence, *Crusader Castles*, 14.

It is not enormous; but the carvings on its 3 portals are as fine as the best of all Greek work. Till yesterday I would put no sculptors near the Greeks of the Vth cent. Today the French of the early middle ages *may* be inferior, but I do not think so: nothing in imagination could be grander than that arrangement of three huge cavernous portals, (30 odd feet deep), of gigantic height, with statues everywhere for pillars, bas-reliefs for plain surfaces, statuettes & canopies for mould-ings. The whole wall of the cathedral is chased & wrought like a Florentine plaque, and by master hands! . . . Chartres besides has the finest late xvi & early xvii bas-reliefs in the world, and is beautiful in its design & its proportions. (*HL*, 80–81)

This is Lawrence's criticism of specifics (as opposed to his recounting of the effect of the whole), and it will be seen that his attention is claimed entirely by the wrought work of the portals and the flawlessly detailed and compre-hensive wrought work of the walls. His enthusiasm for them is shared by others: Henry Adams says that "the portal of Chartres is the type of French doors; it stands first in this history of Gothic art; and, in the opinion of most Gothic artists, first in the interest of all art." (69). E. H. Gombrich writes that "there is a . . . feeling of lightness and weightlessness in the sculptures that flank the porches like heavenly hosts. . . . The master who worked for the northern porch . . . made each of his figures come to life. They seem to move, and look at each other solemnly, and the flow of their drapery indicates once more that there is a body underneath" (142).

A Gothic cathedral, in addition to being the pride of a town, was its center and meeting-place, and the scene of activities that today would be considered purely secular. The iconography of Chartres is comprehensive in subject matter partly, of course, for religious reasons. The cathedral, which is dedicated to Our Lady, embodied and supported the faith of the people. The illiterate would recognize each figure by its symbols; for example, Moses holds the tablets on which were inscribed the commandments and the column with the brass serpent with which he cured the people (Gombrich, 143). It is comprehensive because Mary was patroness of the seven liberal arts, because Chartres had an important center of learning in its cathedral school, and because the preferences of individual, noble, and corporate donors (the local guilds) were necessarily taken into account. Lawrence would have had no need to be embarrassed by his judgment that "Chartres is Chartres:—that is, a gallery built by the sculptors to enclose a finer collection than the Elgin marbles" (80).

Apparently Lawrence devoted no time to the architecture of the cathedral, even though Fleming tells us that "the parts beyond the transepts" of Chartres Cathedral had expanded "to unprecedented proportions" (188–89) because of the large choir and sanctuary and the chapels (some of which contained prestigious relics). But Lawrence comments neither on these architectural peculiarities, nor on the alleged imperfections of the cathedral (Fleming, 184, 186). Lawrence is probably showing the influence of Ruskin's *Seven Lamps of Architecture* here. In the "Preface to the Second Edition" (1855), Ruskin writes:

> Artistical and rational Admiration.—I found, finally, that this, the only admiration worth having, attached itself *wholly* to the meaning of the sculpture and colour of the building. That it was very regardless of general form and size; but intensely observant of the statuary, floral mouldings, mosaics, and other decorations. Upon which, little by little, it gradually became manifest to me that the sculpture and painting were, in fact, the all in all of the thing to be done; that these, which I had long been in the careless habit of thinking subordinate to the architecture, were in fact the entire masters of the architecture; and that the architect who was not a sculptor or painter, was nothing better than a frame-maker on a large scale. (Cook and Wedderburn, 10)

Nor, as George Bernard Shaw observed, does Lawrence comment on the stained glass (Mack, 61). Such criticism, however, is unduly severe: Lawrence was under no obligation (in a holiday letter) to be complete. His exaltation at what he saw rings true despite the letter's careful phrasing:[13] "I was absolutely exhausted, drenched to the skin (it had poured all day) and yet with a feeling I have never had before in the same degree—as though I had found a path (a hard one) as far as the gates of Heaven, and had caught a

13. Lawrence lived in an age that had a different attitude to letter-writing from that of today. He usually made a rough copy, which was later corrected and recopied.

glimpse of the inside, the gate being ajar. You will understand how I felt though I cannot express myself. Certainly Chartres is the sight of a lifetime, a place truly in which to worship God" (*HL*, 81).

Perhaps it was Lawrence's exhaustion that intensified his state of exaltation. We must remember that this young man was already somewhat hostile to the seemingly hypocritical and guilt-ridden Evangelicalism that pervaded the home of his Bible-saturated parents. Genesis 28:17 quoted Jacob on awakening from his dream at Bethel, "How awe-inspiring this place is! This is nothing less than a house of God; this is the gate of heaven!" Matthew 7:14 reads, "But it is a narrow gate and a hard road that leads to life, and only a few find it." It would have been in the medieval tradition to muse in such scriptural allusiveness; Lawrence's background also gave him the ability, if not usually the wish, to see his experiences and feelings in Biblical terms.

For his graduation in 1910, Lawrence took advantage of a new regulation that allowed him to present, in addition to his final examination papers, a thesis not longer than twelve thousand words. This thesis was entitled "The Influence of the Crusades on European Military Architecture to the End of the Twelfth Century"; as we have seen, it helped earn its author a First Class degree. Lawrence's work was in direct opposition to the generally accepted view of the time, represented by C. W. C. Oman and E. G. Rey. Lawrence claimed that "the Crusading architects were for many years copyists of the Western builders."[14] In other words, the Crusaders did not take back to Europe from Byzantine examples their knowledge of engineering and fortification, but brought it with them to the East from their native lands. The dispute has still not been finally settled; however, it seems that Lawrence, with characteristic force, originality, and self-confidence, overstated his case. Modern experts agree that there was more mutual influence than Lawrence admitted. Certainly Lawrence contributed to the change in opinions that has taken place since the days of Oman and Rey, but much remains to be learned about the chronology and development of castle building. As the definitive statement on the development of twelfth-century military architecture, *Crusader Castles* is not acceptable. But as evidence of remarkable reading,

14. *Crusader Castles*, 56. This book, first published in 1939, is a verbatim printing of the thesis, with Lawrence's later penciled comments also reproduced. A second volume reproduces letters written home when Lawrence was collecting material.

traveling, and the ability to master ideas and handle them to suit a purpose, it is eminently so. *Crusader Castles* is in many ways *the* work on which we should judge Lawrence's intellectual growth, both in nature and extent.

When it has been admitted that the thesis is not a last word, when accusations of misrepresentation about castles visited have been taken into account,[15] and when we have realized that Lawrence had the use of H. Pirie-Gordon's plans, made from a tour of the previous year, then we can extrapolate from the work's revealing virtues. *Crusader Castles* is obviously the product of a young man who has seen firsthand what he reports and who has the gift (already demonstrated at Château Gaillard) of envisaging the lives of the people whose work he was studying in unacademic quotidian terms. "Most admirable latrines," he remembered of Saone [Sahyun] in a marginal note, "with as usual a strong draught through them," and he knows which loop-holes in the face of a wall can be effectively shot through and which cannot (T. E. Lawrence, *Crusader Castles*, 33, 36). Above all, Lawrence is sufficiently sure of his grasp of the topic to interpret, in consistently fluid and self-confident prose, a mass of complex and technical detail in a way that supports his thesis (he had made up his mind before leaving Europe, of course). Robin Fedden describes Chastel Pelèrin (Athlit),[16] a fortress flanked on three sides by the sea, as follows:

> On three sides the rocky promontory, wading deep into the waves, offered in itself a strong protection to a garrison who were also masters of the sea. On three sides therefore the Templars confined themselves to building a single massive wall rising almost from the water's edge, with one or two rectangular towers. . . . Wisely the main defences were piled up on the landward side of the promontory. They were still impressive, and this largely by reason of the cyclopean stones of which they were built.
>
> The series of defences that protect the landward face of Chastel Pèlerin are complex, and represent perhaps the fullest Crusader

15. Desmond Stewart, *T. E. Lawrence*, 61. Stewart says that Antioch and Urfa were not visited.
16. Athlit is the name of the present-day village. The castle was called Chastel Pelèrin (Castrum Peregrinorum) because it was built, in 1218, with the aid of pilgrims.

development of that conception of fortification associated with Byzance.[17]

Lawrence, however, first writes of the two military orders into whose hands the ownership of almost all the large castles devolved—because the cost of their upkeep was too great for the vast majority of feudal lords—that each added to or rebuilt its acquisitions in its own styles:

> The Templars, always suspected of a leaning toward Eastern arts and heresies, took up the mantle of Justinian, as represented by the degenerate fortresses in Northern Syria, and amplified it, in making it more simple. The Hospitallers, in harmony with their more conservative tradition, drew their inspiration from the flourishing school of military architects in contemporary France. (T. E. Lawrence, *Crusader Castles*, 42)

He then writes about Chastel Pelèrin:

> The characteristics of the Templar style will be grasped at once if a plan (49) of Château Pélérin [*sic*] (Athlit) their chief stronghold be considered. They held possession there of a narrow promontory of rock and sand, eminently defensible according to mediaeval ways. Yet here the Templars, working in 1218, threw aside all the carefully arranged schemes of flanking fire, all the covering works, all the lines of multiple defence which were being thought out meanwhile in Europe. At Athlit they relied on the one line of defence—an enormously thick wall, of colossal blocks of stone, with two scarcely projecting rectangular towers upon it. These were the keeps, the master towers of the fortress, and instead of being cunningly arranged where they would be least accessible they are placed across the danger line, to bear the full brunt of the attack. One would expect them to be unusually massive, but they are, in true Byzantine style, of thin walls, compared with their curtain, and the hoard, which was just

17. Robin Fedden, *Crusader Castles*, 57–59. A plan of Chastel Pelèrin may be found in Fedden, 58. Plan 49 of Lawrence's *Crusader Castles* is of Chastel Pelèrin.

then being generally adopted, is not made use of to repair the weakness. The projection of these towers is very slight, insufficient to rake an enemy busied on the face of the curtain, and the little in front is not of a force to be held alone. The strength of Athlit was brute strength, depending on the defenceless solidity of the inner wall, its impassible height, and the obstacle to mining of a deep sea-level ditch in the sand and rock before the towers. The design is simply unintelligent, a reworking of the old ideas of Procopius, only half understood. Justinian, except in rare exceptions, had not intended his fortresses to stand alone, as the last refuge in a conquered country: they were temporary defences to assist the unrivalled Greek field-army. Given unlimited time and labour, anyone can make a ditch so deep and a wall so high of stones so heavy as to be impregnable: but such a place is as much a prison for its defenders as a refuge: in fact a stupidity. Such is Athlit. (T. E. Lawrence, *Crusader Castles*, 42–43)

Fedden, then, takes it as a matter of course that the weak—the landward—side of the castle (the Crusaders always had command of the sea) should be heavily defended; we may assume that the admiration with which he elsewhere writes of the ingenuity and labors of the Crusaders applies here to "first, a solid masonry glacis, and a ditch or moat, 80 feet wide and 20 feet deep, which could be flooded from the sea at either end" (59), and then two lines of defense behind that.[18] Lawrence, however, is positively scathing about the Byzantine-inspired castle: Château Pelèrin is a "stupidity." He writes of the castle, with its "unintelligent" design, in a tone reminiscent of the scorn that he will later manifest toward army officers who prefer bayonet-charges, conventional armies, and Foch to imaginative, skillful guerrilla war. Lawrence has to denigrate the château. He must maintain that the splendid erections still standing in the Middle East derive from Europe; that the military engineers of genius were Western; in particular that his admired Richard was in the forefront of intelligent castle-building.

There is no evidence that Richard borrowed anything, great or small, from any fortress which he saw in the Holy Land: it is not likely that

---

18. Fedden does criticize one thinly built tower. This does not affect my argument.

he would do so, since he would find better examples of everything in that South of France which he knew so well. There is not a trace of anything Byzantine in the ordinary French castle, or in any English one: while there are evident signs that all that was good in Crusading architecture hailed from France or Italy. (T. E. Lawrence, *Crusader Castles*, 56)

This sophisticated handling of rather arcane material is a tribute to Lawrence's intelligence. It is also a tribute to his knowledge of the theories of castle development. That his research had an emotional dimension is shown by his attachment to Richard. The enterprise of researching and writing the thesis had been engrossing: " 'Eureka.' I've got it at last for the thesis: the transition from the square keep form: it really is too great for words" (*Letters*, 61). It had involved physical and personal adventure, a flexing of the literal and metaphorical muscles.

Lawrence's B.A. thesis thus is something of a triumph. Not only is it a precocious work of learning still treated with respect by experts today, but it also represents the successful imposition of a view that its holder finds comfortable and heartening onto a large amount of technical detail of absorbing interest, and hence, by extension, onto chaotic life itself, which— challenges, threats, promises, and all—was just opening before Lawrence. This imposition does no violence to the understanding of author or reader.

I·I·I

LAWRENCE
AND THE
MEDIEVAL REVIVAL

"He lived," wrote Vyvyan Richards of Lawrence's Oxford period, "in a world of old things, castles, churches, memorial brasses, pottery, and books—books—books" (Richards, 21). Having discussed Lawrence's travels in search of artifacts from the Middle Ages, I turn now to his reading in medieval and neomedieval literature. Lawrence was one of the world's great readers. From boyhood to disillusioned maturity he read omnivorously and commented frequently on what he found. An early letter shows him fitting together his experience and memories of his reading, explaining one in terms of the other. (It contains, in fact, Lawrence's first surviving literary allusion—the first of hundreds, some of them embedded, unacknowledged, in the text of *Seven Pillars*.) "The moon was full and glorious. . . . I cannot say whether the cloud effects or the reflection on the water were the best but the ensemble was perfect and left nothing to be desired. I never before understood properly Tennyson's 'Long glories of the Autumn moon' but I see his reason now for mentioning it so often" (*HL*, 5). Apparently the young Lawrence was no better at remembering the lines that caught his imagination than the older Lawrence, who admitted that he was never sure of quoting correctly even the simplest of his long-favourite poems. The words "And the long glories of the *winter* moon" (my emphasis) are to be found in "Morte D'Arthur" (line 192) and "The Passing of Arthur" (line 360). Tennyson nowhere uses Lawrence's version.

Lawrence may not have been able to quote from memory, but he obviously know Tennyson well by the time he was eighteen. "One of his prizes at school was for an essay on Tennyson, whom he had selected for special study" (Mack, 24). It seems that a Tennyson volume accompanied him on the 1906 trip; in other letters written during this period, he quotes passages of two to five lines, from four of the *Idylls of the King* (namely "Balin and Balan," "Lancelot and Elaine," "Guinevere," and "The Passing of Arthur") and from "The Palace of Art" and "The Dead Prophet."[1] "I used nearly to live on [Tennyson,] once," he later wrote, describing "Morte D'Arthur" as "splendid" and "The Palace of Art," "The Lotus-Eaters," "Saint Simeon Stylites" and "parts of *The Princess*" as "good as good can be. . . . Even I have read *Becket*, & *Harold*, and *Maud*."[2]

The titles of some of these poems and plays notwithstanding, Tennyson was not a writer of the medieval revival in the same central way that other favorites of Lawrence were. The reader of *Idylls of the King* comes across much that is externally "medieval": tournaments, swords, shields and armor, heraldry, the rules of knighthood. Tennyson, however, although he did his homework for the *Idylls*, reading Welsh history and literature, visiting Wales, and even learning some of the language (Turner, 159), had no great knowledge of or interest in the medieval world. The *Idylls* are not inspired by a conviction that man had in the Middle Ages a knowledge or attitude to life since tragically lost (unlike certain writings of Ruskin and Morris). They are rather an allegorical treatment of contemporary developments in religion

1. *HL*, 20, for "Balin and Balan," lines 332–36. In *HL*, 32–34, eighteen quotations are found (Lawrence describes his activities and the scene before him by quoting appropriate lines). The sixth quotation is from "The Palace of Art" (lines 21–24), as is the eighth (lines 70–72); the tenth is from "The Passing of Arthur" (lines 95–97); the twelfth from "The Dead Prophet" (lines 21–24); the fourteenth from "Lancelot and Elaine" (lines 1002–3); and the fifteenth from "Guinevere" (lines 236–42). The first, second, thirteenth, and eighteenth are from Shelley's *Alastor* (lines 308–10, 86–87, 337–39, and 334–35, respectively). The fourth and fifth quotations are from Shelley's "Hymn to Intellectual Beauty" (stanza 7); the seventh from his "Stanzas Written in Dejection, Near Naples" (lines 12–13); and the tenth from his "A Summer Evening Churchyard" (lines 1–4). The sixteenth and seventeenth quotations consist of lines from Milton's *Paradise Lost* (Book 3, line 11, and Book 4, lines 606–9, respectively). The third quotation has successfully defied the efforts of research.

Desmond Stewart is thus mistaken in claiming that Lawrence "transcribed from memory no less than forty-seven lines from Tennyson's *Idylls of the King*" (33). The lines would have been copied from the books the literary young man carried with him on his tour. Similarly the lines from Shelley's *Julian and Maddalo* in a letter of 1908 would almost certainly have been copied as well (Stewart, 33).

2. British Library Add. MS 45904. Letter of 8 May 1928 to Charlotte F. Shaw.

and science perceived by Tennyson as harmful to man's spiritual well-being (Turner, 152–54). One knight of Tennyson's Round Table, Tristram, attributes the decline of the Order to unrealistically high ideals (Ricks, 1722).

> a doubtful lord
> To bind them [the knights] by inviolable vows,
> Which flesh and blood perforce would violate;
> For feel this arm of mine—the tide within
> Red with free chase and heather-scented air,
> Pulsing full man. Can Arthur make me pure
> As any maiden child?
>   ("The Last Tournament," lines 682–88)

The materialists are always with us and are always to be fought with absolute ideals: in Tennyson's words, with a "sword bathed in Heaven." This doctrine would have appealed to the young Lawrence.

The "nowhere" and "no time" of Tennyson's Camelot is as good a means of illustrating allegorically the dangers of life in Victorian England, and the way to combat them, as any other, indeed, better than most because there already exists a series of tales about Camelot readily susceptible to editing and change. Tennyson was enchanted by Malory, and bowdlerized his tales to suit his own preoccupations and the taste of his respectable audience.

If Tennyson would not see revived the spirit of what he saw as "a time / That hovered between war and wantonness, / And crownings and dethronements" (Ricks, 1756), he is yet at the center of the nineteenth century's annexation of the knightly ethos and its transformation into the code of the gentleman. As will be seen, this code was to give the postwar Lawrence endless trouble, causing some to shower him with what he considered ill-deserved and inappropriate praise, and providing a framework for the criticisms of others. Mark Girouard has pointed out "how the code of mediaeval chivalry, and the knights, castles, armour, heraldry, art and literature that it produced, were revived and adapted in Britain from the late eighteenth century until the 1914–18 war" (preface). The revival produced not merely new tellings of old stories and new representations of old scenes, but "ideals of behaviour, by which all gentlemen were influenced, even if they did not consciously realise it" (Girouard, preface). The public schools, the Boy Scout movement, the "muscular Christians," the more exalted of the workers for Empire: all were at least partly inspired by the "return to Camelot" and its ethos.

The revival of chivalric interests helped encourage in Lawrence and his contemporaries more important coincidences of thought and language than the three about to be cited. But they are interesting and significant, and set Lawrence in his time. First, Lawrence did not, unlike Charlie Lamb, the son of a Sussex baronet, decide "shortly after his seventh birthday in 1823 that he was going to write the history of his guinea-pigs, Minnikin, Pin and Toby. *Ivanhoe* had come out four years earlier; Charles Lamb's father had written an epic in twelve cantos, *The Dragon Knight.* . . . Minnikin, Pin and Toby were gradually transformed into guinea-pig heroes of chivalry. As Charles Lamb grew older, his history grew and multiplied" (Girouard, 89). But Lawrence's elder brother does recall that "when we were small and shared a large bedroom, he used to tell a story which went on night after night without any end. It was a story of adventure, and successful defence of a tower against numerous foes, and the chief characters were Fizzy-Fuz, Pompey, and Pete— fur animal dolls that my brothers had. Long pieces of rhyme telling of the exploits and achievements were composed by him, and this was before he was nine!" (*BHF*, 31). Secondly, Lawrence did not, as far as I know, ever describe himself and his siblings or colleagues as a "band of brothers"— unlike Nelson, who "in 1799 . . . quoted from Henry V's speech before Agincourt and called the officers serving under him at the battle of the Nile a 'band of brothers.' The phrase was to be re-used over and over again in the nineteenth century; in 1802 Scott applied it to his volunteer friends in the Edinburgh Light Dragoons" (Girouard, 41). But there was not lacking some-body to do it for him. In a rather sentimental account of the Lawrences' childhood, his friend Ernest W. Cox writes, "Here then was an ideal family of boys, a very band of brothers—united, conscientious, strong in character, clean alike in limb and in life" (*BHF*, 37). Finally, Lawrence, not having been killed in the first years of the war, and not having come from the correct social class, did not elicit "a flood of chivalrous epithets" in 1915, unlike Julian and Billy Grenfell ("amongst the heroes and saviours of England . . . perfect gallant knight . . . shining radiant knight" [Girouard 287–88]). But there is a similarity of perception and phrasing between Lady Barrington's response to Billy Grenfell and the response to Lawrence of Mrs. Fontana (the wife of the British consul in Aleppo). The former was "I never forget seeing Billy once at Westminster Abbey after the King's Funeral. He was standing against the Dryden Monument, and a shaft of sunlight came down on his head; and I thought what a beautiful picture of manly youth. . . . He looked like a young knight who would ride into battle with joy" (Girouard, 287). The latter was "I am glad [Robert Graves] passed on my memory of [Lawrence's] youthful beauty and colour. Surely there were others who observed it? It is odd how vividly and how often I remembered that bright hair—all through the war when one wondered if it had been trampled into mud yet— and after, as if it were something significant in itself" (Mack, 92).

Mrs. Fontana is responding here, no doubt unconsciously, to a tradition in what Paul Fussell calls "Victorian iconography"; in such a tradition, "to be fair-haired or (better) golden-haired is . . . to be especially beautiful, brave, pure, and vulnerable. For Victorian painters of Arthurian themes, the convention was that Galahad, Tennyson's 'bright boy-knight,' was golden-haired" (Fussell, 275). Lawrence here benefits from "The equation of blondness with special beauty and value [that] helps explain the frantic popularity of Rupert Brooke, whose flagrant good looks seemed an inseparable element of his poetic achievement" (Fussell, 276).

The question of why the nineteenth century so interested itself in medieval life and art, why it attempted to reproduce what it saw as their characteristic forms and spirit, is a difficult one. The scholars who studied medieval papers in the seventeenth century had contemporary political and religious, rather than literary, applications in mind (Ker, "Literary Influence," 220). Lawrence's favourite, Anthony à Wood, wrote of his "tender affections and insatiable desire of knowledge . . . ravish'd and melted downe by the reading of" William Dugdale's *The Antiquities of Warwickshire* in 1656 (Aldis, 382). Dugdale represents a more "scientific" approach to the study of history than that of his predecessors: he relied upon primary sources such as charters, registers, muniments, genealogies, monumental inscriptions, and heraldry. The school of which he is a member, based at Oxford, traces its beginnings to the opening there of Sir Thomas Bodley's library, which, since 1602, had been accumulating materials and extending its collections (Aldis, 341–42). Lawrence later wrote critically of the sort of history that is based on respect for and fidelity to documents. But the medievalism of later centuries would

have been impoverished had it not been for the conservation of Dugdale and
his fellow scholars.

However, the continuing rise of medievalism in the next century has much
to do with the inevitable human reaction against established modes of
treating conventionally approved subjects. Dryden, Pope, and Dr. Johnson,
being accepted by the majority, must be found wanting by more adventurous
spirits, or at least by those who considered themselves so. For example,
Horace Walpole bought Strawberry Hill in Twickenham in 1747 and over the
years transformed it into a miniature Gothic castle. It was in this inauthentic
but influential building that he wrote *The Castle of Otranto* (1764), which
today reads absurdly, but which manifests an enthusiasm for medieval
paraphernalia and thrilling pseudomedieval horrors. Walpole was a wealthy
dilettante; but men like Hurd, Gray, and Percy were more weighty. Bishop
Hurd produced his most famous phrase in a lukewarm assessment of the
neo-Classical school and a defense of Spenser: "What we have gotten by this
revolution, you will say, is a great deal of good sense. What we have lost, is a
world of fine fabling; the illusion of which is so grateful to the *Charmed
Spirit* that in spite of philosophy and fashion *Faery* Spenser still ranks highest
among the Poets; I mean with all those who are either come of that house,
or have any kindness for it."[3] Gray wrote imitations of Norse, Provençal,
Welsh, and medieval Spanish poetry, and his *The Descent of Odin* and *The
Fatal Sisters* are the conscious product of literary research into northern
heroic poetry.[4] Bishop Percy provided the best known of the anthologies of
traditional folk poetry, *Reliques of Ancient English Poetry* (1765). Chandler
reports that his comments on the poems are almost as important as the
poems themselves, for they helped encourage the idealization of chivalry
(17). Percy wrote that

> that fondness for going in quest of adventures, that spirit of challeng-
> ing to single combat, that respectful complaisance shown to the fair
> sex . . . are all of Gothic origin, and may be traced to the earliest times
> among all the Northern nations. These existed long before the feudal
> ages, though they were called forth and strengthened in a peculiar

3. *Cambridge History of English Literature,* 10:240.
4. Alice Chandler, 14; *Cambridge History of English Literature,* 10:220–21.

manner under that constitution, and at length arrived to their full
maturity in the times of the Crusades, so replete with romantic
adventures. (Quoted in Chandler, 17)

We shall see in Chapter 5 that Lawrence's mentor W. S. Blunt considered
that "Knight-errantry, the riding forth on horseback in search of adventures,
the rescue of captive maidens, the succour rendered everywhere to women
in adversity, all these were essentially Arabian ideas" (Blunt and Blunt, xiv).
Obviously Blunt is remembering and contradicting Percy. We do not presume
to say whether chivalry's origin is Gothic or Arab, but plainly it is to be found
in the mysterious past of a vigorous and *different* people—a people who
knew the secret of performing noble deeds in a meaningful universe in a
way that we eighteenth- (or nineteenth- or twentieth-) century Englishmen
do not.

Percy in his turn had an influence on *Lyrical Ballads*. The reader of
"Christabel" and "Kubla Khan" experiences imaginatively a world very
different from that which surrounds him in everyday life, as, indeed, does
the reader of "La Belle Dame Sans Merci" and "The Eve of St. Agnes." The
medieval world becomes a symbol of alien, challenging, and, perhaps, more
rewarding modes of being.

But men more practical than poets looked to the medieval world as a
source of remedies for present imperfections. Those who were horrified by
the conditions of the working classes chose to see the Middle Ages as a
period in which competition and exploitation had little place. Feudal society,
it was felt, held lord and peasant in a mutually beneficial relationship: the
lord received laborors and soldiers; the peasants received security. Those
who were disgusted by laissez-faire economics and utilitarian doctrines
emphasized what they considered a medieval belief: noblesse oblige. Those
who were dismayed by the Church's apparent inefficacy looked back to an
age of general piety, when the Church fulfilled a valuable social role.

The psychological need for belief in an almost unchanging world that
cherished values for which the nineteenth century seemed to have no place
was strong after the tumultuous changes of 1789 and the succeeding eighty
or so years: the upheavals caused by the French Revolution and its subsequent
wars, the rate of industrial development, and, in 1859, the shock given to
orthodox Christianity and man's self-esteem by Darwin's theories of evolu-

tion. "The world into which Pre-Raphaelitism"—a movement that took some of its inspiration from Dante, Malory, and Froissart—"was [born was] far from pleasant" wrote D. S. R. Welland.

> 1848 has been characterized as "the year of great and general revolution." At the beginning of the year there was serious apprehension of a French invasion. Then in February revolution broke out in Paris and Louis Philippe was overthrown. Rioting continued sporadically in France, and civil war raged in Hungary, in Poland, and in Italy. This conflict of ideologies and classes throughout Europe is best epitomized by one fact: 1848 saw the publication of the Communist Manifesto by Karl Marx and Friedrich Engels. England was in the grip of the "hungry forties": it was the aftermath of the Industrial Revolution, when working-class unrest had found expression in the Chartist risings. . . . But domestic uneasiness was not only due to political causes: in 1848 the dangers of over-industrialization were emphasized in the grim form of an outbreak of cholera. (21)

Immersion in medieval study or imaginings could be an escape from the unrelenting present, a search for the key to its improvement, or even a token of faith in an "ordered yet organically vital universe," where "far from being isolated from nature, mediaeval man was seen as part of it, and his chivalry mirrored its benevolence" (Chandler, 1, 17). So the gentleman antiquaries continued their research. Indeed, Lawrence's father, with his interest in the architecture of castles and cathedrals, was one of them. T. E. himself could easily have joined their ranks, had it not been for the possession of other, more dramatic, talents. Serious scholarly activity at this time unearthed more and more about the literature, language, and social organization of the Middle Ages.

The second of Lawrence's surviving literary allusions takes us to the work of a man who considered the age he lived in spiritually poorer than the medieval epoch. On 17 August 1906, Lawrence reports the purchase of Ruskin's *Stones of Venice*, a four-franc present to himself for his eighteenth birthday (*HL*, 21). Three days later he had decided, "I like his style and subject intensely; his [sic] is most interesting. I am exceedingly glad I bought them for I now have some conception of the right way in which to study architecture, and how to draw the truest lessons from it. Father will be entranced with it" (*HL*, 24). The later letter that quotes twenty-one lines from Tennyson also goes on to give a further verdict: "My Ruskin is better than ever. . . . It gives a most masterly exposition of the meaning and method of Gothic, and he simply smashes the Renaissance styles. No wonder they are going out of fashion after this book" (*HL*, 35).

Ruskin's works did indeed influence the architecture of his time, although Ruskin could not always approve of his own influence. Throughout the second half of the nineteenth century, "to read Ruskin was accepted as proof of the possession of a soul" (Clark, xiii). His books "were to be found lying beside the *Idylls of the King* on the tables of those who did not normally read, but wished to show some evidence of refinement" (Clark, xiii). Ruskin's fame, his interest in architecture, and his praise of the Middle Ages made it inevitable that Lawrence would sooner or later read him. "The Nature of Gothic," a chapter in *Stones of Venice*, makes the social implications of Ruskin's medievalism clear. Ruskin contrasts the work of the craftsman of the Middle Ages (often imperfect but performed to the best of each man's capacity, and with pleasure) with the production of the modern workman (superficially and mechanically perfect but the result of soulless toil). What Lawrence read in Ruskin he never forgot. Ruskin's contrasts occur, in a transmuted form, in that account of a struggle waged by enthusiatic amateurs, *Seven Pillars of Wisdom* (see Chapter 9).

Lawrence's main architectural interest seems to have been the military (he enjoyed trying to adduce the reasons for this or that feature of the castle before him), but, as we have seen, he could be enthusiastic about ecclesiastical work too. The interest in architecture was enduring. After the war he wrote that "Something in the Norman style strikes me as so logical & unanswerable. It's not argument, a proposition, like the pointed work, which stands only by stress & balance. Norman, Romanesque rather, is a plain statement."[5] This remark (suggested by "glorious" Ely Cathedral) clearly shows a sympathy with architecture and the unconscious forces and attitudes behind it. Ruskin was praising the "pointed work," on the grounds that, in northern climates, it is functional, and the product of a secure faith that could be content in simplicity. The decadence of Venetian architecture is an

5. British Library Add. MS 45903. Letter of 27 September 1924 to Charlotte F. Shaw.

indication of the decadence of modern civilization, architectural beauty being impossible without communal health. Nineteenth-century England could imitate the external forms admired by Ruskin, but to no avail; the link between faith and pleasingness is not to be sidestepped. In the "Preface to the Third Edition" (1874), Ruskin remembers being "startled" by suddenly coming across in England

> a piece of Italian Gothic in the style of its best time.
> The architect had read his third part of the *Stones of Venice* to purpose; and the modern brickwork would have been in no discord with the tomb of Can Grande, had it been set beside it at Verona. But this good and true piece of brickwork was the porch of a public house, and its total motive was the provocation of thirst, and the encouragement of idleness. (Cook and Wedderburn, 11–12)

The "truest lessons," in Lawrence's words, to be learned from Ruskin would lead the student back in time, or at least to a land that did not "mimic the architecture of Christians to promote the trade of poisoners" (Cook and Wedderburn, 13).

It is not surprising that Lawrence praised Ruskin's style; its somewhat self-conscious eloquence was then fashionable. Shortly after Ruskin's death in 1900, another Victorian giant, Sir Leslie Stephen, wrote

> The cardinal virtue of a good style is that every sentence be alive to its fingers' ends. There should be no cumbrous verbiage: no barren commonplace to fill the interstices of thought: and no mannerism simulating emotion by fictitious emphasis. Ruskin has that virtue in the highest degree. We are everywhere in contact with a real human being, feeling intensely, thinking keenly, and, even when rhetorical, writing, not to exhibit his style or his eloquence, but because his heart burns within him.[6]

6. Sir Leslie Stephen, 84–85. This essay first appeared in the *National Review* in April 1900.

The young Ruskin (like the young, and mature, Lawrence) may have had a weakness for "purple patches," but this venial fault is redeemed by the quality of his thought, writes Stephen.

Lawrence must have read Ruskin assiduously. The letter describing Chartres, already quoted, echoes Ruskin's sentiments in *Stones of Venice*. "The middle ages," writes Lawrence, "were truer that way [in the matter of worship] than ourselves, in spite of their narrowness and hardness and ignorance of the truth as we complacently put it: the truth doesn't matter a straw, if men only believe what they say or are willing to show that they do believe something" (*HL*, 81). Ruskin made a distinction between "the calculating, smiling, self-sustained, self-governed man, and the believing, weeping, wondering, struggling, Heaven-governed man;—between the men who say in their hearts 'there is no God,' and those who acknowledge a God at every step" (Cook and Wedderburn, 190).

But the number of hours Lawrence spent reading Tennyson and Ruskin does not compare with those immersed in William Morris. His devotion to Morris was lifelong, and, as he himself came to realize, could not be justified only by reference to Morris's ability or importance.

> Morris was a great poet: and I'd rather have written The Well at the World's End or The Roots of the Mountains or John Ball or The Hollow Land than anything of the 19th Cent. except War and Peace or Moby Dick. Sigurd and The Dynasts and Paradise Lost and Samson and Adam Cast Forth [by C. M. Doughty] are the best long poems in English. And Morris wrote 50 perfect short poems. Why, the man is among the very great! I suppose everybody loves one writer, unreasonably. I'd rather Morris than the world.[7]

> [T]he charm and comfort of imperfection makes up for most of the failures of the world. We admire the very great, but love the less: perhaps that is why I would choose to live with the works of William Morris, if I had to make a single choice. My reason tells me that he isn't a very great writer: but then he wrote just the stuff I like.[8]

---

7. British Library Add. MS 45903. Letter of 23 March 1927 to Charlotte F. Shaw.
8. British Library Add. MS 45904. Letter of October 1929 to Charlotte F. Shaw.

After the war—and especially after he had begun translating the *Odyssey*, a work he considered spuriously archaic—Lawrence saw that his love for Morris was a personal predilection. But there is no such separation of emotion and intellect in the many prewar references to Morris, where the heart and the mind are committed equally.

There are remarkable similarities of personality and interest between Morris and Lawrence. Both men reacted to (more or less) the same society— industrial, competitive, and manifestly unjust—in (exactly) the same way; namely, by escape into a preindustrial society where the only competition was purportedly for honor and where lack of material or political equality did not imply exploitation. Both dreamed of adventure and excitement in a neomedieval elsewhere even as children: Lawrence's tales of Fizzy-Fuz, Pompey, and Pete have already been referred to; and Morris "invented and poured forth endless stories, vaguely described as 'about knights and fairies,' in which one adventure rose out of another and the tale flowered [*sic*] on from day to day over a whole term" (Mackail, 17). These dreams led on to the sagas and chivalric adventures of the Middle Ages. Both men loved Oxford's architecture, both rubbed brasses. Both eventually found a more "primitive" people whom they saw (although Lawrence was later to become disillusioned) as remembering and living according to the spirit of their medieval epics and romances; who were stoic in the face of nature's, and man's, harshness; and who had nothing to do with the considerations governing life in nineteenth-century England. Morris found the people of Iceland; Lawrence, of course, the Bedouin. Lawrence, indeed, makes his point quite explicitly through one of his Arab warrior chieftains. He (Lawrence) had gone back into the desert to find a lost man. Eventually the two of them

> regained Nasir and Nesib in the van. Nesib was vexed with me, for perilling the lives of Auda and myself on a whim. It was clear to him that I reckoned they would come back for me. Nasir was shocked at his ungenerous outlook, and Auda was glad to rub into a townsman the paradox of tribe and city; the collective responsibility and group-brotherhood of the desert, contrasted with the isolation and competitive living of the crowded district. (*Seven Pillars* [1976], 198)

Both hated injustice and oppression and did what they could to relieve it, but in significantly different ways. Both were interested in the aesthetics of printing (Lawrence being very much under the influence of Morris). Both enjoyed working with their hands: Morris dyed, wove, and embroidered; Lawrence (acknowledging the twentieth century here at least) took pleasure in tinkering with his motorcycles and aeroplanes. Finally, both were described by their friends as apparently sexless: Wilfrid Scawen Blunt found Morris "absolutely independent of sex considerations" (Rickett, 63–64), and a male friend of Lawrence's who had been in love with him later wrote, "I realise now that he was sexless—at least that he was unaware of sex" (Knightley and Simpson, 29).

It is fortunate that Lawrence's enthusiasm for one of Morris's writings, the aforementioned *Sigurd the Volsung*, was fired while he was out of Oxford, in Carchemish. The letters written home during the first four months of 1912 make frequent mention of "the best poem I know," as Lawrence solicits the opinion of each member of his family. *Sigurd* is now dated, and seems (to adapt the older Lawrence's phrase about the *Odyssey*) "Wardour-Street English" (Wardour Street being the London street where fraudulently antique furniture acquires its antiquity). But this retelling of the story of Siegfried— of his winning of the elf-gold and the losing of his love Brynhild through trickery—attempts to re-create the world of high-minded adolescence before involvement in the world and loss of innocence, and hence, happiness. Or, as Mackail put it, "at the root of the dream is a separation between the boundless desires of the heart and the limitations of the world" (330).

Morris here produced, as his young admirer was later to do, a long account of conspicuously heroic actions written in an artificial and mannered style and vocabulary that at first annoy but gradually win over the reader. The world of *Sigurd* is not far from the golden age, before "Earth grows scant of great ones, and fadeth from its best, / And fadeth from its midward and groweth poor and vile" (Morris, *Sigurd*, 6). Lawrence, in *Seven Pillars* (1976), will have the notably anachronistic chieftain Auda, who "saw life as a saga" (171), echo this sentiment: "My father . . . was master, greater than Auda; and he would praise my grandfather. The world is greater as we go back" (273). But in 1912 Lawrence did not know of the events that were to give him an opportunity to match his ideals and dreams against the outside world. Sigurd's aspiring innocence is Lawrence's: "And the light of life smote Sigurd, and the joy that knows no rest, / And the fond unnamed desire, and the hope of hidden things" (Morris, *Sigurd*, 106). Lawrence's identification with the poem and its yearning for absolutes—of strength, valor, and wisdom—is revealed by a comment in a letter home: "I hope *Sigurd* is not kept carefully [at the Oxford home]: a good book like that should be put in the best place where it may have the widest influence on the lives of the people it meets" (*HL*, 191). He realizes, however, that *Sigurd's* philosophy points away from Georgian England: "[R]emember the tale itself is Norse, and it is perhaps the most near to us of all the Norse tales—the one we can best assimilate and enjoy—better, of course, if one knows a simple people, as I happen to know the Arabs" (*HL*, 198).

Lawrence admired Morris's celebration of heroic stoicism and physical courage. But there is another explanation of why Morris wrote "just the stuff I like." Both men had a liking for what Dorothy M. Hoare calls "langourous music . . . prisoned . . . from air" (32). Of D. G. Rossetti's poem "The Bride's Prelude," Morris said "That is *pure* poetry."

> Within the window's heaped recess
> The light was counterchanged
> In blent reflexes manifold
> From perfume-caskets of wrought gold
> and gems the bride's hair could not hold
>
> All thrust together: and with these
> A slim-curved lute, which now,
> At Amelotte's sudden passing there,
> Was swept in somewise unaware,
> And shook to music the close air.
>   (Rossetti, 194)

(Here the music is *literally* "prisoned . . . from air.") Lawrence quotes from De la Mare's "Arabia":

> Sweet is the music of Arabia
> In my heart, when out of dreams
> I still in the thin clear mirk of dawn

> Descry her gliding streams;
> Hear her strange lutes on the green banks
> Ring loud with the grief and delight
> Of the dim-silked, dark-haired Musicians
> In the brooding silence of night.
>
> (*Minorities*, 198)

Lawrence said "[it] is the ne plus ultra of minor poetry."[9] (He actually misquotes one line as "dark-skinned, dim-silked musicians," but the incorrect form also evokes the exotic, the dreamlike.)

Morris's praise of "The Bride's Prelude" and Lawrence's praise of a poem that gains its similar effects in the same manner help make it clear how much the latter was of his period in some ways. Graham Hough has said of the "decorative Keatsian poems like 'Rose Mary,' 'The Bride's Prelude,' and 'The Staff and Scrip'" that "they are the least adapted to modern taste. They seem overloaded and too merely poetical, without relevance to anything but previous literature. They bring up in an acute form the whole question of what is called poetry of escape, poetry that seems to do nothing to interpret the experience of its author or the life of its time" (6). The balance of escapism and commitment in the art of the Pre-Raphaelites can be delicate. The first appeal of medievalism may have been its contrast with the dreary, money-grubbing present. "For Burne-Jones the Middle Ages was essentially 'such stuff as dreams are made on,' and his pictures of it are coloured by 'a light that never was on sea or land,' so that at times it becomes little more than an irritating affection—'Wardour Street medieval,' as one modern critic has not undeservedly called *King Cophetua and the Beggar Maid*" (Welland, 39). But late nineteenth-century medievalism was not always factitious and the dream could become didactic. Morris's *News From Nowhere* (1890) is, literally, a dream: the narrator falls asleep and dreams of finding himself in a better England that is a revealing mixture of a medieval past and a communistic future.

Lawrence's escapist dreams also imply ameliorating action. "The Staff and Scrip" appears *in toto* in *Minorities*, his collection of favorite poems. C. Day Lewis finds in this collection a "taste . . . founded on what T. E. most liked at

---

9. British Library Add. MS 45903. Letter of 21 April 1927 to Charlotte F. Shaw.

his most impressionable age . . . a faintly Ninetyish-plus-Edwardian flavour" (T. E. Lawrence, *Minorities*, 14). However, even when the impressionable age was long past, Lawrence soaked in Morris's pseudomedieval prose tale *The Well at the World's End* (1896) as in a comforting hot bath (real hot baths being another Laurentian weakness, incidentally). His reaction to *The Well*, a tale of the search for eternal life that creates a dream "other" world, where pain is not, or where it is muffled, stylized, and does not discomfort the reader, could not be more revealing. "I sleep for two or three hours at a time in its pages. It is like a river of quietness over my head. . . . *The Well* should be read in such a form [i.e., the Chiswick Press edition]. I am trying to keep it free from the stains of our ordinary living here. Morris could not have been an airman."[10]

Neither Morris nor Lawrence was the timid maiden aunt these lines imply. Lawrence's gratitude for his pleasant dreams leads him to sentimentalize his hero. Morris certainly found relief in the world he created from the "real" one ("I know well the tendency at Queen Square to make life comfortable: anything rather than face death or a fact" said a friend [Hough, 128]), but he did become involved in politics. So, very differently, did Lawrence. Lawrence too had notions of what the world should be, notions derived from a native idealism and the reading of elevated literature. He attempted to put them into practice but was obliged occasionally to retreat from the world's incorrigible imperfection back to the literature, for further strength and comfort. "In my saddlebags was a *Morte d'Arthur*," he wrote at one of the desert campaign's lowest points. "It relieved my disgust" (*Seven Pillars* [1976], 385).

The first phase of the cycle of inspiration through literature, *engagement*, and retreat can be observed in a letter written seventeen years before the one quoted above. It is remarkably similar in content (down to the admiration for fine printing and the naming of a Morris prose romance), but the tone is more aspiring, more hopeful, unaware of man's capacity for intransigent evil.

> And it is lovely too, after you have been wandering for hours in the
> forest with Percivale or Sagramors le desirous, to open the door, and

10. British Library Add. MS 45903. Letter of 21 July 1927 to Charlotte F. Shaw.

from over the Cherwell to look at the sun glowering through the valley-mists. Why does one not like things if there are other people about? Why cannot one make one's books live except in the night, after hours of straining? . . . One needs books that will be worthy of what you are going to put into them. What would you think of a great sculptor who flung away his gifts on modelling clay or sand? Imagination should be put into the most precious caskets, & that is why one can only live in the future or the past, in Utopia, or the Wood beyond the World. . . . [I]f you can get the right book at the right time you taste joys—not only bodily, physical, but spiritual also. (*HL*, 110–11)

Here, then, we have the germ of Lawrence's impulsion to action in the desert, the link between the somewhat precious aspects of his medievalism and his studies of military fortification with their accompanying exercises in physical hardihood. That interests in fine printing, in such poems as Rossetti's "The Stream's Secret" (*HL*, 126), and in the aesthetics of medieval cathedrals coexisted with a capacity for military leadership and accomplishment is a principal source of Lawrence's enduring popular fascination. If he were just an aesthete or just a soldier he would be less generally interesting. His reluctance to accept the world about him and desire to escape in dream and idealistic action resulted from immersion in the Middle Ages.

Lawrence has taken us from the nineteenth-century revival to the works of the medieval period proper. We should now make some assessment of Lawrence's reading thereof.

I · V

LAWRENCE'S EARLY
MEDIEVAL READING

EARLY in 1920 Robert Graves met Lawrence at a guest-night at All Souls. The friendship between the two men developed to the point that Graves eventually became Lawrence's first biographer (unless we count the American journalist Lowell Thomas, whose sensational and unreliable account *With Lawrence in Arabia* came out in 1925). Lawrence did much to help Graves, who admits himself that "Two-thirds of the book was a mere condensation of *Seven Pillars* material" (*RGLH*, 1:47). Most of the rest of *Lawrence and the Arabs* (1927) came from Lawrence, who supplied notes and answered questions. Some of the notes concerned his earlier reading. "At Jesus read history, officially: actually spent nearly three years reading Provençal poetry, and Mediaeval French chansons de geste. When time came for degree wasn't prepared for exam" (*RGLH*, 1:48). Lawrence helped the military historian Basil Liddell Hart in the same way, if not to the same extent, and told Hart, a later biographer, that "I also read nearly every manual of chivalry. Remember that my 'period' was the Middle Ages, always" (*RGLH*, 2:50).

These claims went unexamined until Richard Aldington prepared his vitriolic *Lawrence of Arabia: A Biographical Enquiry*. Aldington's reaction to the man he came to regard as "phoney from start to finish" (MacNiven and Moore, 7), a "lazy little bastard (literally!)" (Benkovitz, 80), and a "filthy little lying bugger" (MacNiven and Moore, 20) resulted in a book that caused one of the twentieth century's more impressive literary storms. Friends of Lawrence like B. H. Liddell Hart rallied to his defense and attempted to rebut

Aldington's arguments in some detail. However Aldington, whose research had begun in 1951, was a formidable adversary:

> Is there anyone in Oxford left who would know about this French-Provençal claim? I looked through the list of his library [*BHF*, 476–510], which contains no Provençal texts, and a few chansons de geste in translations of modern French 're-writes' . . . and among them several books which have pre-war dates in his writing and are mentioned in the letters as bought during the French tours. (He is supposed to have lost a lot of books and posted many in bank letter boxes to get rid of them.) . . . The lack of French mediaeval texts—not a dozen—is surprising if he were such a scholar, but then he may have lost or sold them. (Benkovitz, 41)

A year later:

> A TEL query. Among other "thrasonical brags" he says he "read all the Manuals of Chivalry." Where are they? Perhaps he merely means the romans in langue d'oil (which I suspect he read in translation, there being several such and hardly any texts in his library) or perhaps Froissart? I am teased with a half-memory that Caxton issued a Boke of Chevalry . . . frm [*sic*] the Frenysshe. . . . I see Caxton did a Book of Curtesye and The Book of Good Manners, so perhaps Lawrence meant them. But are they "manuals of chivalry"? Could one say that of Christine de Pisan even? You will rightly infer from this that I strongly suspect even L's alleged erudition to be largely bogus.[1]

Let us take Lawrence's claims in the order in which Aldington here approaches them. The first of the paragraphs quoted above eventually appeared in the *Biographical Enquiry* (47): the same points are there made in more careful phrasing. Aldington observes that Lawrence makes only one reference to Provençal literature, "when he tells his younger brother, Wil-

---

1. *A Passionate Prodigality*, 57. The first ellipsis is present in the text. Benkovitz identifies the *Boke of Chevalry* as "possibly *The Order of Chivalry* (1484) or Christine de Pisan's *Fayttes of Armes and of Chyvalrye*, which Caxton translated and issued in 1489" (58, n. 4).

liam, 'if you can read history and Bertrand together you would not dream of following Ezra Pound.' 'Bertrand' of course is Bertrand de Born (whose castle Lawrence afterwards visited)[2] and the other reference presumably to Ezra Pound's poem *Altaforte*" (47).

Lawrence's claim of immersion in the poetry of the Provençal troubadours is indeed puzzling, and not only because of the paucity of references to it, or the absence of texts at Clouds Hill. It is true that Lawrence was at Oxford (1907–10) when Provençal literature was nearer the forefront of the general educated consciousness than it is now. Hugh Kenner, author of *The Pound Era: The Age of Ezra Pound, T. S. Eliot, James Joyce and Wyndham Lewis,* writes that there existed then a public (prepared by the work of Rossetti) for an inexpensive bilingual Dante, which went through many reprintings; and that H. J. Chaytor's *The Troubadours of Dante* (1902) "offered as much 'as any one is likely to require who does not propose to make a special study of Provençal.'" Kenner commented further that Pound's note to his 1908 poem "Na Audiart" ("Anyone who has read anything of the troubadours knows . . .") was "not swank"; Pound, in common with many of his contemporaries, read the troubadours avidly, and provided versions of Provençal poems in *Personae* (1909) and *Exultations* (1909)—both of which Lawrence possessed (76–77). Provençal scholarship had recently provided Carl Appel's *Provenzalische Chrestomathie* (1895), "a magnificent self-contained textbook with a grammar and as elaborate a glossary as one might require" (Kenner, 78), and important editions of several of the poets. Furthermore, Bertrand de Born had appeared memorably in Maurice Hewlett's *Richard Yea-and-Nay* (1900), a *vie romancée* of Coeur-de-Lion. Lawrence idolized Richard, of course, and thought Hewlett's novel "a masterpiece" (*HL*, 193). (He was later to lift one of its better phrases for *Seven Pillars*.) Remembering that Pound came to Oxford to lecture on Cavalcanti at the invitation of Will, T. E.'s younger brother, we see a strong current of interest in Provençal that might have carried Lawrence along with it.

If it did, however, it did not carry him so strongly that it left a discernable trace in his own writings. Even the more casual of *Seven Pillars*'s readers must note its author's obsession with chivalry, but one searches in vain for any interest in or reference to the one subject commonly associated with the

---

2. A mistake. Lawrence had already visited the castle.

Provençal poets (including those like Bertrand who also wrote about contemporary politics and the joys of war): courtly love. Lawrence is not interested in the relations between the sexes, and is most certainly not interested in the perfection of one particular woman or the nature of true love. "[F]rom end to end of it there was nothing female in the Arab movement, but the camels" (*Seven Pillars* [1976], 163). Women make few appearances in *Seven Pillars*, and Lawrence is hardly infatuated: Auda abu Tayi is surprised in his tent with a new wife, and "To gain ground with him, I began to jeer at the old man for being so old and yet so foolish like the rest of his race, who regarded our comic reproductive processes not as an unhygienic pleasure, but as a main business of life" (*Seven Pillars* [1976], 272). One group of women is greeted "with a humour I little understood—till I saw that, beside their legitimate profits of handicraft, the women were open to other advances" (*Seven Pillars* [1976], 409). Arabs may tell "love tales" around the hearth or the villagers may have "love verses" (*Seven Pillars* [1976], 151, 179), but with these tales and verses Lawrence has little to do.

Lawrence fought for two years with a people who might plausibly be presented as living a sort of nomadic equivalent of the knightly good life, complete with champions who distinguish themselves in the search for honor and women who are worthy objects of their love. The most revealing indication of Lawrence's attitude towards the latter is his reaction to a verse translation of early medieval Arabic poetry by Lady Anne Blunt and Wilfrid Scawen Blunt.

W. S. Blunt is noted by Girouard as another anachronistic knight-errant, whose political activities in Ireland and Egypt were prompted by motives that "could genuinely be described as chivalrous." In 1874 he visited the Arabs of Algeria and contrasted "their noble pastoral life on the one hand with their camel herds and horses, a life of high tradition filled with the memory of heroic deeds, and on the other hand the ignoble squalor of the Frank settlers with their wine shops and their swine" (Girouard, 271). In 1903 Blunt and his wife published a translation of *The Seven Golden Odes of Pagan Arabia, Also Known as the Moallakat.*[3] Legend states that these pre-Islamic poems were "set down in golden manuscript and hung up in the Kaaba at Mecca"

---

3. Lawrence wrote home from Cairo asking for a copy of this book on 20 February 1915 (*HL*, 303).

(Blunt, xvi), hence their name of "Golden Odes" or "Suspended Poems." I shall show later how Blunt's portrayal of the chivalrous courts of the Arabian peninsula influenced *Seven Pillars* and how Lawrence found in the *Moallakat* a justification for the fantasies he projected onto the Arabs (for fantasies, to some extent, they must have been). Suffice it to say here that Blunt insists in his introduction on the Arabic origin of chivalry and the importance of woman to that chivalrous society.

> The Arabs, therefore, had in their womenkind the material of a high romance, and they built on it the whole scheme of chivalry which we are accustomed to consider an exclusively Christian condition of things, but which in fact mediaeval Europe imitated and developed on lines of its own from the original Arab model, brought through Africa into Spain. Knight-errantry, the riding forth on horseback in search of adventures, the rescue of captive maidens, the succour rendered everywhere to women in adversity, all these were essentially Arabian ideas, as was the very name of *chivalry*, the connection of honourable conduct with the horse-rider, the man of noble blood, the cavalier. . . . Devotion to a woman nobly born . . . is the theme their poets love to dwell on. . . . It is the keynote initially struck of every poem of the Moallakat.
>
> . . . .
>
> There is no part of the earth's surface where love exists under such strenuous and enduring conditions as the Arabian desert, where the souls of man and woman are knit so closely by the immense isolation of their lives, where either becomes so dependent on the other by the constant pressure of material dangers. (Blunt, xiv)

Here then is Lawrence's chance. Here is the vindication for any love theme he may wish to introduce, and he does have something to say about love in the isolated desert. But there is one important difference between the two accounts. The following lines, arguably the most notorious in *Seven Pillars*, are much quoted, but must be quoted once more.

> The Arab was by nature continent; and the use of universal marriage had nearly abolished irregular courses in his tribes. The public

women of the rare settlements we encountered in our months of wandering would have been nothing to our numbers, even had their raddled meat been palatable to a man of healthy parts. In horror of such sordid commerce our youths began indifferently to slake one another's few needs in their own clean bodies—a cold convenience that, by comparison, seemed sexless and even pure. Later, some began to justify this sterile process, and swore that friends quivering together in the yielding sand with intimate hot limbs in supreme embrace, found there hidden in the darkness a sensual co-efficient of the mental passion whcih was welding our souls and spirits in one flaming effort. (*Seven Pillars* [1976], 9)

Blunt has the "souls" of a man and a woman "knit" together by the dangers and isolation of desert life; Lawrence has the "souls and spirits" of men "welded" together. Blunt is romantic (in one sense of that word) and heterosexual; Lawrence is political and homosexual.[4]

However, Lawrence's treatment of Blunt's comments about Arab love tells us even more about his attitude to heterosexual relationships. "Devotion to

4. Some mention should be made of the story first published by John E. Mack in *A Prince of Our Disorder*. It is an account (64–67) of Lawrence's alleged prewar proposal of marriage to a childhood friend, Janet Laurie, a proposal which was rejected. The story has not been considered credible by other Lawrence scholars. Desmond Stewart is reminded of the standard story of Algernon Swinburne's rejection by his cousin "Boo," and writes sardonically of the "unreliability of memory" (30n.). Jeffrey Meyers refers to "this absurd tale [which] is contradicted by everything we know about Lawrence's revulsion to homosexuality [*sic*, for heterosexuality]" ("Faithful are the Wounds," 506).

However, even if the story does not generally convince, it does provide more evidence of the pervasiveness of the Provençal ethos, at least in its chaste nineteenth-century form. E. F. Hall told Mack that Lawrence "worshipped [Janet] from afar" (Mack, 66). Perhaps—impelled less by heterosexual feelings than by an attitude toward life shaped by reading (and a feeling that this is what one does)—Lawrence did indeed make something like a proposal. (It should also be borne in mind that a woman known since childhood would be less sexually intimidating—more like a sister—than one met for the first time as an adult female.) Certainly the only other suggestion of Provence implies an idealistic, or credulously anachronistic, attitude on Lawrence's part. Asked by Robert Graves whether "troubadour" love was, in fact, always honorable ("whether it had ever happened, for instance, that two lovers, kept apart by rank or marriage, simulated a mystical bond as cover for mere sexual adventure"), Lawrence replied that he "thought not; its validity would immediately have been challenged by other men and women who had experienced true love themselves" (Graves, *Poetic Craft*, 191–92).

a woman nobly born," writes the elder man "of their own noble race and people, is the theme their poets love to dwell on, and always stands foremost in their scheme of romance. *It is the keynote initially struck of every poem of the Moallakat*" (Blunt and Blunt, xiv, my emphasis). Blunt here refers to the conventional opening of each of the Golden Odes, described by one ninth-century writer as follows:

> I have heard from a man of learning that the composer of Odes began by mentioning the desert dwelling-places and the relics and traces of habitation. Then he wept and complained and addressed the desolate encampment, and begged his companion to make a halt, in order that he might have occasion to speak of those who had once lived there and afterwards departed. . . . Then to this he linked the erotic prelude, and bewailed the violence of his love and the anguish of separation from his mistress and the extremity of his passion and desire, so as to win the hearts of his hearers and divert their eyes towards him and invite their ears to listen to him, since the song of love touches men's souls and takes hold of their hearts, God having put it in the constitution of his creatures to love dalliance and the society of women, in such wise that we find very few but are attached thereto by some tie or have some share therein, whether lawful or unpermitted.[5]

Blunt's description of the preoccupations of "Bedouin troubadours" (as he calls them) is a little shorter but no less intense.

> It is almost always the woman loved and lost that is mourned by them with the most passionate longing, for whom they perform their most glorious deeds, and whom they celebrate in their most enduring songs, the recollection of a short connubial season spent in the enormous solitude of the desert in some shut valley of the desolate hills green for those few sweet weeks of Spring and love, then lost and left unbeautiful forever. . . . In the open plain with its wild, parsimonious beauty, every bush and stone, every beetle and lizard,

---

5. Ibn Qutaiba (d. 889) in R. A. Nicholson's translation, quoted in A. J. Arberry, *Seven Odes*, 15.

every rare track of jerboa, gazelle or ostrich on the sand, becomes of value and is remembered, it may be years afterwards, while the stones of the camp-fires stand black and deserted in testimony of the brief season of love. (Blunt, xiv–xv)

Blunt writes incidentally of "the memorial stones of their encampments so touchingly remembered" (xvi).

Perhaps the first ode best illustrates in quotation what Ibn Qutaiba and Blunt were writing about.

> Weep, ah weep love's losing, love's with its dwelling-place
>   set where the hills divide Dakhuli and Haumali.
> Tudiha and Mikrat! There the hearth-stones of her
>   stand where the South and North winds cross-weave the sand-
>   furrows.
> See the white-doe droppings strewn by the wind on them,
>   black on her floors forsaken, fine-grain of pepper-corns.
> Here it was I watched her, lading her load-camels,
>   stood by these thorn-trees weeping tears as of colocynth.
> Here my twin-friends waited, called to me camel-borne:
>   Man! not of grief thou diest. Take thy pain patiently.
> Not though tears assuage thee, deem it beseemeth thee
>   thus for mute stones to wail thee, all thy foes witnesses.
> What though fortune flout thee! Thus Om Howeyrith did,
>   thus did thy Om Rebabi, fooled thee in Masali.
> O, where these two tented, sweet was the breath of them,
>   sweet as of musk their fragrance, sweet as garanfoli,
> Mourned I for them long days, wept for the love of them,
>   tears on my bosom raining, tears on my sword-handle.
> Yet, was I un-vanquished. Had I not happiness,
>   I, at their hands in Daret, Daret of Juljuli?
>
>   (Blunt and Blunt, 4)

In this instance, too, Lawrence remembered his mentor's words. A half-paragraph in *Seven Pillars* (1976) owes its existence to the conventional opening of the *Moallakat* odes. But in this case as in the first it is in the difference between source and transmuted version that the interest lies.

> These tailings of valleys running into Sirhan were always rich in grazing. When there was water in their hollows the tribes collected, and peopled them with tent-villages. The Beni Sakhr with us had so camped; and, as we crossed the monotonous downs they pointed first to one indistinct hollow with hearth and straight gutter-trenches and then to another saying, "There was my tent and there lay Hamdan el Saih. Look at the dry stones for my bed-place, and for Tarfa's next it. God have mercy upon her, she died the year of samh, in the Snainirat, of a puff-adder." (*Seven Pillars* [1976], 322)

Lawrence's lines are suggested by one of literature's classic expressions of a perennial emotion: poignant grief at the memory of lost, early love. Ibn Qutaiba, the ninth-century Arab, and W. S. Blunt, the twentieth-century Englishman, along with the poets who are their common source and inspiration: all surrender imaginatively. Lawrence, however, being one of those who do *not* "love dalliance and the society of women," one of those who are *not* "attached thereto by some tie," takes this promising situation and positively vulgarizes it, producing something not very far from the wry domestic comedy of the long-married: "God have mercy on her, she died the year of Samh, in the Snainirat, of a puff-adder." (Note the faint ludicrousness of the manner of Tarfa's death and its reporting.) Lawrence had little sympathy with the bliss of young heterosexual love. We shall see later that he borrows and homosexualizes another "medieval" account of idyllic and fugacious young love, when he uses the relationship of Daud and Farraj as an objective correlative for his memories of prewar Carchemish and Dahoum.

If Lawrence remembered any of the seven odes more than another when writing his lines, he remembered Zoheyr's, that is, the fourth.

> Here our hearth-stones stand, ay, blackened still with her cooking-pots,
> > here our tent-trench squarely graven, grooved here our camel trough.
>
> (Blunt and Blunt, 30)

Zoheyr's "hearth-stones" and "tent-trench squarely graven" suggest Lawrence's significantly anonymous Arab's "hearth," "straight gutter-trenches," and "dry stones."

We have wandered rather far from Aldington's doubts vis-à-vis Lawrence's learning. We may share the biographer's puzzlement at his subject's claim about Provençal literature, but it is much easier to find correspondences of interests, if not explicit references in letters and the recollections of friends, when we come to the *chansons de geste*. Shortly after Lawrence's death the magazine of his former college reprinted some reminiscences of the then Dean of Christ Church: "I remember a rare occasion when he came to a meeting of the College Literary Society: a paper was read on the Chanson de Roland. When it was over Lawrence spoke for about twenty minutes in his clear, quiet voice, ranging serenely about the epic poetry of several languages. It was all first hand: you felt that he had 'been there" (Edwards, 345). Lawrence carried the *Chanson de Roland* with him on his arduous 1911 walking tour (T. E. Lawrence, *Oriental Assembly*, 51). The epic poem tells the celebrated story of the bloody, steadfast resistance of Charlemagne's rear guard, treacherously caught in the passes of the Pyrenees by a numerically superior force of "pagans"; of the contrast between the fanatical Roland and the more reasoning Oliver; and of their eventual heroic deaths and Charlemagne's defeat—for the moment—of the enemy. It presents a world in which the important virtues are physical courage, physical prowess, and completeness and strength of conviction.

In the world of the *Chanson* there is no place for what Lawrence was to call "doubt, our modern crown of thorns" (*Seven Pillars* [1976], 16). Written in the ardor of a Crusading age (probably toward the end of the eleventh century), the *Chanson* recounts the transcendentally sanctioned exploits of Christian warriors, who must protect the faith at all costs.

> Paien unt tort e chrestïens unt dreit.
>
> (line 1015)
>
> [Pagans are in the wrong and Christians are in the right.]
> (Brault translation)

Ferez i, Francs, nostre est li premers colps!
Nos avum dreit, mais cist glutun unt tort.   AOI
                                        (lines 1211–12)

[Strike, Franks, the first blow is ours!
We are in the right and these wretches are in the
wrong.]
                                        (Brault translation)

Divine approval of and support for the actions of Roland and the men under
his command—the killing of many thousands of pagans, whose souls are
then dragged off to Hell—is made clear by Archbishop Turpin.

Clamez vos culpes, si preiez Deu mercit!
Asoldrai vos pur voz anmes guarir.
Se vos murez, esterez seinz martirs,
Sieges avrez el greignor pareïs.
Franceis decendent, a tere se sunt mis,
E l'arcevesque de Deu les beneïst:
Par penitence les cumandet a ferir.
                                        (lines 1132–38)
[Say your confessions and pray for God's mercy!
"I will absolve you to save your souls.
If you die you'll be holy martyrs,
You'll have seats in highest Paradise."
The French dismount, they knelt to the ground,
And the Archbishop blessed them in God's name.
For a penance, he commands them to strike.]
                                        (Brault translation)

It is also manifested by such divine interventions as the Almighty's sending
three angels to bring Roland's soul up to Heaven when he finally succumbs
to death; and by his protracting the daylight, which enables Charlemagne to
complete his rout of the enemy hordes.

Lawrence could not have failed to take the point that the eleventh-century
Christian warrior knew his place in the world, or rather the universe. But the

winning and keeping of that place involved the practice of a ferocious and unflinching physical courage. The long-standing critical debate on Roland's *desmesure* (summarized in Brault, 10–15) has centered on who is "right" in the oliphant scene: Roland, who considers that to blow the oliphant would be an admission of failure and bring shame on him and his descendents; or Oliver, who urges the recall of the main army, and represents a courage as great but more realistic, more prepared to compromise. Brault has claimed that "Roland has no fault or flaw and makes no mistake" (xiii). However unsympathetic he may sometimes be to us, he embodies submission to the will of God, and as perfect a discharge of feudal and Christian obligations as can be attained.

But the world of the *chansons* combines this martial service to God with detailed descriptions of the inevitable results of fighting: physical exhaustion, and cruel, ghastly wounds usually resulting in death. The warriors of the *chansons* need a strong arm as well as a strong faith; the result of meeting someone stronger is clearly described in *Roland* and elsewhere.

> [Oliver] vait ferir un paien, Malun.
> L'escut li freint, ki est ad or e a flur,
> Fors de la teste le met les oilz ansdous,
> E la cervele li chet as piez desuz
> Mort le tresturnet od tut. VII.C. des lur
>
> (lines 1353–57)
>
> [Oliver goes to strike a pagan, Malon,
> He smashes his shield, ornamented with gold and a flower design,
> He knocks both eyes out of his head
> And his brains spill down over his feet,
> He tumbles him over dead with seven hundred of their men]
>
> (Brault translation)

> Defors sun cors veit gesir la buele,
> Desuz le frunt li buillit la cervele.
>
> (lines 2247–48)
>
> He sees his entrails spilled outside his body,
> His brain is oozing out beneath his forehead.
>
> (Brault translation)

Tels set cenz homes trovent de lur terre,
Entre lur pez trainant lur bowele;
Par mi lur buches issent fors lur cerveles
E de lur escuz se courent sur l'erbe;
Trubles unt les vis e palles les meisseles,
Turnez les oilz qui sistrent as testes;
Gement e criant cels qui les almes i perdent.

(McMillan, 1, 25)

They found seven hundred of their fellows, their entrails trailing between their feet, brains coming out of their mouths and running down the shields on to the grass; their faces were contorted and their cheeks pale, their eyes turning back in their heads, they moaned and cried as their souls departed from them. (Muir, 89)

The world of the *Chanson de Roland* and that of *Seven Pillars* may be compared in several ways, but Lawrence was eventually to decide that he possessed neither a strong arm nor a strong faith, whatever may have been his outlook as he unnecessarily walked himself into exhaustion in the summer of 1911.

The *chansons de geste* are certainly not the "manuals of chivalry" that Aldington wondered about when writing the *Biographical Enquiry*. Granted, one reference in *Roland* shows that a code is beginning to develop:

Li quens Rollant . . .
Dunc ad parled a lei de chevaler
(lines 751–52)
[Count Roland . . .
spoke as a true knight]
(Brault translation)

Nonetheless, the "connection of honourable conduct with the horse-rider, the man of noble blood, the cavalier" (to echo Blunt) would later become more elaborate, eventually overelaborate, decadent, and rococo. Aldington's difficulties with the "Manuals of Chivalry" ("Where are they? Perhaps he merely means . . .") are difficulties of definition. Caxton's translations, Christine de Pisan's original *Le Livre des Faits d'Armes et de Chevalerie*, and such works as Honoré Bonet's *L'Arbre des Batailles* (c. 1387)—itself one of Christine's sources—may, or may not, properly be described as "manuals of chivalry," if we admit that such things ever existed. One cannot prove that Lawrence ever read them, although one suspects that he did. It is, however, possible to show that Lawrence did read three more or less overtly didactic works, works that extolled and inculcated the ethos of chivalry.

One of these works is relatively slight. Shortly before the outbreak of war, Lawrence's brother Will wrote home from India, where he was teaching, asking that a passage from one of T. E.'s books be copied out and sent to him, for "a popular exposition of chivalry." (It is, incidentally, additional evidence to support Girouard's thesis that the brother who most resembled T. E.—"They were like twins" (*HL*, 394)—should be telling the ruled or rulers or both in the empire's most prized possession about chivalry.) "[F]ind a book in *Everyman's Library* called *Mediaeval Stories and Romances* or some such name, look at the end of it for a story called 'Sir Guy de Tabarie,' and copy out for me what Sir Guy says to Saladin about the Rule of Chivalry. Just a short piece of the style of Tennyson's 'Sir Gareth' 'live pure, right wrong, etc' " (*HL*, 555).

"Sir Hugh de Tabarie" (Mason, *Aucassin and Nicolette*, 85–90) is a six-page tale about the hero's brief stay in Saracen captivity. Sir Hugh is persuaded to explain to Saladin "in what fashion a man was made knight of the Christian chivalry" (Mason, *Aucassin and Nicolette*, 86). He trims Saladin's hair and beard; causes him "to enter within a bath," that he may leave it symbolically "pure of all stain and villainy"; lays him in a bed to represent the rest in Heaven to be won by chivalrous efforts; clothes him in white for bodily cleanliness and then red for the blood he must shed in defense of God and His Church; gives him brown shoes to represent the earth to which he will return, and a white belt for chastity and golden spurs for eagerness in battle. Then comes the sword and its three lessons, the explanation of which provides the paragraph Will had remembered.

> Courage, justice and loyalty. The cross at the hilt of his sword gives courage to the bearer, for when the brave knight girds his sword upon him he neither can, nor should, fear the strong Adversary

himself. Again, sire, the two sharp edges of the blade teach loyalty and justice, for the office of chivalry is this, to sustain the weak against the strong, the poor before the rich, uprightly and loyally. (88)

Sir Hugh feels he cannot give his captor the accolade, the blow upon the neck with the sword. The story ends with Saladin providing half of the sum he had himself fixed as the Christian knight's ransom, while the Saracen lords give so generously toward the rest that Sir Hugh presently rides away free.

A number of points should be made about this story. It appears in a popular collection, led off by the well-known *Aucassin and Nicolette*, and with an amiable Introduction in which the translator writes, "Not being a scholar myself, I have no pretension to write for scholars. My object is more modest. I have tried to bring together a little garland for the pleasure of the amateurs of beautiful tales. To me these mediaeval stories are beautiful, and I have striven to decant them from one language into another with as little loss as may be. To this end I have refined a phrase, or, perhaps, softened an incident here and there" (xvi–xvii). We need not share Aldington's opinion of Lawrence's scholarship simply because the latter bought some of the Everyman series.[6] But we should note that Lawrence's attitude to foreign languages in particular was pragmatic, not ambitiously scholarly or rigorous. He unblushingly read translations[7] and cheerfully wrote Greek without accents and French with the wrong ones. Maurice Larès writes that Lawrence's French reveals "une ignorance grammaticale et un manque de rigueur affligeants" (304).

Second, the English into which Mason translates his tales now seems dated and coy. "Sir Hugh" alone includes "I am more fain," "vesture," "vermeil," "cincture," "girded withal," and "glaive." Lawrence was to introduce some late-nineteenth-century archaisms into *Seven Pillars*; some phrases from his translation of the *Odyssey* (which he came to consider spuriously archaic) would not be out of place in Mason's volume. Third, although heavy with

6. Lawrence also probably possessed Mason's Everyman translation of Marie de France, *French Mediaeval Romances From the Lays of Marie de France*.

7. A. W. Lawrence remembers his brother reading translations, including *Huon de Bordeaux* and *The Four Sons of Aymon* (*BHF*, 585).

symbolism and moral uplift, the story makes no attempt at tedious specificity (Christine de Pisan addresses herself mostly to specific military problems). Lastly, the emphasis on the sword—that sword which the Church tried to insist should be used only in her defense or the defense of the weak, and laid back on the altar at the death of its possessor—justifies and exalts righteous war. The sword makes literal and figurative appearances in *Seven Pillars*; indeed, the words "the sword also means clean-ness & death" were stamped on the cover of the 1935 edition, this phrase being a slight misquotation of one in a postwar letter (*Letters*, 372).

The second didactic work is Antoine de la Sale's *Le Petit Jehan de Saintré*, "a xv Cent. novel of knightly manners—very good" (*HL*, 110), which Lawrence read in 1910. *Le Petit Jehan*, which tells of the education in courtesy and chivalry of a young page, is the product of an old man living at the end of the chivalric age. (La Sale was born c. 1386 and died c. 1460; *Jehan* dates from c. 1459.) We are now very far from the bloody endurance of *Roland*; Jehan grows up in a rich, polished, and self-conscious society, which seems to have forgotten the raison d'être of chivalry and to regard it and its adjuncts (such as heraldry) as a superior social game. La Sale, a former tutor of the princely, with a sentimental esteem for the chivalric tradition and a gentle, scholarly interest in heraldry—chapter 58 consists largely of a list of the names and arms, properly blazoned, of the knights who allegedly accompanied Saintré on Crusade (but one cannot easily imagine blood and brains dripping down *these* shields)—presents a society fossilized into ceremonious observance of "knightly" rites. Money and ostentation are more important than valor and martial competence. When Saintré leaves Paris to seek adventure and honor, he is part of a gorgeous procession of trumpeters, knights, squires, and officers of arms, who see him off. Saintré buys most of them dinner at Bourg-la-Reine, where he lodges the first night, "Et au matin leur donna cinquante escuz"[8] [and in the morning gave unto them fifty crowns] (Gray, 130). A certain Polish knight is ambitious for honor, but money, apparently, he already has.

8. J. Marie Guichard, ed., *L'Hystoyre et Plaisante Cronique du Petit Jehan de Saintré et de la jeune Dame des belles Cousines*, 95. I have not been able to examine the edition read by Lawrence and found in Clouds Hill at his death, but that too reproduces the text established by Guichard.

[Il] portoit, pour emprise d'armes à cheval et à pié, deux cercles d'or: l'ung au dessus du coulde du bras senestre, et l'aultre au dessus du coup du pié, tous deux enchainez d'une assez longue chayne d'or, et ce par l'espace de cinq ans, se, entre deux, il ne trouvoit chevalier ou escuyer de nom et d'armes, sans reproche, qui le delivrast des armes qui s'ensuyvent. (Guichard, 136)

[He] wore, as challenge to combats on horseback and on foot, two bracelets of gold, the one above the elbow of his left arm, and the other above his ankle, the two chained together with a middling long chain of gold; and this for the space of five years, unless in the mean while he should find a knight or squire of blood and coat-armour, without reproach, to deliver him by arms, as hereafter followeth. (Gray, 174)

The knight's detailed challenge stipulates that the loser of the prescribed combats on horseback must give the winner "ung dyamant, sur la place, du pris de trois cens escus ou au dessus;" the loser of "les poulx des lances a pié" gives a ruby of the same value; and so on.

Yet one can see the appeal Lawrence found in the "very good" book. La Sale is credulous, naive, and perhaps a little foolish—and about seventy years old. But there is nothing shameful in his obvious longing for "[le] bon temps . . . dont l'en tenoit assez plus de compte que l'en ne fait aujourd'hui" (Guichard, 219, 127) [the good times . . . (when) men held such matters (of chivalric ceremony) of more account than they do at this present time] (Gray, 254, 164). Nor is there anything shameful in his belief that "par ainsi escouter et retenir les nobles hystoires, exemples et enseignements, pourrez acquerir la pardurable joye de paradis, honneur en armes, honneur en sens, et honneur en richesses, et vivre liement et honnorablement" (Guichard, 72) [by thus reading, hearkening to and remembering noble histories, ensamples and teachings, you may acquire the everlasting joys of Paradise, honour in arms, honour in wisdom and honour in riches, and live worshipfully and cheerfully] (Gray, 105), although there is much that is dangerous. The woman who becomes his paramour instructs Saintré in love, honor, and the social graces; Saintré and Lawrence take in what she says.

The third "manual of chivalry" is of even later date. There are no references in Lawrence's writings to *The Right Joyous and Pleasant History of the Feats, Gests, and Prowesses of the Chevalier Bayard, The Good Knight Without Fear and Without Reproach, By the Loyal Servant*, to give it its full title. But a copy of the Newnes's Pocket Classics edition, translated by Sara Coleridge, was found at Clouds Hill with the inscription "T.E.L. Beyrout 1911" (*BHF*, 478). Bayard is almost the eponym of fearlessness and chivalrous scrupulousness, and his exploits in France and Italy are well known. The Loyal Servant's account of his life provides examples of luxurious ritual similar to those in *Saintré*,[9] but Bayard spent much of his career in action and his achievements cannot be denied. Unfortunately, the most significant part of his story may be the manner of his death. Retreating slowly before the enemy while brandishing his sword, Bayard was struck by a stone, discharged from an early form of artillery, the *hacquebouze*. When this can happen, the end of chivalric war is nigh, as Bayard himself seems to have realized: "It appeared that Bayard foresaw the kind of death that awaited him. He hated the arquebusiers to such a degree that he never pardoned any who fell into his hands, 'it being a great heartsore to him (says one of our old writers) that a valiant man should be slain by a paltry pitiful ragamuffin.' "[10]

Lawrence agreed. " 'The Battle of Crécy—1346—was the beginning of the end,' he once told [Robert Graves]. 'Those two primitive cannon we used against the French eventually sacrificed the most honourable element in war—hand-to-hand fighting—to the practical advantage of scientific slaughter.' "[11] Lawrence, in fact, went further, and considered armor unfair. "Such imputed dignities [titles such as "Prince" and "Bey"], like body armour in a duel, were no doubt useful; but uncomfortable, and mean, too" (*Seven Pillars* [1976], 354). In the 1922 edition he makes the same point more strongly: "and larding me with titles, which always seemed to me a cowardice—like

9. Cf. Coleridge, 50, with its suggestion of a tourney as a means to honor.

10. "Notes by the French Editors," Coleridge, 354. Also in Coleridge, there occurs an incident in which German knights refuse to attack a breach made by artillery—on the grounds that they are gentlemen.

11. Graves, *Poetic Craft*, 198. But cf. Oman: "We need not pay much heed to the statements of Villani and the *Grandes Chroniques de France* that the English had two or three small cannon in their front line, which scared the Genoese and the horses of the men-at-arms. It is most unlikely that cannon could have been brought across France with the field army at such an early date: we do not find them used in the field for many years later. Moreover no English chronicler mentions them" (611n).

body-armour in a duel" (194). This is an idealistic and anachronistic attitude indeed: Lawrence insists on the supreme value of individual skill, strength, and courage, and their validity as arbiters in disputes.

But, the *Moallakat* excepted, we have so far been dealing with relatively minor works. What ideas about chivalry does Malory hold? What does the impressionable young reader pick up from his writings? As a young man Lawrence possessed the Everyman edition of Malory, with an Introduction by the principal of his college, John Rhys, that discussed the Welsh origins of the Arthurian cycle. It is on record that when the Winchester MS was discovered in 1934 an aircraftman on a motorcycle showed interest in the discovery (Bennett, vi–vii). The best-known and most influential version of the matter of Britain (paradoxically written by one who in his own life outraged in acts of theft, rape, and attempted murder the ethos he so memorably enshrined), the *Morte d'Arthur* has become institutionalized in England as the most complete, pleasing, and uplifting account of the rise and fall of Arthur's kingdom, extracts from which are considered suitable both for schoolboy reading and for public recitation at the death of kings.

Malory presents a world in which knighthood imposes certain obligations: one must not fight at an unfair advantage ("When the knight saw that, he alit, for him thought no worship to have a knight at such avail, he to be on horseback and he on foot" [Malory 1:41]); one must show mercy ("Thou new-made knight, thou hast shamed thy knighthood, for a knight without mercy is dishonoured" [1:79]); one must keep one's promise even at the risk of one's life (Arthur, refusing to surrender because he has promised to fight "to the uttermost, by the faith of my body, while me lasteth the life," says that he "had lever to die with honour than to live with shame" [1:103]). Something like a formulated code exists. When Arthur "stablished all his knights, and them that were of lands not rich, he gave them lands," he also "charged them never to do outrageousity nor murder, and always to flee treason; also, by no means to be cruel, but to give mercy unto him that asketh mercy, upon pain of forfeiture of their worship and lordship of King Arthur for evermore; and always to do ladies, damosels, and gentlewomen succour, upon pain of death. Also, that no man take no battles in a wrongful quarrel for no law, nor for no world's goods" (1:89–90). When the code is outraged, Lancelot speaks with genuine anger: "What? . . . is he a thief and a knight and a ravisher of women? he doth shame unto the order of knighthood, and contrary unto his oath; it is pity that he liveth" (1:165). Lancelot himself embodies a kind of excellence, although a flawed one. Sir Hector's lament over his brother's body expresses the code in its late-medieval, courtly-military form.

> Ah Launcelot . . . thou were head of all Christian knights, and now I dare say . . . thou Sir Launcelot, there thou liest, that thou were never matched of earthly knight's hand. And thou were the courteoust knight that ever bare shield. And thou were the truest friend to thy lover that ever bestrad horse. And thou were the truest lover of a sinful man that ever loved woman. And thou were the kindest man that ever struck with sword. And thou were the goodliest person that ever came among press of knights. And thou was the meekest man and the gentlest that ever ate in hall among ladies. And thou were the sternest knight to thy mortal foe that ever put spear in the rest." (2:400)

The single qualification here—"thou were the truest lover *of a sinful man* that ever loved woman"—refers, of course, to Lancelot's adultery with the wife of his chief and friend. P. E. Tucker, in "Chivalry in the *Morte*," has written that Malory found his sources' preoccupation with love, if not quite so alien as Lawrence found the subject, then at least sufficiently distasteful to be changed in his own version. Malory, increasingly disturbed at his growing realization that Lancelot is not only "the greatest exemplar of knighthood" (Bennett, 72), but also Guinevere's lover, and constitutionally unable to believe that his fervor in the latter role inspires his prowess in the former, eventually evolves a new way of telling an old tale. The victories that Lancelot wins are in spite of, not because of, his love for Guinevere; he has promised to be her knight "in right *other in wrong*" (my emphasis) as he tells her twice. His failures in the quest for the Holy Grail are not due to the sins of unchastity and homicide, as in the French source, but to an instability of purpose caused by privy thoughts of Guinevere. This aspect of Lancelot's private experience during the quest is Malory's addition: "And if I had not had my privy thoughts to return to your love again as I do, I had seen as great mysteries as ever saw my son Galahad, outher Percivale, or Sir Bors" (2:272).

Whether Lawrence read Malory sufficiently closely to pick up his differences from the *Queste del Saint Graal*, which we know him to have carried and, presumably, read, during the 1909 walk, is difficult to decide. The point is finally unimportant, partly because Lawrence has already shown his ability to leave or change that which does not appeal to him, partly because Malory retains enough of the spirit of his original to make it clear that virginity is of the highest value in the quest, despite the acts of physical love frankly acknowledged in previous stories. (The values of the quest story, coming toward the end of the book, immediately before the catastrophe, tend to overwhelm, for example, the desires of Sir Gareth and Dame Lyonesse.) Lawrence will have taken pleasure in knightly adventures, knightly courtesy, and vigorously described battles; he will not have been offended by Sir Percivale's stabbing himself in the thigh after the near loss of his virginity. In fact, Sir Percivale's words ("Sithen my flesh will be my master I shall punish it" [2:204]) would have reminded him of the Egyptian cenobite attitudes he always found so sympathetic.

Reading Malory in the desert during the war, Lawrence must often have seen coincidences between actions and beliefs on the printed page before him and the actions and beliefs of the living men around him. Most important, Malory's knights and Lawrence's Arabs both show an interest in reputation and honor, terms often subsumed by the earlier writer, and sometimes by the later, under the word *worship*. In little matters, an unfailing courteous formality of speech, especially in greetings, is natural to Malorian knights and twentieth-century Arabs, but rings strangely in modern occidental ears. The words of Sir Percivale and "an olde man" on meeting ("Sir," says the former, "ye be welcome." "God keep you," replies the latter. "And of whence be ye?" [2:200]) might almost have been translated word by word from the Arabic. Lawrence would have heard almost those exact expressions thousands of times. In greater matters, family and clan are important to Malory's characters and Lawrence's companions in a way they are no longer important to us. Kin confers privileges and exacts obligations. Lawrence, in a humorous mood, writes home from prewar Carchemish describing typical problems:

> And then there is the case of the good and so privileged workman, who brings each day a new one of his seven brethren and 49 cousins, all afire to work (our wages are so good) and the case of the man

embroiled with the overseer, both parties calling Allah to witness that
the other is entirely in the wrong ("And if I did strike him with a pick-
handle," said Abdo Jadur, "where is the harm? Is he not the son of my
sister's aunt at law?") (*HL*, 170–71)

Such men would have understood when the ties of kinship demand revenge.
Sir Lamorak's and Sir Gaheris's dispute is most readily understood if set out
in dramatic form:

> SIR LAMORAK. Ah, Sir Gaheris, knight of the Table Round, foul and evil
> have ye done, and to you great shame. Alas, why have ye slain your
> mother that bare you? with more right ye should have slain me.
> SIR GAHERIS. The offence hast thou done . . . notwithstanding a man is
> born to offer his service; but yet shouldst thou beware with whom
> thou meddlest, for thou hast put me and my brethren to a shame,
> and thy father slew our father; and thou to lie by our mother is too
> much shame for us to suffer. And as for thy father, King Pellinore,
> my brother Sir Gawaine and I slew him.
> SIR LAMORAK. Ye did him the more wrong . . . for my father slew not
> your father. . . . and as yet my father's death is not revenged.
> SIR GAHERIS. Leave those words . . . for an thou speak feloniously I will
> slay thee. But by cause thou art naked I am ashamed to slay thee.
> But wit thou well, in what place I may get thee I shall slay thee; and
> now my mother is quit of thee. (2:14)

Conversely, Sir Lamorak and Sir Gaheris would have understood the suicidal
actions of Tallal after the massacre at his home village of Tafas (*Seven Pillars*
[1976], 504–7). Sometimes medieval literature did give Lawrence an accurate
idea of what he would find in the Middle East.

· V ·

THE
IMPACT
OF
W. S. BLUNT

In the last chapter of *The Return to Camelot: Chivalry and the English Gentleman* (275–93), Mark Girouard describes how the outbreak of the First World War was greeted with something approaching joy by a people who saw in it an antidote to "old hysterical mock-disease" (the phrase is from the lines about the Crimean War in Tennyson's *Maud*). The ideals of chivalry implied struggle, and the metaphor of the fight—against impurity within oneself and unrighteousness in others—inevitably falsified real armed struggle. In blissful, idealistic ignorance, people looked forward to a glorious and God-approved victory, accompanied by cavalry charges, over the German bully. For the first time in a century (the Crimean and Boer and various minor colonial wars not, apparently, having impinged greatly on the general consciousness, or taught any lessons) the youth—especially the educated youth—of the nation could prove themselves. Lawrence's youngest brother remembered the mood: "The whole world was their oyster and seemed sure to go on being so till the end of time. . . . Rupert Brooke's 'Now, God be thanked Who has matched us with His hour' expressed the general relief of [my brother] Frank's friends at having something big enough to do, when the war started."[1]

The poem A. W. Lawrence refers to is "1914: Peace." Cognate with those

1. A. W. Lawrence to John E. Mack, 1 November 1968. Quoted in Mack, 130. F. H. Lawrence was an undergraduate at Jesus College at the outbreak of war, when he was given his commission. He was killed in France on 9 May 1915.

such as W. E. Henley's *Song of the Sword*, and Herbert Asquith's "The
Volunteer" (Girouard, 276, 284), the poem continues:

> And caught our youth, and wakened us from sleeping.
> With hand made sure, clear eye, and sharpened power,
> To turn, as swimmers into cleanness leaping,
> Glad from a world grown old and cold and weary,
> Leave the sick hearts that honour could not move,
> And half-men, and their dirty songs and dreary,
> And all the little emptiness of love!
>
> (Mack, 486)

T. E. Lawrence himself wrote at the time that "Not many dons have taken
commissions—but 95% of the undergraduates have taken or applied for
them."[2]

The rest of Girouard's chapter and the literary history of the war show
how these elevated expectations of chivalric fighting were disappointed by
the mud, squalor, and slaughter of Flanders. But if the three of Lawrence's
brothers who fought in France knew a war that had less and less to do with
color, excitement, and individual courage and skill, and more and more to
do with bloody stalemate, barbed wire, and mustard gas, then T. E. himself
did not, as E. M. Forster recalled.

> He has also contributed to sociology, in recording what is probably
> the last of the picturesque wars. Camels, pennants, the blowing up of
> little railway trains by little charges of dynamite in the desert—it is
> unlikely to recur. Next time the aeroplane will blot out everything in
> an indifferent death, but the aeroplane in this yarn is only a visitor,
> which arrives in the last chapters to give special thrills. A personal
> note can still be struck. . . . Because it was waged under archaistic
> conditions, the Arab revolt is likely to be remembered. It is the last
> effort of the war-god before he laid down his godhead, and turned
> chemist. (170)

2. T. E. Lawrence to James Elroy Flecker, 3 December 1914. Houghton Library, Harvard
University. Quoted in Mack, 130.

When, after the war, the American publicist Lowell Thomas gave a series of lectures that concentrated on a romanticized version of the campaign, he found ready listeners. Thomas had failed to find in Europe any material that would help persuade the United States to enter the war, but Lawrence and the Arabs could be represented as everything that the combattants of France so obviously were not. Although much of Thomas's appeal is to the infatuation with the "mystery of the East," he realized too that the British public had been stunned by the contrast between what they had expected and what they had experienced. Lawrence benefited from the gratitude of starved appetites suddenly satisfied, as the prewar reverence for gallantry and chivalrous gentlemen again found what seemed a worthy object.

But this is to anticipate. Lawrence, like the rest of his generation, entered the war not knowing whether he would survive it. He entered it sharing the patriotism of the rest of the country, intensified in his case not only by his years of chivalric reading and the aspirations of the educated young, but also by the compensatory impetus toward exemplary conduct provided by his mother. When Mrs. Lawrence took the death of Frank badly, T. E. reminded her of the obligation to keep a brave face.

> [I]n any case to die for one's country is a sort of privilege.
>
> There, put that aside, & bear a brave face to the world about Frank. In a time of such fearful stress in our country it is one's duty to watch very carefully lest one of the weaker ones be offended: and you know we were always the stronger, & if they see you broken down they will all grow fearful about their ones at the front. (*HL*, 304)

So the house (the hothouse, one is tempted to say) sent three sons to France (two of whom died there) to fight in a twentieth-century conflict that mocked the juxtaposition of war and glory. T. E. Lawrence, however, was more fortunate. He fought in a part of the world that, especially at the beginning of the war, was relatively unaffected by European civilization.

In 1920 Lawrence was to publish an article that noted in part the changes wrought in the Middle East by the interests and presence of European powers.[3] "The Changing East" rehearses some of the themes of *Seven Pillars*

---

3. "The Changing East," reprintd in T. E. Lawrence, *Oriental Assembly*, 67–97.

of Wisdom, such as the way in which nationalism replaced religion as the faith worth fighting and dying for. Europe, writes Lawrence, had the chance to progress gradually over hundreds of years. In the matter of transport, for example, she developed in stages, from pack-horses to solid wheels to springless wagons, on to the culmination of the aeroplane. Asia made the same leap in a generation, "from saddle-donkeys to Rolls-Royce cars, from blood-mares to aeroplanes" (73). More to the point is the replacement of antique arms by more scientific and deadly weapons. "We grew by slow stages of muskets from bows to automatic guns: it took us five hundred years. The marauder of the desert laid away his spear just before the war, and to-day goes out on his raids with a Maxim. . . . The Asia of Kinglake and Lamartine is wholly gone. Our eyes show us this, and some of us, the mediaevalists, lament it" (73–74).

Lawrence the medievalist knew in 1920 that one of the few societies in the world that until then could legitimately be portrayed as anachronistically "medieval" was no more. We must examine how he depicts that society in the mannered and ambitious *Seven Pillars*, and what justification there is for the depiction in Lawrence's own less fraught works and in the writings and recollections of others. It will be enlightening to deal with the sword, which was the symbol of war, the badge of the warrior (or officer class)—and, in the Middle East up to the end of the First World War, a weapon actually to be used.

Although the sword may have been a mere symbol elsewhere (in *August, 1914*, Solzhenitsyn describes swords flapping uselessly in their scabbards against officers' legs, the real fighting being performed with more modern weapons), it was very much a fact in the region Lawrence calls Western Asia. In a report written for the Arab Bureau—the group of specialists in Cairo who concerned themselves with the Arabs and their relations with each other and the outside world—he records that "before this war they [Hejazi tribesmen] had slow old muskets, and they have not yet appreciated fully the uses of a magazine rifle. They would not use bayonets, but enjoy cutting with swords" (T. E. Lawrence, *Secret Despatches*, 32). This information is supported by W. S. Blunt, who, writing thirteen or so years earlier, observes of the words "His hand became cut by the bowstring" in the *Golden Odes* that "It is not easy to ascertain at what date the bow ceased to be used in Bedouin warfare, nor the reason of its having ceased. It is not that the bow had been replaced by fire-arms, for among the great fighting tribes firearms are still practically unknown, or were so a generation back" (64). Blunt also writes: "The sword is only used by the Bedouins when dismounted. Fire-arms thirty years ago were almost unknown among the great horse-owning tribes of Nejd, but are now more common, to the growing detriment of their horse-breeding. In the hill-country of Hejaz [where Lawrence fought at the beginning of the campaign] and Yemen match-locks [Lawrence's "slow old muskets"] have long been in use" (60). In the notes to the *Moallakat*, Blunt describes another antique arm: the lance. "The Bedouin rider carries his lance, a hollow bamboo cane fourteen to sixteen feet long, over his shoulder in time of peace, the point of it behind him and the butt, which is also shod with iron, but bluntly, in front. When fighting he reverses it, using it not under-handed as our European lancers do, but over-handed, brandished and shaken above his head. Thus the Norman knights are represented in the Bayeux tapestry").[4] Lawrence does not write of Arab lancers in *Seven Pillars*, but his comment above about "laying away spears" is suggested by Blunt. The sword, however, does appear literally and metaphorically in *Seven Pillars*, as will be seen. What it implies about Arab society is both vindicated by the reports of W. S. Blunt the traveler and partially inspired by W. S. Blunt the poet.

Let us examine the source before coming to the work of the apt pupil. Lawrence had written home from Cairo for *The Seven Golden Odes of Pagan Arabia, Also Known as the Moallakat* in February 1915, three months before Frank was killed by some form of bullet and eight months before Will was shot down in an airplane. The poems provided external sanction for Lawrence's view of the Arabs as a people who act in the best chivalric traditions, and whose struggle is for a noble end. This view of the Arabs is itself the product of Lawrence's profound need to idealize life, or his actions, or himself.

It would not be true to say that the need was lifelong. But the Blunts' obscure little volume, which disappointed their hopes of a success as great as that of FitzGerald's *Rubáiyát of Omar Khayyám* forty years previously, did play a part in another Western popularization of the mysterious East. As will

---

4. Blunt, 59–60. Plate 6 of Marc Bloch's *Feudal Society* (vol. 2) is a representation of part of the Bayeux tapestry in which both styles can be seen.

be shown in some detail, phrases and ideas from the book were in Lawrence's mind when he came to write *Seven Pillars*, but he also remembered the *Moallakat* in the talks he and Lowell Thomas had about the articles the latter was writing and the biography of Lawrence he would eventually undertake. The style of the following extract from Thomas's *With Lawrence in Arabia* (1925) is unmistakably the author's. But there can be no doubt about the source of his information. The quotation constitutes a sort of poor man's guide to the *Golden Odes* and the part played by poetry and poets in Arab life.

> Certain statesmen of world prominence choose detective stories for their moments of relaxation; Prince Feisal, in the lull between campaigns, refreshes himself for renewed battle and the cares of state with classical Arabic poetry. His favourite poet is Imr el Kais, the most renowned of all Arab bards, who lived just before Mohammed, and who wrote about camels, the desert, and love. Among Feisal's other favourites are Ibn Isham, Ibn el Ali, Zuhair, Zarafa, Al Harith, and Mutanabbi, great writers of the Middle Ages, when Arabian learning and culture penetrated to the most remote corners of Europe. Mutanabbi's couplet must have struck a responsive chord in Feisal's heart:
>
> > "Night and my steed and the desert know me—
> > And the lance-thrust and battle, and parchment and pen."
>
> I also saw him frequently reading the works of Antara, the famous poet who wrote a huge epic of his own life filled with tales of raids and love lyrics. The recent war of liberation inspired many new poets to arouse the people by means of patriotic songs. Even the humblest camel-driver improvised songs built around Lawrence, Feisal, and that celebrated warrior, Auda Abu Tayi. (54)

Imr el Kais is the author of the first of the poems ("the jolliest of the seven," in Lawrence's opinion [*Letters*, 584]). Zuhair wrote the third, Tarafa (misheard, misnoted, or mistyped by Thomas as "Zarafa") the second, and Al Harith the last. "Ibn Isham" is no doubt Ibn Hisham, who, in the ninth century, prepared a recension of the oldest extant biography of the Prophet, that of the eighth-century Ibn Ishaq. "Ibn el Ali" suggests no likely candidate to Arabic scholars. Thomas may have misheard, or even shamelessly invented. Mutanabbi (Aḥ-mad Ibn Al-Husain [Abū Ál-Taiyib]) is the Arab poet of the tenth century, "universally esteemed the greatest of all the Arab poets" (Arberry, 1). Lawrence may well have read him or may have remembered the lines as the motto to Richard Burton's *Personal Narrative of a Pilgrimage to Al-Madinah and Meccah*. The first edition (1855–56) has the couplet in Arabic only; the Memorial Edition of 1893 translates it too.

الـلّيـلُ وَالْخَيـلُ وَالْـبَيـداءُ تَعْرِ فُنِـى

وَالـسّيـفُ وَالـضّيـفُ وَالْـقِرْطَاسُ وَالـقَلَمِ

Dark and the Desert and Destriers me ken,
And the Glaive and the Joust, and Paper and Pen.
(Al-Mutanabbi)

These lines are particularly famous; as legend has it, they led directly to Al-Mutanabbi's death. It was the quoting of this couplet by his servant that caused the poet to stand and fight the robbers who had stopped them—a fight in which, in August 965, he was killed (Arberry, 14).

Antara (or Antar) is a half-historical, half-legendary hero of a great body of folktales, like King Arthur in the Occident. Lawrence probably knew Terrick Hamilton's partial translation, *Antar, a Bedoueen Romance* (London: Murray, 1819; 1819–20; 1820). The work has left no trace on *Seven Pillars*, however. Lawrence knew that he had spent time among people who regard poetry with the greatest respect: Arabs traditionally congratulate one another on the birth of a son, the birth of a foal, and the appearance of a poet. Readers of *Seven Pillars* (1976; all subsequent references, unless otherwise noted, will be to this edition) will remember that at the capture of Eshref Bey "the Iman . . . intoned an ode in praise of the event. . . . The poem was creditable as the issue of only sixteen minutes, and the poet was rewarded in gold" (115–16); that Auda abu Tayi's first experience of dynamite moves him "to a rush of hasty poetry on its powerful glory" (189); and that Abdulla, indeed, is criticized for excessive interest in the local poets and their productions.

So, in 1920, in discussions with Thomas in the Wimbledon house the journalist had rented, Lawrence, in the throes of the first versions of his own chivalric desert tale, remembered the *Golden Odes*. But even by 1928, when the effort to idealize had been abandoned, and he had, to use his own solecism, oscillated from one asymptote to the other (16n), he was still able to send an account of the poems to a soldier friend. The account is better than Thomas's as an introduction.

> We call them The Moallakat—the things that were hung up—presumably at Mekka in the great temple before Mohammed came.[5] They are seven in number and quite peculiar in form. Imr el kais wrote the jolliest of the seven: but Lebid is good, and Antar, and parts of Tarafa. It was Tarafa who likened Death to a blind camel lounging[6] about in the dark.
>
> . . . .
>
> There is a good translation, into English poetry, by Wilfrid Blunt, a great old man who died lately. His wife, Lady Anne, was an Arabic scholar. She made a prose translation: and Wilfrid, who could speak some Arabic, and liked Arabs, put them into very fine verse. . . .
>
> *The Moallakat* are pagan: pre-Moslem desert verse; sometimes warlike, sometimes sententious, sometimes prosy, sometimes humourous. There is a queer vividness and sense of life about e.g. Amr el Kais' one. Whether the seven poems were really written by seven poets or not, Heaven only knows. They are on one model; and feel much the same to me: but are vastly different in spirit. . . .
>
> . . . Blunt has done well. . . . *The Moallakat* . . . are formal

---

5. Not so, apparently. "Every Arab schoolboy is taught that this name (which in everyday language means 'suspended') was applied to these poems because there was a custom in pre-Islamic Mecca for the prize-winning poems in poetical competitions held at the fair of 'Ukāẓ to be written down and hung up in the Ka'bah. This tale is certainly a fable, invented in order to explain the name on the basis of the commonest sense of the word. As Nöldeke and others have pointed out, there are many early authorities who have provided us with an extremely detailed description of life in Mecca during the Prophet's youth, yet not one of them contains the slightest allusion to a custom of this sort." El Tayib, 111.

6. *Sic*, for *lunging*. See *RGLH*, 1:76.

performances. Imr and his girl ate a camel by the pools of Jelajil and
pelted each other with strips of its fat! As formal a story as the deed
was informal.

The seven poems put together wouldn't make fifty pages of medium
print. Quite short. (*Letters*, 584–85)

Blunt, remembered by Lawrence as "like a careless work of art in well-worn
Arab robes . . . my Master Arabian" (T. E. Lawrence, "Introduction" to *Arabia
Felix*, xv), prefaces the poems with a twenty-page introduction, in which he
describes their historical and social background. We have already seen that
Blunt claims an Arabic origin for chivalry, "which we are accustomed to
consider an exclusively Christian condition of things, but which in fact
mediaeval Europe imitated and developed on lines of its own from the
original Arab model, brought through Africa into Spain" (Blunt, xiv). Pre-
Islamic Arabian poetry represents for Blunt the original wellspring of pure
chivalry, lived as well as written, superior not only to the medievalisers of
the late nineteenth century, but also to the writers of the European Middle
Ages themselves. And the authors of the seven suspended odes were the best
of this pristine best.

> In their own land the *Poets of the Ignorance*, for such is the name
> given them by Islamic writers, were sometimes themselves princes or
> of princely family. They were at least free gentlemen of blood and
> lineage, undebased by toil and ignoring the "dignity of labour." They
> were warriors and knights errant, the heroes of their own romances,
> prompt with sword and spear, horsemen and camel-riders, tent-
> dwellers from their childhood and inured to physical hardships of all
> kinds. Outdoor doers of wild deeds, these valourous desert song-
> masters were no mere decadents, the "idle singers of an empty day,"
> but men determined to live every hour of their gay lives, to enjoy
> every joy within their reach to their pleasure's uttermost. Here we
> find nothing of the Ossianic gloom of our own archaic bards, nothing
> of the superstitious doubts and conscience-stricken terrors of medi-
> aeval Europe in fear of things beyond the grave, nothing of the
> theological limitations of the later Moslem verse. All with them is
> frankly, inspiritingly, stupendously hedonistic. (Blunt, xi)

It was William Morris who described himself as the "idle singer of an empty day." The belief of Blunt and his disciple that the *Moallakat* poets represent refreshing water straight from the pure source of the stream is so strongly held that it carries the reader along, and it is with something approaching shock that one reads A. J. Arberry's "For my own part I find many signs in the *Mu'allaqāt* of an already well-advanced literary tradition; occasionally they even show slight symptoms of decadence" (251).

Blunt offers specific examples in the biographical notes preceding each poem and the explanatory or textual notes at the end of the collection. It is surprising to a non-Arabist to note the extent to which the northern Arab courts of Hira and Ghassan (founded after "the historical dispersion of the Yemenite clans in the second century of the Christian era" [Blunt, ix]) resemble the courts of Western Europe, six or more centuries later— especially in their manner of fighting. For example, the little story of Imr el Kais, author of the first ode, and "a certain valourous Jewish chieftain, El Samueli" would, in its emphasis on the supreme importance of one's word and one's honor, and the inescapable connection of the two, fit easily into the world of *Sir Gawain and the Green Knight*. Imr el Kais has had to flee to the latter's desert fortress, taking with him "five suits of armour inherited from his ancestors, to each of which a name had been given, as long afterwards to their swords by the heroes of Christian chivalry" (2). El Samueli advises Imr el Kais to seek support in his dispute from the emperor in Constantinople, where he is eventually murdered due to a love-intrigue with the emperor's daughter. "[B]eing pressed by the Emperor's vassal, El Harith, King of Ghassan, to deliver up the five suits of armour which had been left in his charge . . . El Samueli refused, although at the cost of his son's life, whom El Harith had seized as hostage" (2–3).

The description of arms in the sixth ode, by Ibn Kolthum, could be from a *chanson de geste*.

> Nay, ye know of our valour, our hands with your hands,
>   fights how fierce with the spears, with the arrows singing.
> Helmets ours are of steel, stout shields from Yemen,
>   tall the swords in our hands and poised for striking.
> Mail-coats ours; in the sun you have seen them gleaming;
>   hawberks wide for our swords, of a noble wideness.

> Ay, and after the fight, you have seen us naked,
>> creased the skin of our limbs like leathern jerkins,
> Seen the bend of our back, where the armour pressed us,
>> scored with waves, like a pool the South-wind blowing. (42)

El Harith, author of the seventh ode, goes on to provide those accurate descriptions of wounds that are a feature of the *chansons* already noted.

> Them we drove back with wounds like the outrushing
>> streams when goat-skins are pricked; it was thus their blood
>> flowed;
> Drove them back to Thahlana its strong places,
>> scattered, drenched in their gore where the thigh wounds
>> spouted.
> Struck we stern at the lives of them; then trembled
>> deep our spears in their well, like a long-roped bucket. (47)

So Blunt describes the Arabs of the Ignorance as a people who admire honor and martial prowess. The point is not whether he is right, but whether he is plausible and convincing. Among the scholars who support Blunt is Wacyf Boutros Ghali, in his *La Tradition chevaleresque des Arabes.* The reader of this work soon realizes that its francophile, arabophile, and teutophobe author should be approached with caution. But Boutros Ghali also can make a case that "Les seuls biens de l'Arabe étaient la gloire, la famille, le cheval et les armes" and that "cette chevalerie arabe n'était pas l'apanage exclusif d'une classe ou d'une caste—elle était le *modus vivendi* de tout un peuple" (Ghali, 34, 38). Many of his examples are taken from the *Moallakat.*

Lawrence, who viewed the Arabs at their moment of change from a medieval world to a modern one (the process much hastened by war and by Lawrence himself), chose to concentrate on the archaic aspects of the society before him, as had Blunt. What he took from Blunt when he wrote *Seven Pillars* was sometimes incidental: the phrasing of the rejection of the systems of transliteration for changing Arabic characters into the Roman alphabet is typically Laurentian; but the idea was Blunt's first.

> (Blunt) The system of transliteration followed in the rendering of the
> Arabic names throughout the volume is that usually adopted by
> geographers and historians, no attempt being made by means of dots
> and symbols to distinguish accurately between the various forms of
> Arabic consonants. Such symbols, useful as they are in works of
> erudition, would, the translators think, only confuse the general
> reader, for whose assistance simple accents have been placed on the
> syllables of each word where the stress in speaking naturally falls.
> (Blunt, 51)

> (Lawrence) Arabic names won't go into English, exactly, for their
> consonants are not the same as ours, and their vowels, like ours, vary
> from district to district. There are some "scientific systems" of translit-
> eration, helpful to people who know enough Arabic not to need
> helping, but a washout for the world. I spell my names anyhow, to
> show what rot the systems are. (xii)
>
> Arabic names are spelt anyhow, to prevent my appearing an adher-
> ent of one of the existing "systems of transliteration." (534)

But what Lawrence took from Blunt was often more central, for example,
his perception of the Arab. Blunt writes in his introduction to his glimpse of
a lost and chivalric world:

> The primitive Arabs, just as are still their true Bedouin descendents,
> were rank materialists. They believed in neither heaven nor hell, nor
> in any life beyond the one they were enjoying. Of religion they
> understood nothing but a vague monotheism, tempered with just
> enough idolatry to make oath by, but not enough to modify their
> lives. They were the least superstitious of mankind, the least influ-
> enced by fetish fears and hobgoblin terrors. (xi)

Blunt, a womanizer with religious difficulties, projects onto the Arabs his own
hedonism. We have already seen his comment that "these valourous desert
song-masters were . . . men determined to live every hour of their gay lives,
to enjoy every joy within their reach to their pleasure's uttermost." Lawrence,
of a different cast, spends most of chapter III in his introduction ("Founda-

tions of Revolt") to more than a glimpse of a lost and chivalric world in claiming that "Semites" (including Arabs) are "almost . . . monopolists of revealed religions. . . . The common base of all the Semitic creeds . . . was the ever present idea of world-worthlessness" (17). Even so, some of Lawrence's lines are suggested by Blunt's.

> They were a limited, narrow-minded people, whose inert intellects lay fallow in incurious resignation. Their imaginations were vivid but not creative. . . . They invented no systems of philosophy, no complex mythologies. They steered their course between the idols of the tribe and of the cave. The least morbid of peoples, they had accepted the gift of life unquestioningly, as axiomatic. To them it was a thing inevitable, entailed on man, a usufruct, beyond control. Suicide was a thing impossible, and death no grief. (*Seven Pillars*, 16)

"Primitive" Arabs were "the least superstitious of mankind," writes Blunt, and uninterested in religious argument. The "convictions" of "Semites" are "by instinct," writes Lawrence: they are "The least morbid of peoples." (*Seven Pillars*, 17, 16)

Similarly, Blunt's view of the Arabs as "a nervous, excitable people" whose courage "of a different quality, perhaps, from that admired among ourselves," requiring "encouragement from onlookers and from their own voices . . . defiance before the battle, immoderate boasting afterwards" (Blunt, 25) is more than echoed in Lawrence's "The first great rush round the Mediterranean had shown the world the power of an excited Arab for a short spell of intense physical activity; but when the effort burned out the lack of endurance and routine in the Semitic mind became as evident" (*Seven Pillars*, 20). It is also reflected in such comments as "This well-peopled province . . . had suddenly changed its character from a rout of casual nomad pilferers to an eruption against Turkey, fighting her, not certainly in our manner, but fiercely enough. . . . There was among the tribes in the fighting zone a nervous enthusiasm common, I suppose, to all national risings" (*Seven Pillars*, 74).

By the time Lawrence writes of Azraq that it was "steeped in an unfathomable pool of silence and past history, instinct with strange knowledge of wandering poets, and champions, and lost kingdoms, all the crime and chivalry and dead magnificence of the legendary desert-courts of Hira and

Ghassan, whose most sober story read like Arthur come again" (*Seven Pillars* [1922], 179),[7] he has made a whole series of references to Blunt and Blunt's translated stories revolving round these "desert-courts." By this same time the Arab revolt has progressed so far north that Lawrence is actually riding near Azraq (fifty-five miles almost due east of Amman). He is within the historical areas of Hira and Ghassan, and can point out the sites to his English fellow soldiers: "We pretended that the raid was become a tour, and talked of Roman remains and of Ghassanide hunting-places" (*Seven Pillars*, 458); "In the afternoon, tired, we came to Kusair el Amra, the little hunting lodge of Harith, the Shepherd King, a patron of poets; it stood beautifully against its background of bosky rustling trees" (*Seven Pillars*, 458); "[The Englishmen] asked me with astonishment who were these Kings of Ghassan with the unfamiliar halls and pictures. I could tell them vague tales of their poetry, and cruel wars: but it seemed so distant and tinselled an age" (*Seven Pillars*, 458–59).[8]

The last comment refers to the increasing mechanization of the war, and Lawrence's occasional guilt at "introducing the throbbing car, and its trim crew of khaki-clad northerners, into the remoteness of this most hidden legendary ["mediaeval" in 1922 version] place [Azraq]" (*Seven Pillars*, 447). But before "the tide of life which had left [Azrak] a thousand years ago" (*Seven Pillars*, 459) flowed back into the Middle East from Mecca to Damascus, and flowed back with an unrelenting force that makes the earlier stages of Lawrence's war feel almost as strange to us as those of the Kings of Ghassan, Lawrence could legitimately see the *Moallakat* reflected in early twentieth-century Hejaz. Blunt can tell of the author of the first Golden Ode and a "*rival* poet . . . *capping* verses in praise of their horses" [my emphasis] (Blunt, 2). Lawrence can write of the two wings of a tribe of the march, each with its poet, that "before [the right wing] could brandish it [a "single invented couplet"] a fourth time the poet of the left wing broke out in his solo, an extempore reply, to the couplet of his *rival* on the left, in the same meter, in answering rhyme, and completing or *capping* his sentiment" (*Seven*

7. For explanation of the differences between the 1922 and 1976 versions, see *Seven Pillars*, 1976, x.

8. Lawrence again is a little overenthusiastic. "Kusair el Amra" [Qasr 'Amra] is Ummayyad, "constructed between A.D. 705 and 715, during the reign of Caliph Walid I" (Harding, 156).

Pillars [1922], 63, my emphasis). The life story of, for example, Tarafa, author of the second ode, "a wild Bedouin youth—such as may be found not uncommonly at the present day in Arabia—imaginative, impulsive and perverse, embroiled in constant quarrels, hot-tongued and violent handed" (Blunt, 9–10), could be transferred in substance (if not exactly in style) to *Seven Pillars* and the reader would feel no incongruity. The life story of, to cite what is perhaps the best example, Abdulla, "surnamed el Nahabi, or the Robber" (*Seven Pillars*, 366) could be removed from *Seven Pillars* into one of Blunt's seven introductory biographies (again in substance) and the reader would sense very little foreign matter; el Nahabi is just such a youth as Blunt describes. (Only Blunt's word "imaginative" might give us pause, and the emphasis on the seaminess of some of Abdulla's career is Laurentian rather than Bluntesque. Lawrence, incidentally, is plainly enchanted by Abdulla, the "perfect retainer," who becomes one of the two leaders of his bodyguard.) In the same way there is a great similarity between Antar, author of the fifth ode, "the hero of the medieval romance which bears his name . . . the true prototype of the Knights errant of our own Age of Chivalry" (Blunt, 31), and Auda abu Tayi, "the greatest fighting man in northern Arabia" (*Seven Pillars*, 131), who possesses "an immense chivalrous name" (131) and who "had come down to us like a knight errant" (169). Apart from his love for Abla, Antar's life was "an unbroken sequence of raids, battles, and reprisals, and as long as he lived there could be no peace with the enemy" (Blunt, 31). Auda, writes Lawrence, "had been wounded thirteen times; whilst the battles he provoked had seen all his tribesmen hurt and most of his relations killed. He himself had slain seventy-five men, Arabs, with his own hand in battle. . . . His sub-tribe had been reduced from twelve hundred men to less than five hundred, in thirty years, as the standard of nomadic fighting rose." Furthermore, "Auda raided as often as he had opportunity, and as widely as he could. He had seen Aleppo, Basra, Wejh, and Wadi Dawasir on his expeditions: and was careful to be at enmity with all tribes in the desert, that he might have proper scope for raids" (170).

Lawrence never ventures to compare himself directly to a *Moallakat* warrior. He would, however, like to see himself as belonging to the same world; he does claim virtue by association, and also ascribes such virtue to the admired Nasir. The reader is invited to compare these two passages, the first from Tarafa's ode, the second from *Seven Pillars* (my emphasis).

Here on my swift-foot camel I laugh at love's bitterness.
Ship-strong is she, my naga, my *stout-timbered* road goer,
          footing the long-lined path-way—a striped cloak—in front of us.
Steel tempered are her sinews. *She runs like an ostrich-hen,*
          one which has fled defying the ash-plumed proud lord of her.
                                                   (Blunt and Blunt, 11)

Nasir led us, riding his Ghazala—a camel *vaulted and huge-ribbed as
an antique ship*; towering a good foot above the next of our animals,
and yet perfectly proportioned, *with a stride like an ostrich's*—a lyrical
beast, noblest and best bred of the Howeitat camels, a female of nine
remembered dams. Auda was beside him, and I skirmished about
their gravities on Naama, "*the hen-ostrich,*" a racing camel and my last
purchase. (*Seven Pillars*, 218)

Lawrence has also remembered two lines from the second stanza of El
Harith's ode: "Mount I light on my naga. No hen ostrich / swift as she, the tall
trotter" (Blunt and Blunt, 45). Hence in Lawrence's version, "towering a good
foot above the next of our animals," "I skirmished about their gravities," and
"the hen-ostrich." In fact, the paragraph quoted above is a reminiscence and
combination of the two poets' descriptions of their camels. The author of
Seven Pillars reassures himself that the world of the Poets of the Ignorance
and his own have much in common.

But the most significant reference to the *Moallakat*—significant both in
length and in its implication—has not yet been detailed. Just as the manner
of his death at the hands of an arquebusier is perhaps the most historically
suggestive event of le chevalier Bayard's military career, so is it Lawrence's
reproduction (in a not casually altered form) of some lines in Tarafa's ode
that tells us most about Lawrence's love of the old chivalric ways, of his regret
at their inevitable passing away, and of his role in causing them so to do.

Blunt has remarked of the odes of Ibn Kolthum and El Harith that

to those well acquainted with contemporary Arabia they possess an
extreme interest, as proving how little the Bedouin world has changed
either in its political ideas or even in its political position during the
last fourteen hundred years. There is hardly an idea expressed by

either . . . that might not today be heard in the mouths of rival tribe-
sheykhs who have journeyed to Hail to lay their disputes before Ibn
Rashid. The only difference at the present day would be that the rival
declamations would no longer be in verse. (Blunt, 38)

These two odes deal with intertribal warfare and boast of the prowess of the
poet's own tribe. (The quotations already made from Ibn Kolthum's and El
Harith's odes will give some idea of the whole.) This is the world that is most
seriously weakened, but not destroyed, by "Some Englishmen . . . [who]
believed that a rebellion of Arabs against Turks would enable England, while
fighting Germany, simultaneously to defeat her ally Turkey" (7)—in other
words, by nationalism, T. E. Lawrence, and those doing the same work as he.
When Lawrence writes of the "political ideas" (Blunt's words) of the Arabs
he writes not of intertribal warfare, but of "their familiar understanding of
intense political nationality" (*Seven Pillars*, 69). Even though "The Semites'
idea of nationality was the independence of clans and villages, and their idea
of national union was episodic resistance to an intruder" (*Seven Pillars*, 70),
the old world that Blunt recognized as late as 1903 is made difficult, if not
impossible, by involvement in an undeniably twentieth-century war, even if a
largely nineteenth-century idea is being made use of.

The lines from Tarafa's ode that appear in so sadly altered a context in
Seven Pillars describe what makes life worth living for the poet.

> Time will not wait for us.
> And, truly, but for three things in youth's day of vanity,
> fain would I see them around me the friends at my death-
> bedding,
> As first: to outstrip the sour ones, be first at the wine-bibbing,
> ay, at the blink of day-dawn when mixed the cup foams for me;
> And next, to ride their champion, who none have to succour them,
> fierce on my steed, the led one, a wolf roused and thirst-stricken;
> And third, to lie the day-long, while wild clouds are wildering,
> close in her tent of goat's hair, the dearest beloved of me.
> O noble she, a tree-stem unpruned in her maidenhood,
> tall as a branch of Khirwa, where men hang their ornaments.
> 'Tis thus I slake my soul's rage, the life-thirst so wild in me.
>   (Blunt and Blunt, 13–14)

The demands of a serious nationalist effort endanger all that.

> [C]hancing to look across the valley, [Abd el Kerim, a "young Beidawi Sherif"] saw the hollows beneath and about us winking with the faint camp-fires of the scattered contingents. He called me out to look, and swept his arm round, saying half-sadly, "We are no longer Arabs but a People."
>
> He was half-proud too, for the advance on Wejh was their biggest effort; the first time in memory that the manhood of a tribe, with transport, arms, and food for two hundred miles, had left its district and marched into another's territory without the hope of plunder or the stimulus of blood feud. Abd el Kerim was glad that his tribe had shown this new spirit of service, but also sorry; for to him *the joys of life were a fast camel, the best weapons, and a short sharp raid* against his neighbour's herd: and the gradual achievement of Faisal's ambition was making such joys less and less easy for the responsible. (*Seven Pillars*, 112, my emphasis)

Tarafa's "life-thirst" demands pleasures that are a little different from Abd el Kerim's "joys of life" (at least as represented by Lawrence). But this is not the first time we have seen the latter convert Blunt's sexual pleasures into (or at least combine them with) the pleasures of war; and Lawrence, let us remember, was usually teetotal.

Wilfrid Scawen and Lady Anne Blunt could scarcely have imagined that their somewhat recherché little book would so influence a man whose fame as an Arabophile so greatly eclipses theirs, and whose influence in the Arab world, at a decisive moment, was used to push forward that family—the Hashemites—who most appealed to his love for the ethos admired and explicated by the Blunts. Lawrence bound himself to the cause of the Hashemites—the "Sherifian" cause—with an often puzzling firmness. Other British officials, noting the increasing strength of rival Ibn Saud and the obstinacy of the Sherif of Mecca, were able to adapt to perceived realities. Lawrence stood by Husain and his family, immediately quitting the scene when two of the sons had been provided with thrones, largely due to

Lawrence's strenuous efforts. Kathryn Tidrick has written that "He seems to have conceived his own destiny as being intimately linked with [the Hashemites']" (176); and that Lawrence's Sherifian policy fused the nationalist and the aristocratic principles in a manner which Blunt, the supporter of the Irish and the Egyptians, the almost stereotypically patriarchal squire of his country house Crabbet, would have entirely supported (117). The illegitimate son of an Irish baronet, with years of chivalric, neochivalric, and pseudochivalric reading behind him, saw the descendants of the Prophet as the only Arabs with the necessary prestige to surmount factionalism and internecine feuding. For it was not only to "the tribes [that] the Sherif and his sons were heroic," in Lawrence's words (*Seven Pillars*, 68). A hitherto overlooked passage in *Seven Pillars* makes clear the closeness with which Lawrence identified with Husain and his sons. Lawrence means to describe the four sons of Sherif Husain and their powerful father. He also describes the five sons of Thomas Chapman and their powerful mother (and, of course, knows that he does so).

> Soon they hardened, and became self-reliant, with that blend of native intelligence and vigour which so often comes in a crossed stock. Their formidable family group was admired and efficient, but curiously isolated in their world. They were natives of no country, lovers of no private plot of ground. They had no real confidants or ministers; and no one of them seemed open to another, or to the father, of whom they stood in awe. (69)

What family but the Lawrences, three of the five sons, T. E. in particular, showing evidence of remarkable ability or potential, manifested a self-reliant "blend of native intelligence and vigour?" What sons provide a better example of "crossed stock" than the offspring of the Irish baronet and the Scottish nursemaid? "Their formidable family group was admired and efficient, but curiously isolated in their world"—does this sentence better describe the Hashemites in Mecca or the Lawrences in North Oxford? It is the Lawrences who, moving after the elopement from country to country and region to region, before finally settling in Oxford in 1896, were "natives of no country, lovers of no private plot of ground." In the last sentence above we have to substitute "mother" for "father," but we need make no other change.

Lawrence's heroic dreams created three Arab thrones, one of which quickly disappeared and one of which is still with us. According to H. V. F. Winstone, the dreams helped bedevil for decades British relations with the then more obscure Arab who rapidly grew to dominate the peninsula, who ejected the Hashemites from the Hejaz in 1925, and who gave his family name to the kingdom that is now assiduously courted by the West.[9]

9. Victor Winstone, "Lawrence and the Legend that Misfired." *Times* (London), 6 November 1982, p. 8, cols. 7–8. H. V. F. Winstone develops this view of Lawrence in *The Illicit Adventure*.

V·I

CHIVALRY
AND THE
NOMADIC CODE

Although some chivalric references in *Seven Pillars* are inspired by the Blunts, Lawrence sometimes explicitly quotes chivalrous rules observed by the Arabs, what he calls "the nomadic code of honour . . . the desert law" (318).

> This bitter taste of the Turkish mode of war [i.e., the rape and slaughter in Awali, a suburb of Medina] sent a shock across Arabia; for the first rule of Arab war was that women were inviolable: the second that the lives and honour of children too young to fight with men were to be spared: the third, that property impossible to carry off should be left undamaged. The Arabs with Faisal perceived that they were opposed to new customs. (64)

> Arab rules of war forbad to kill men in cold blood. ([1922], 168)]

> The Howeitat were very fierce, for the slaughter of their women on the day before had been a new and horrible side of warfare suddenly opened to them. In all their history were only two remembered instances of a woman intentionally harmed in life or body, and they had been brought up to execrate the authors of these outrages in passionate songs. (236–37. Second sentence only in 1922 edition.)

The Turks are not, to say the least, chivalrous enemies, and *Seven Pillars* contains more than one account of bloody massacre, Turk and reciprocal Arab. But the elements of medieval conflict at its best are present in the "last of the picturesque wars." Lawrence thought he saw medieval ideals being put into practice, and is supported by A. C. Kirkbride, a fellow British officer mentioned in *Seven Pillars*, whose straightforward and soldierly accounts (*A Crackle of Thorns; An Awakening*) of the war and his role in it do not suggest a book-reading romantic. "Lawrence once told me that his idea of waging war was based on the professional condottieri of medieval Italy. This is to say, to gain one's objectives with a minimum of casualties *on both sides*. . . . T. E. L. had a horror of bloodshed. . . ." Kirkbride, in the same letter, writes that the Ageyl certainly adhered to this code.[1] Lawrence's descriptions of the Ageyl (108–9, 368) concentrate more on the consequences of their being townsmen (rather than nomads), their foppishness in dress, and their great skill with camels than their aims and principles in war. He does say, however, that "being mercenaries, [they] would not do well unless paid, and for lack of that condition had fallen into disrepute" (368). One standard authority has a more cynical explanation of the bloodlessness of *condottieri* engagements: "The soldiers who fought under the *condottieri* were almost entirely heavy-armoured cavalry and were noted for their rapacious and disorderly behaviour. With no goal beyond personal gain, the armies of the *condottieri* often changed sides, and battles usually ended with little or no bloodshed."[2] Nonetheless, Lawrence's idealistic view has found support. *Condottieri*, writes Geoffrey Trease, were rather like present-day lawyers or football-players, who earn their living by engaging in a series of contests. Today's enemy may be yesterday's friend—and perhaps the friend of tomorrow. "[O]bviously the condottiere was looking for a livelihood, not a hero's grave, and having done his best he was not going to fight on to the death." An established ransom system meant that surrender held no terrors. But "there *were* desperate battles and heroic exploits and forlorn hopes that were crowned with success. Condottiere warfare had its conventions but it never became either a ballet or a game of chess" (18).

1. Kirkbride to Basil Liddell Hart, 8 December 1962. Bodleian Reserve MSS G56. Quoted in Mack, 239. Emphasis in original.
2. "Condottieri," *Encyclopedia Britannica: Micropaedia,* 1974 ed.

The war in the desert can still be personal, individual, archaic, and therefore occasionally merciful: Faisal, a "confirmed smoker," sends pack-animals loaded with cheap cigarettes to a tobaccoless enemy garrison (372–73); his brother Abdulla writes an exultant letter to the Turkish commander Fakhri Pasha telling him of an important capture of Turkish booty and leaving it where it will be found and passed on (115); Lawrence himself refrains from shooting a temporarily unarmed Turk he accidentally comes across: "At a safe distance I glanced back. He put thumb to nose, and twinkled his fingers at me" (408); such battles as took place early in the war were preceded by screamed insults: "To my ears they sounded oddly primitive battles" (66)

Perhaps the best indication of the nature of *Seven Pillars*'s world is the sword, which we have already seen reported as being still in use as a weapon. Lawrence the creative artist makes much of the antique weapon. It appears in action, most notably during the battle of Tafileh, when Hamd el Arar, "a melancholy, courtly, gallant cavalier" (377) "took the occasion . . . fittingly. Before riding off he devoted himself to the death for the Arab cause, drew his sword ceremoniously, and made to it, by name, a heroic speech" (381). (The very next sentence, incidentally, is evidence of the clash of two epochs taking place in the Middle East in 1917–18: "Rasim took five automatic guns with him: which was good.") We read in the *Chanson de Roland* that Charlemagne named his sword Joyeuse and Roland named his Durendal. Malory records the naming of Arthur's sword Excalibur. Sometimes the carrying of a sword is ceremonial: the slave who leads Lawrence to Faisal at their slightly precious first meeting has a "silver-hilted sword in hand" (62). Sometimes it seems a combination of the ceremonial and the martial: poor Ashraf (plural of "sherif," one descended from the Prophet) "wore rusty-red tunics henna-dyed, under black cloaks, and carried swords. Each had a slave . . . to help him with rifle and dagger in the fight" (113). In the delightful description of a tribal feast, "one of the chief Howeitat eating with us would draw his dagger, silver hilted, set with turquoise, a signed masterpiece of Mohammed ibn Zari, of Jauf" to cut meat, the mention of the name leading Lawrence to add one of his rare explanatory footnotes: "The most famous sword-smith of my time was ibn Bani, a craftsman of the Ibn Rashid dynasty of Hail. He rode once on foray with the Shammar against the Rualla, and was captured. When Nuri recognized him, he shut up with him in prison ibn Nari, his own sword-smith, swearing they should not come out till their work was indistinguishable. So ibn Zari improved greatly in the skill of his craft, while remaining in design the better artist" (207).

More important are the metaphorical and symbolic uses of the sword. (One becomes a little surprised that Lawrence never feels he can risk *glaive*.) Shortly after finishing *Seven Pillars* he wrote to a friend: "The sword was odd. The Arab movement was one: Faisal another (his name means a flashing sword): then there is the excluded notion, Garden of Eden touch: and the division meaning, like the sword in the bed of mixed sleeping, from the *Morte d'Arthur*. I don't know which was in your mind, but they all came to me—and the sword also means clean-ness, and death."[3]

Aldington took up the last point and complained, in a passage dealing with Lawrence's alleged appeal to Puritan prejudice in his use of the word "clean," that "He praises 'the sword'—i.e. the archaic symbol for War, with all its filth and degradation—as 'clean' " (330). Lawrence, as will be shown in more detail later, was more than aware of the "filth and degradation" of war, but for him the sword stood for war at its best, war as a trial of courage and prowess, for the old times when endeavor could be heroic—war as he thought he sometimes experienced it even in the twentieth century in an "Ancient and artificial [society] like this of the Sherifs and feudal chieftains of Arabia" (162), rather than war as Aldington had experienced it on the Western Front. There are worse ways of settling disputes in a post-lapsarian world than single combat without benefit of armor. If one's view of heterosexual relations is Lawrence's, then one can see "the sword in the bed of mixed sleeping" as representing stern duty or noble chastity rather than ease or shameful pleasure. The first two remarks in Lawrence's letter—"The Arab movement was [a sword]: Faisal another (his name means a flashing sword)"—are best explained by reference to the text of *Seven Pillars*.

Throughout his book Lawrence insists on the nobility of the Arab cause: the warriors who attained freedom for the Arabs "achieved a deathless thing, a lucent inspiration to the children of their race" (29). It is proper that the sword, with its connotations of antique glory, should be associated with it. Toward the end of the campaign Lawrence distinguishes the Arab fight from the efforts of the mechanized and regimented British: "I could feel the taut power of Arab excitement behind me. The climax of the preaching of years

---

3. *Letters*, 372. The reference to the "bed of mixed sleeping" is to the Tristram story.

had come, and a united country was straining towards its historic capital. In confidence that this weapon, tempered by myself, was enough for the utmost of my purpose, I seemed to forget the English companions who stood outside my idea in the shadow of ordinary war" (468). Lawrence has maintained throughout *Seven Pillars* that the Arab struggle is taking place in a region that is more than geographically removed from the Western Front. Nevertheless, the twentieth century changes the nature of war even in Arabia:

> The printing press, and each newly-discovered method of communi-cation favoured the intellectual above the physical, civilization paying the mind always from the body's funds. We kindergarten soldiers were beginning our art of war in the atmosphere of the twentieth century, receiving our weapons without prejudice. To the regular officer, with the tradition of forty generations of service behind him, the antique arms were the most honoured. As we had seldom to concern ourselves with what our men did, but always with what they thought, the diathetic [here meaning propaganda] for us would be more than half the command. In Europe it was a little set aside, and entrusted to men outside the General Staff. In Asia the regular elements were so weak that irregulars could not let metaphysical weapons rust unused. (148)

Even here, the spirit of the sword invests, transforms, the modern weapon of propaganda.

The Turks have lost control of their former empire because martial virtues are out of date in the world they have chosen to inhabit. They would emulate the warfare of the Western Front; they, unlike the Arabs, have accepted, even embraced, modern inventions, and found themselves in a world too complex. "The sword had been the virtue of the children of Othman, and swords had passed out of fashion nowadays, in favour of deadlier and more scientific weapons. . . . Their administration had become perforce an affair of files and telegrams, of high finance, eugenics, calculations" (29–30). The same point is made even more strongly in "The Changing East":

> [O]f his former dominion the Turk kept only the sword—and he tried to change even his sword, which he handled as well [as] or better than

any race in Europe, for rifles and big guns and aeroplanes, and in such newfangled things his factor of efficiency soon dropped. He found that they put a premium on brains, and accordingly the meaner races, who used their wits before their hands, gained steadily on him. In the old days a few rusty horsemen had held Tripoli and Albania, and Arabia and Syria, and Mesopotamia and Armenia in subjection. Now each province demanded a substantial garrison. (*Oriental Assembly*, 80–81)

The Arabs have *not* accepted such a world. We have already seen that they adhere to the old virtues. War in Arabia is not war in Europe. In Book 1 Lawrence is gradually initiated into the strange other world that is Arabia, a land to which the twentieth century (and the machine-gun; and our moral relativism) is alien, but where Roland (with Durendal; and his "Paien unt tort e chrestiens unt dreit") would feel at home: "the noon sun in the East, like moonlight, put to sleep the colours. There were only lights and shadows, the white houses and black gaps of streets" (40). Much later in the campaign, when Lawrence is weary and disillusioned, when, indeed, "my will, the worn instrument which had so long forged our path, broke suddenly in my hand and fell useless" then "sunset was fierce, stimulant, barbaric; reviving the colours like a draught . . . while my longings were for weakness, chills and grey mistiness, that the world might not be so crystalline clear, so definitely right and wrong" (435). The phrase that immediately precedes the first quotation is significant, and its provenance noteworthy: "the heat of Arabia came out like a drawn sword and struck us speechless." We owe this to Lawrence's memory of Maurice Hewlett's *Richard Yea-and-Nay*: "At Acre, by the time September was set, the sun had put all the air to the sword, so that the city lay stifled" (297).

But not all Arabs are possessed by the spirit of Arabia. From Lawrence's first meeting with him at Jeddah in the early stages of the revolt to the last casual mention nearly four hundred pages later, Prince Abdulla is represented as nothing so strongly as a selfish and negligent medieval knight or lord. If Faisal is a constant inspiration, "the heedless burning torch which would set fire to everyone upon the path," then his brother is a constant failure. Abdulla approaches his first meeting with Lawrence and Storrs "on a white *mare* . . . *softly* with a *bevy* of *richly*-armed slaves" (41, my emphasis).

Later it will be reported as his habit to surround himself with a "*bevy* of *silk-clad* fellows . . . when he would be *easy*" (164, my emphasis). "[N]othing was futile in the atmosphere of higher thinking and responsibility which ruled at Faisal's [camp]." Abdulla, on the other hand, "passed his merry day in the big cool tent accessible only to friends, limiting suppliants or new adherents or the hearing of disputes to one public session in the afternoon. For the rest he read the papers, *ate carefully, slept.* . . . [H]e would sometimes ride a little, or shoot a little, and *return exhausted to his tent for massage*; and afterwards reciters would be introduced to soothe his aching head. He was fond of Arabic verses and exceptionally well read" (161–62, my emphases). Abdulla is interested in the war in the West, and has "learned by rote the courts and ministries of Europe, even to the name of the Swiss president." It is here that Lawrence remarks—and it is not by chance that he remarks it *here*, for, as I shall show, his mind is running on his medieval reading—that it is to the advantage of England's reputation that "we still had a King," for "Ancient and artificial societies like this of the Sherifs and feudal chieftains of Arabia found a sense of honourable security when dealing with us in such proof that the highest place in our state was not a prize for merit or ambition" (162). Abdulla's life of slothful ease in court (he even has a "court jester" [144], a "court fool" [162], who is rewarded with three months' pay after his master has shot a coffeepot off his head three times from twenty yards) is paralleled by his lack of interest in keeping the field: at one stage Lawrence rides off to ask "why he had done nothing for two months" (133). As a military leader, Abdulla "graciously [permits] anything not calling upon his own energies" (165).

Lawrence's criticism of the prince becomes explicitly harsh.

> Time slowly depressed my first, favourable, opinion of Abdulla's character. His constant ailments, which once aroused compassion, became fitter for contempt when their causes were apparent in laziness and self-indulgence, and when he was seen to cherish them as occupations of his too-great leisure. His casual attractive fits of arbitrariness now seemed feeble tyranny disguised as whims; his friendliness became caprice; his good humour love of pleasure. (162–63)

The Abdulla of Lawrence's epic, whose very virtues ("kindness," "charm," "merryness") are used to damn him, is rhetorically conceived to act as a foil to the grave and noble Faisal. He is literary in source and didactic in intent. He exemplifies some passage from one of Lawrence's "manuals of chivalry," perhaps the following, from Honoré Bonet's *Tree of Battles*:

> Next, he [the good knight] should be very discreet and measured in bodily delights and should not keep his body too delicately nourished, for otherwise he will be of little worth in war. For this reason we say that the chivalry of today is by no means of the valour of former times, for according to the old laws knights ate beans and bacon and coarse meats; they lay hard and wore harness most of the time; they dwelt outside cities and liked the air of the open country and willingly kept the field; and they did not usually dispute as to which was the best wine but drank clear water, because they could endure all hardship and labour. (213)

Abdulla is deliberately shown to be guilty of every charge here, with the exception of the last. Even here his abstention is not necessarily matter for praise, as "inherited religious prejudice was allowed rule over the keenness of his mind because it was less trouble to him than uncharted thought" (163).

It is, perhaps, the greatest criticism of Abdulla that he reacts inappropriately to his father's Rolandesque threat, absurd as the old man is, "to put himself at the head of his own people of Mecca, and to die fighting before the Holy City" (43). "Abdulla, smiling a little, asked, to prevent such a disaster, that a British brigade . . . be kept at Suez" (44). Lawrence has begun to form his opinion of the prince even at their first meeting, and chooses his words carefully in its expression. "I became more and more sure that Abdulla was too balanced, too cool, too humorous to be a prophet: especially the armed prophet who, if history be true, succeeded in revolutions. His value would come perhaps in the peace after success. During the physical struggle, when singleness of eye and magnetism, devotion and self-sacrifice were needed, Abdulla would be a *tool too complex* for a simple purpose" (42, my emphasis). It is as difficult to imagine Abdulla being a sword (as the "armed prophet" Faisal is, etymologically and symbolically) as to imagine Roland making a joke.

The Abdulla of *Seven Pillars* is no doubt the product of Lawrence's honest observation, but we may suspect too that Lawrence the artist has felt justified in producing a truth paradoxically greater than literalness. We may compare Lawrence's impressions of Abdulla with those of the late General Sir John Glubb ("Glubb Pasha"), the Englishman who commanded the Arab Legion (the precursor of the present-day Jordanian Army) from 1939 until his dismissal by King Hussein in 1956.[4] Glubb, also a devotee of the chivalric code, recognized the Arabs' respect for it (see his "Arab Chivalry"). Glubb greatly admired Abdulla, who in postwar settlements became prince of Transjordan and later ruler of the Hashemite Kingdom of the Jordan. He served him loyally and wept at his funeral. Two fascinating passages from his *A Soldier with the Arabs* compare directly with observations made by Lawrence. "[R]eciters would be introduced to soothe [Abdulla's] aching head," writes the Arab's earlier English brother-in-arms in criticism. "He was fond of Arabic verses and exceptionally well read." Glubb tells the following story:

> Abdulla was an all-round man, a man of culture. In November 1948, while the Israeli offensive against the Egyptians was in progress, I visited the King in his warm winter residence in the Jordan valley, a thousand feet below sea-level. I found him sitting in a chair in his drawing-room, looking out at the wide scrub-covered plain of the Jordan valley, falling away to the deep blue Dead Sea between its craggy precipitous mountains.

4. In early 1985 four soldiers of the Royal Green Jackets rode seven hundred miles on camelback across Jordan to commemorate the fiftieth anniversary of Lawrence's death. The leader of the expedition, Captain Charles Blackmore, reported of Anglo-Jordanian relations that "The consistent feeling was a strong liking and respect for the English. Without a doubt this stemmed from the work of one man, General Sir John GLUBB K.C.B., C.M.G., D.S.O., M.C. ('Glubb Pasha'). His name and work is a legend amongst the Bedu (he was responsible mainly in the '30s to '50s for raising the Jordanian Army and police force, establishing a chain of desert police forts to end camel raiding, and eventually bringing a new life and prosperity to the Bedu); as a result any Englishman was highly thought of. There were many long and genuinely told stories of the greatness of 'Glubb Pasha' recounted around campfires in the evening. The legacy of his achievements has undoubtedly brought a close bond from the Jordanians to the English. His memory has eclipsed that of Lawrence." C. D. Blackmore, 22. Cf. Charles Blackmore, 87–88.

After greeting me, he said: "What do you think of this?" and he read out two verses of poetry. I could not catch the words.

"I am sorry, sir," I said, "I did not understand it."

He read it out again and once more I was obliged to make the same answer. The King smiled.

"Of course you didn't," he said. "It isn't Arabic, it's Persian. This is what it means in Arabic:

> " 'Hafidh compared thy ringlets to daggers,
> Hafidh was right!
> And those daggers
> Are plunged in my heart.' "

"Very pretty," I said.

The King sighed and put his book down on a little table beside his chair. "Well, Pasha," he said, "I suppose you don't want to talk about poetry. You want to tell me about wars and battles." (274–75)

Here the joke is on Glubb, as Glubb perfectly well realizes. But one can imagine how the story of the conversation held "while the Israeli offensive against the Egyptians was in progress" would fall from Lawrence's pen.

The second anecdote is more serious. Glubb too fought a modern war in a medieval setting. After remarking that "There was something strangely moving to me in seeing my own soldiers on these historic walls [of the Old City of Jerusalem], their rifles thrust through mediaeval loopholes, shaped long ago to the measurement of cross-bows," Glubb goes on to tell how

> One morning during this early fighting [between Arabs and Jews] in Jerusalem, I was summoned to the palace. The King had that hollow sunken expression which he wore in times of anxiety.
>
> "I conjure you by God to tell me the truth," he said. "Can we hold Jerusalem, or will the Jews take it?"
>
> "If God wills, they will never take it, sir!" I answered.
>
> "I want you to promise me," the King went on, "that if you ever think the Jews will take Jerusalem, you will tell me. I will not live to see them in the Holy Places. I will go there myself and die on the walls of the city."
>
> "If God wills, that will not happen," I said. (127)

Glubb is a writer of transparent honesty, and of a literal honesty that Lawrence neither attempted nor desired. His story of Abdulla's response to the possible fall of Jerusalem—very different from his response to the possible fall of Mecca—has been quoted to cast another light on his master and to provide more evidence that Lawrence allows his rhetorical purpose to color somewhat his portrayal of Abdulla.

Although we should not be trapped into thinking that Glubb's story must be "disproved" if Lawrence is to be defended, the critic who considers Lawrence to have been more an ambitious artist than a narrator of quotidian fact will make three points. First, thirty years separate Abdulla's smile at the thought of his father's Rolandesque death from his vow to die on Jerusalem's walls if the city fell. People often become less "merry" as the years progress. Second, he himself would have borne the shame of defeat if all Jerusalem had fallen, instead of merely being the son of the defeated as in the case of Mecca. Third, it would have been less offensive to the devout Moslem Abdulla for Mecca, the holiest city of Islam, to fall to his coreligionists the Turks than for Jerusalem, the second holiest city in Islam (containing "The Dome of the Rock and the Aqsa Mosque from which the Prophet Muhamad had ascended to Heaven" [Glubb, *Soldier*, 127]) to fall to the Jews.

Abdulla is not a "flashing sword," although Faisal is. Faisal carries a great burden of significance, which bids fair to crush the life from him. On one occasion Lawrence refers us back explicitly to the source of his inspiration: "He called back Mirzuk and lowered the tent-flap: a sign that there was private business to be done. I thought of the meaning of Faisal's name (the sword flashing down in the stroke) and feared a scene" (88). The name *Faisal* is derived from the root *faṣala*, which means both to divide and to settle, the sword representing power. On another occasion Lawrence reminds us of the Arab's name (and implicitly compliments his generalship) when writing of military intuition—"and the greatest commander of men was he whose intuitions most nearly happened"—that "It could be ensured only by instinct (sharpened by thought practicing the stroke) until at the crisis it came naturally, a reflex" (146). At the very end of the campaign, Faisal, "large-eyed, colourless and worn," is likened to a "fine dagger" (529). If Abdullah is a negligent lord, then Faisal, before the writing of *Seven Pillars*, had reminded Lawrence of Coeur de Lion: "Looks like a European and very like the monument of Richard I, at Fontevraud" (T. E. Lawrence, *The Essential T. E. Lawrence*, 89).

V·I·I

LAWRENCE'S LITERARY MEDIEVALISM

To leave the sword for the shield, or at least what is emblazoned upon the shield, is to realize anew how learned a medievalist and how ingenious a writer Lawrence was. C. F. C. Beeson, a childhood friend, writes that a study of heraldry had made its jargon part of Lawrence's idiolect (BHF, 53). Oxford, indeed, is a happy hunting-ground for one with an interest in the subject. The city, university, and college arms provide numerous examples—almost textbook examples—of the elements of heraldry: fields, ordinaries, and charges; canting arms and marshalings. For example, the entrance gateway of Christ Church shows the arms of college benefactors, kings and commoners. Lawrence, furthermore, was growing up at a time when the study of heraldry was again becoming intellectually respectable. We know that he read not only genuine medieval works but also the poetry of Tennyson and the Pre-Raphaelites, who inherited something of the Romantic attitude toward heraldry. Tennyson, whom Lawrence the schoolboy had selected for special study and quoted in letters, could incorporate, more or less correctly, heraldic terms into poetry.

> [Merlin] found a fair young squire who sat alone,
> Had carved himself a knightly shield of wood,
> And then was painted on it fancied arms,
> Azure, an eagle rising or, the sun
> In dexter chief; the scroll, "I follow fame."

> Gawain saw
> Sir Lancelot's azure lions, crown'd with gold,
> Ramp in the field.[1]

When Lawrence read *Le Petit Jehan de Saintré* in 1910 he would have learned about the duties of heralds and improved his knowledge of explicitly French heraldic language. Chapter 58 of that work consists largely of a list of men whom La Sale claims accompanied Saintré on crusade and their coats of arms, described in proper technical language. To take an example almost at random, "Le vidame de Chartres, d'or à trois faisses de sable, à ung orle de six merlectes de mesmes, et crye: Merle" (177). In fact there are many heraldic references scattered throughout *Le Petit Jehan*.

How then does Lawrence apply his learning? The Arabs did bear before them a plain crimson flag (*crimson* is Lawrence's word, and nonheraldic). The flags are referred to as *banners* and the men who carry them called *standard-bearers*, somewhat inconsistently (*Seven Pillars*, 121). This deliberate "error"—a banner being a coat of arms depicted on a square or rectangular flag, and a standard being a swallow-tailed flag bearing badges and motto, with the arms themselves (or St. George's or St. Andrew's cross in the case of an English or Scottish knight) perhaps in the hoist—will be paralleled in Lawrence's indifferent, and anachronistic, use of *herald* and *pursuivant* in his translation of the *Odyssey*. (A pursuivant is a junior version of a herald, but Lawrence uses both words, often of the same man, to denote a messenger.) But with that exception heraldic language must be used in *Seven Pillars* in a transferred sense, not describing concisely and accurately lines and shapes on a shield but lines and shapes in the writer's surroundings. Herein lies Lawrence's originality. He is rare indeed in using a family of somewhat arcane words or phrases outside their usual contexts to such suggestive effect. Lawrence's war is fought on historic ground, not only around Hira and Ghassan but also under "the old Crusader fort of Monreale . . . very noble against the night sky" (374, 393). He would have us link two wars, one fought with shields and swords and one with rifles and armored tenders, both in idealistic endeavor. Not even the most unbending purist could object to Lawrence's borrowings as abusing heraldic language. They

---

1. "Merlin and Vivien," lines 470–74; "Lancelot and Elaine," lines 658–60 in Ricks, 1608, 1639.

create resonances for any reader of *Seven Pillars* who has the slightest knowledge of heraldry: "[T]he Turks had dug trenches and stoned up an elaborate outpost of engrailed sangars [a sangar being a stone breastwork]" (283). Lawrence meant by *engrailed* to indicate the shape of "curvilinear indentations" referred to by the *OED* and denoted by the word in modern blazon. He may be remembering line 113 of Tennyson's "The Palace of Art" ("Or over hills with peaky tops and engrail'd"), a poem he thought "as good as good can be."[2]

His use of *diaper* is in effect preheraldic.

> [H]e entered the station yard, carefully for fear of the mines, whose trip and trigger wires diapered the ground. (417)

> I felt restless as the dusty sunlight which splashed a diaper over the paths, through chinks in the leaves. (494)

Diaper originally referred to a textile of Byzantine or Levantine make, so woven that light reflected a pattern from its surface. In modern blazon it denotes an accessory decoration of the shield. Again, Lawrence may be remembering Tennyson; lines 144–49 of "Recollections of the Arabian Nights" read:

> Six columns, three on either side,
> Pure silver, underpropt a rich
> Throne of the massive ore, from which
> Down-drooped, in many a floating fold,
> Engarlanded and diapered
> With inwrought flowers, a cloth of gold.
> (Ricks, 210)

For both Lawrence and Tennyson romance is to be found in the Middle East and the medieval period—and especially in collocations of the two.

Lawrence's most ingenious borrowing is "We lurched across plots of grass, between bars and fields of rough stone, in our two tenders and two armoured cars" (475). The juxtaposition of *bars* and *fields* makes a heraldic reference undeniable; ordinaries (simple geometrical charges, a bar being a horizontal

---

2. British Library Add. MS 45904. Letter of 8 May 1928 to Charlotte F. Shaw.

band) do theoretically stand out in relief from the field (i.e., the surface on which they are imposed).

Heraldic bars appear in two other places in *Seven Pillars*. On both occasions they are used in the same sense as in the first example, that is, to describe an unnaturally neat rise and fall in ground level.

> Less-used roads for hundreds of yards were like narrow ladders across the stone-fields, for the tread of each foot was filled in with clean yellow mud, and ridges or bars of the blue-grey stone remained between each stepping place. (187)

> Afterwards we marched again more slowly, as it seemed for hours, and the plain was still barred with deceitful dykes, which kept our attention at unprofitable stretch. (313)

A *mural crown* is a form of crown or coronet, represented as consisting of stones like those used in the building of city or fortress walls. La Sale tells us that "Les Romains ainsi qu'ilz honnoroient de couronnes ceulx qui faisoient les grans vaillances d'armes, si comme celui qui premier passoit le fossé ou le palis de l'ost aux ennemis, estoit couronné de la couronne Valère, et celui qui premier montoit sur l'eschielle et sur les murs, à l'assaut d'une cité ou chastel ou ville, estoit couronné de la couronne Muralle." ("The Romans were wont to honour with crowns them that did great feats of arms; and that he who first passed the moat or the rampart of the enemy's host was crowned with the Crown Valerian, and he who first mounted upon the scaling ladder or upon the walls, at the assault of a city or a castle or a town, was crowned with the Crown Mural." Antoine de la Sale, *Little John of Saintré*, trans. Irvine Gray [London: Routledge, 1931], 35.)

And Lawrence writes:

> Politically, [Aleppo] stood aside altogether, save in Arab quarters which, like overgrown half-nomad villages scattered over with price-less mosques, extended east and south of the mural crown of its great citadel. (261)

> We went over the ridge and down to the base of the shapely cone, whose mural crown was the ring-wall of the old castle of Monreale, very noble against the night sky. (393)

The use of *crested* is probably suggested by a study of heraldry, a crest being the device worn on top of the helm in jousts and tournaments.

> We turned our camels to the right and advanced towards the rock, which reared its crested domes so high over us that the ropes of our head-cloths slipped back round our necks as we stared up. (295)

> Behind his tall figure the ruins were crested by a motley band, samples from every village and tribe in the Hauran. (489)

Lawrence's use of various forms of *rampant* should not be ignored, although the word can make up part of the vocabulary of those with no knowledge of heraldry. One Arab has been twice demoted in the Turkish Army for "rampant nationalism" (63); a certain type of Englishman becomes the more "rampantly English" the longer he is away from England (271).

A semiheraldic allusion is also present in Lawrence's reference to the men "whose minds all wore my livery" (242). The livery worn by a noble's men would incorporate his heraldic colors (tincture; metal; or stain) and perhaps his badge. Finally, Lawrence once refers to the other side of the shield, to represent "the corruption of our enthusiasm" (371). Of a homosexual encounter involving an Arab and a British soldier there remains only in the 1976 edition the cryptic remark that "Remote from the fighting line, in Akaba, during this pause, we saw the reverse of the shield . . . which made the moral condition of the base unsatisfactory" (371). It is presumably the interracial nature of the incident that makes it unacceptable.

By now the reader has seen evidence to support the view that Lawrence is an intensely "literary" writer. Although Blunt and Blunt sanctioned his view of the Arabs as a martial and chivalrous people who actually lived the ethos he admired, Lawrence's interests had been directed to the Middle East long before. The first (1909) visit had been ostensibly prompted by a quest after material for his B.A. thesis on Crusading military architecture. A letter of 24 January 1911 refers casually to "my [projected] monumental work on the

Crusades" (*HL*, 130), while another of about the same time reveals Lawrence's mastery of the Crusades' military aspects (*Letters*, 93–97). Basil Liddell Hart wrote in the first part of his biography (entitled "The 'Crusader' ") that "[in Lawrence's early years] the idea of a Crusade, the idea underlying it, revolved in his mind, giving rise to a dream Crusade, which implied a leader with whom in a sense he identified himself yet [he] remained as himself a sympathetic observer" (16). Lawrence certainly did so dream and he eventually used Hart's biography to claim that the dream had been realized, at least to some extent. Lawrence exalted the war he fought in by comparing it with the old, glorious one. More specifically, as late as 1933, he makes claims about the true nature of his war—of himself—by comparing himself with Saladin.

Here is Ibn Sheddad, Saladin's biographer, on his former master and friend: "He was well acquainted with the pedigrees of the old Arabs, and with the details of their battles; he knew all their adventures; he had the pedigrees of his horses *at his fingers' ends*, and was master of all curious and strange lore."[3] Here is Lawrence on himself: "When I took a decision, or adopted an alternative it was after studying every relevant—and many an irrelevant—factor. Geography, tribal structure, religion, social customs, language, appetites, standards—all were *at my finger-ends*" (*RGLH*, 2:75). In 'T. E. Lawrence in Arabia and After' (447), Liddell Hart quotes from this letter, thus adding to the myth. Lawrence never arrived at a consistent view of the possibilities of chivalric action in the twentieth century. *Seven Pillars* echoes phrases (or simply quotes without acknowledgment) both from works that take chivalry seriously and from those that mock it. He came back from the East with the news that "the seven pillars were fallen down,"[4] but some years after writing this implicitly linked himself with Saladin.

Lawrence goes on to talk about his expertise with modern weapons that Saladin never dreamt of, but the knowledge needed by the two warriors overlaps even after seven or so centuries. Saladin knew the genealogy and "adventures" of his men. On several occasions Lawrence shows himself aware

---

3. Behâ ed-Dîn, *What Befell Sultan Yûsuf* [i.e., Saladin], 43. Behâ ed-Dîn is usually anglicized Bohadin, just as Salâh ed-Dîn is usually anglicized Saladin. Behâ ed-Dîn is often nicknamed Ibn Sheddad, as he was brought up by his maternal uncles the Beni Sheddâd (xiii). My emphasis.

4. British Library Add. MS 45903–04. Lawrence to Charlotte F. Shaw.

of the importance of one's forebears to the Arabs: the ashraf can so prove themselves because of "the family tree—an immense roll preserved at Mecca, in custody of the Emir of Mecca, the elected Sherif of Sherifs, supposed to be the senior and noblest of all" (24–25); Faisal "seemed never . . . to stumble over a relationship" (90). And "Saladin was a Kurdish nobody. Feisal [Saladin-figure though he be in *Seven Pillars*]—thought himself better than that!" (*RGLH*, 2:101). Family and personal worth are intimately linked, the former setting standards: "Fahad, in courteous fashion, chided me gently for presuming to ride their district on an adventure [Ibn Sheddad's word too] while his father's sons lay in their tent" (322). "My father's son" is here more than an elaborate manner of referring to oneself, for "These sons of Trad, the desert-famous champion of the Beni Sakhr, could not miss an opportunity of following up their father's deeds" (*Seven Pillars* [1922], 176). Lawrence is as aware as Saladin that a knowledge of the desert warriors' family and adventures is important: "Of course I had learnt their histories and families long ago, in readiness for a sudden campaign with them, and so was able, though an interloper, to thrust myself with dignity among such men of worship, without slighting any chance-met warrior by an ignorance of his standing in the scanty desert" ([1922], 252). Consider, furthermore, the second of the "Twenty-Seven Articles," written by Lawrence for the guidance of other British officers who would work with the Arabs: "Learn all you can about your Ashraf and Bedu. Get to know their families, clans and tribes, friends and enemies. . . . Until you can understand their allusions avoid getting deep into conversation, or you will drop bricks." As for "the pedigrees of . . . horses," horses rarely appear in *Seven Pillars*, but we do come across "the pedigree camel given by Ibn Saud of Nejd to King Hussein and by him to Feisal" (194) and "Ghazala—a camel vaulted and huge-ribbed as an antique ship; towering a good foot above the next of our animals, and yet perfectly proportioned, with a stride like an ostrich's—a lyrical beast, noblest and best bred of the Howeitat camels, a female of nine remembered dams" (218). Ibn Sheddad finally writes of Saladin's grasp of "curious and strange lore." Lawrence too inevitably picks up such lore: a letter of 1910 reports his ability to "make Kamreddin, and . . . iron a fez, and all sorts of things," while the reader of *Seven Pillars* closes the book knowing how the Bedu disinfect wounds, their attitude to broken bones, and why one should ride a female camel rather than a male.

Lawrence had sensed "Ibn Shedad's" [*sic*] presence in Azrak, with those of
Diocletian and Harith ([1922], 142). He had learned strategic ideas from
Saladin, a "direct model" ([1922], 137), and seen the similarities between
their tasks and roles. But although he was happy enough to borrow a phrase
or two from Saladin's biographer, when it came to the transcribing of his
experience Lawrence was a more ambitious and gifted writer. *Seven Pillars*
may well be what Lawrence described it as early in the 1922 version: "a
chronicle in the spirit of the old men who marched with Bohemond [a
leader of the First Crusade who helped capture Antioch in 1098] or Coeur
de Lion. It treats of daily life, mean happenings, little people" (12). It is true
too that both Ibn Sheddad and Lawrence are partially inspired by the
necessity of setting down the glorious history they have seen and lived
through; and both feel they have seen men who have kinship with the heroes
of antiquity.

> (Ibn Sheddad) Having seen the goodly days of the reign of our Lord
> the Sultan, it was possible for me to believe certain traditions of the
> men of olden time that are commonly considered improbable and
> fictitious, and to accept as true, anecdotes of noble and benevolent
> men. . . . [T]hese deeds are of such a nature that he who knows them
> cannot keep them concealed, and he who has witnessed them feels
> compelled to pass on to others a narrative of the wonders he has
> seen. (Behâ ed-Dîn, 2)

> (Lawrence) We were wrought up with ideas inexpressible and vapour-
> ous, but to be fought for. We lived many lives in those whirling
> campaigns, never sparing ourselves. . . . [W]e had worked for a new
> heaven and a new earth.
>
> . . . .
> It seemed to me historically needful to reproduce the tale, as perhaps
> no one but myself in Feisal's army had thought of writing down at the
> time what we felt, what we hoped, what we tried (4, 3).

Ibn Sheddad is a less talented writer than Lawrence, and *What Befell Sultan
Yûsuf* is much more a chronicle without literary pretension than *Seven
Pillars*. One chapter is entitled "Arrival of 'Imâd ed-Dîn Zenghi, Prince of

Sinjâr, and of Several Other Chieftains." Like most of Ibn Sheddad's chapters, it consists of one medium-length paragraph, which is worth quoting in full.

> On the 23rd of the month Rabi'a II. (May 30, 1190) Prince 'Imâd ed-Dîn Zenghi, son of Maudûd and Lord of Sinjâr, came into the camp with great pomp and display, followed by an army splendidly equipped in every particular. The Sultan received him with every honour, and drew up his troops in line of battle so as to go out and meet him. The kadis and (government) secretaries were the first from our army to appear before the prince; then came the Sultan's sons, and, finally, the Sultan himself, who at once led his guest to a spot in full view of the enemy, and, after halting there for some time, brought him back to the camp and welcomed him to his own tent. He set a magnificent banquet before him, and presented him with a number of rare and curious things that surpass my powers of description. He had a cushion placed only for him by the side of his own, and a satin cloth laid on the ground of the tent for him to walk upon. Then he ordered a tent to be pitched for him on the extreme left of the left wing, close to the river. On the 7th of the following month, Sinjâr Shah, Lord of Jezîrat Ibn Omar, son of Seif ed-Dîn Ghâzi Ibn Maudûd Ibn Zenghi, came into the camp. He came at the head of a fine army, splendidly equipped. The Sultan received him with the greatest honour, welcomed him in his tent, and then had one pitched for him next to the quarters occupied by his uncle, 'Imâd ed-Dîn. On the 9th of the same month arrived 'Alâ ed-Dîn Knorrem Shah, son of Mas'ûd, Prince of Mosul; he represented his father, whose troops he brought to the Sultan. Salah ed-Dîn showed the greatest joy when he heard of his approach, and rode out a considerable distance to meet him. He made him dismount, and led him into his own tent, where he gave him a magnificent present; then he commanded a tent to be pitched for him between those occupied by his own sons, el-Melek el-Afdal and el-Melek ez-Zâher. (180–81)

Two points should be made before examining Lawrence's description of the arrival of allies. First, Lawrence does not usually condescend to give dates, partly for typographical reasons (he thought figures looked ugly in the text and writing out dates in words was a cheat), partly because that is not the sort of truth he wants. Second, Lawrence would never make such an admission of defeat or indifference as "a number of rare and curious things that surpass my powers of description." Lawrence is always ready with an attempt at describing the "rare and curious," whether it be an object, a custom, or a physical appearance, and his effort is often successful. Lawrence is a much more detailed and precise writer than Ibn Sheddad; he would eschew the Arab's "splendidly equipped in every particular" of the first few lines and describe arms and mounts; he would tell us what was the "magnificent present" of the last few lines. Ibn Sheddad is indeed a chronicler, one who would get down his story before it is too late but who is not stylistically ambitious.

Lawrence's description of very similar scenes is significantly different.

> Then began our flood of visitors. All day and every day they came, now in the running column of shots, raucous shouting and rush of camel-feet which meant a Bedouin parade, it might be of Rualla, or Sherarat, or Serahin, Serdiyeh, or Beni Sakhr, chiefs of great name like ibn Zuhair, ibn Kaebir, Rafa el Khoreisha, or some little father of a family demonstrating his greedy goodwill before the fair eyes of Ali ibn el Hussein. Then it would be a wild gallop of horse: Druses or the ruffling warlike peasants of the Arab plain. Sometimes it was a cautious slow-led caravan of ridden camels, from which stiffly dismounted Syrian politicans or traders not accustomed to the road. One day arrived a hundred miserable Armenians, fleeing starvation and the suspended terror of the Turks. Again would come a spick and span group of mounted officers, Arab deserters from the Turkish armies, followed, often as not, by a compact company of Arab rank and file. Always they came, day after day, till the desert, which had been trackless when we came, was starred out with grey roads.
>
> Ali appointed first one, then two, and at last three guest-masters, who received the rising tide of these newcomers, sorted worshipful from curious, and marshalled them in due time before him or me. . . . Merchants from Damascus brought presents: sweet-meats, sesame, caramel, apricot paste, nuts, silk clothes for ourselves, brocade cloaks, head-cloths, sheep-skins, felt rugs with coloured strands beaten into

them in arabesques, Persian carpets. We returned them coffee and
sugar, rice, and rolls of white cotton sheeting. (344–45)

Note the repeated and varied adverbs or adverbial phrases of time, as
Lawrence builds up his description by adding picture to picture within the
framework of "All day and every day" ("Then . . . Sometimes . . . One day . . .
Always"). Note the two words that are borrowings from admired medieval or
neomedieval authors, "ruffled" being from Morris[5] and "worshipful" from
Malory. Even a phrase like "fair eyes" might be from a Morris prose romance
or a Eugene Mason translation. Note the precisely observed detail in the
description of "rare and curious things": "felt rugs with coloured strands
beaten into them in arabesques." Note the metaphoric use of language at the
end of the first paragraph. It must be admitted, though, that Lawrence's
failings are also present: "fair eyes" would have been rejected by his
contemporaries as a coy nineteenth-century archaism. Although one senses
in the passage a delight in the variety and liveliness of the East, one also feels
that the passage is a little *voulu*.

The same conclusions would be drawn from a comparison of *Seven Pillars*
and, for example, Geoffrey de Vinsauf's *Itinerary of Richard I, and Others to
the Holy Land*, or Le Sieur de Joinville's account of "the chivalric career of
the pious and exemplary Saint Louis of France" (Bohn, iii). Geoffrey and
Joinville too are straightforward chroniclers in a way beneath or beyond the
self-conscious Lawrence. Devoid of literary pretensions, they tell what they
have seen and praise the great men they have followed. They do not carefully
select their words; they start at the beginning and end at the end. They are
noteworthy in that they are not embarrassed by either the glory or the
cruelty of war. Indeed, they are almost unaware of it in a way that is difficult
for Lawrence. What Lawrence selects from their works implies that chivalry
lies in the eye of the beholder.

One of Lawrence's biographers, John E. Mack, finds that his subject's
attitude to the Crusades was always unnaturally technical, that "in his stress
on the military, technical, strategic and tactical aspects of the Crusader castles
he seemed to avoid considering in detail the purposes to which these

5. E.g., ". . . just as Ralph steadied himself and ruffled up to him." *Well at the World's End,*
chapter 4.

structures were put or the real purposes of the Crusader in the East" (45). Only once does Lawrence seem aware of the bloodiness of the Crusades, in a reference to the campaign in southern France against the Albigensian heretics: "The town had been taken, and the Crusaders wanted to kill the heretics, but there were many Catholics in the town as well. What shall we do? they asked the Legate, Peter of Castelnau. 'Kill them all,' said he, 'God will recognise his own,' and some 8,000 were butchered in cold blood. Pleasant people those 13th cent. Crusaders!" (*HL*, 67). The idealistic reader of chivalric adventure certainly finds much to gratify his tastes in Geoffrey de Vinsauf and Joinville. For example, in the former we have Geoffrey's description of the glorious appearance of the Christian army: "You might there see a chosen company of virtuous and brave youth, whose equals it would have been difficult to meet with, bright armour and pennons, with their glittering emblazonry; banners of various forms; lances, with gleaming points; shining helmets, and coats of mail: an army well regulated in the camp and terrible to the foe!" (Bohn, 226). We are told that Coeur de Lion knighted Saladin's nephew, specially sent to him for that purpose (267), and how Saladin's brother honored the Christian warrior's bravery with gifts (324). Joinville describes the splendid appearance of le comte de Jaffa's heraldically decorated galley (391–92), and the manly valor of hand-to-hand fighting, crossbows and ordinary bows not being used (413–14). On the other hand, Geoffrey is quite uncompromising in his recounting of Coeur de Lion's slaughter of the Saracen prisoners at Acre ("King Richard, aspiring . . . to vindicate the Christian religion . . . ordered 2,700 of the Turkish hostages to be led forth from the city and hanged; his soldiers marched forward with delight to fulfill his commands"),[6] and Joinville is capable of reporting Christian acts of cowardice (419).

The best example of taking from a favorite book what one wants brings us back to the text of *Seven Pillars*; it concerns, appropriately enough, the Bedouin. Joinville saw some of them.

> [T]he Bedouins, who are a powerful people, entered the camp of the Saracens and Turks, and seized and carried off whatever they could

---

6. Bohn, 222. Hewlett, a later writer, cannot do this, but he does provide excuses for Richard's behavior (276). Neither Geoffrey nor Hewlett even hints at Richard's homosexuality.

find. . . . [The Saracens] said it was [the Bedouins'] usual custom to fall
on the weakest, which is the nature of dogs; for when there is one
dog pursued by another, and a shouting made after him, all the other
dogs fall on him.

. . . .

They never are armed for combat, for they say, and believe, that no
one can die but at his appointed hour: they have likewise a mode of
cursing, alluding to their faith, when they sware at their children,
saying, "Be thou accursed, like him who arms himself for fear of
death." In battle they use only a sword, made after the Turkish manner,
and are clothed in linen robes like to surplices. They are an ugly race,
and hideous to look at; for their hair and beards are long and black.[7]

Richard Aldington had read this passage and referred to it in his biography
of Lawrence.

The nomad tribes lived chiefly as Gertrude Bell says, "by stealing each
other's washing," which is misleading, as they washed their clothes
but once a year—but what she means is that the camels, sheep, goats
stolen on tribal raids from Tribe B by Tribe A were stolen back again
at the first opportunity. War was a ritual of robbery with violence.
"The Bedouins," says the Sieur de Joinville in the 13th century, "live
out of doors in tents with their wives and children. . . . [ellipsis in
original] they wrap their heads in towels *dont laides gens et hisdeuses
sont à regarder*." And speaking of their plundering the camp of their
nominal rulers, "the Saracens," he explains that "the use and custom
of the Bedouins is always to fall upon the weaker side." Tenacious
holders of old customs, the Bedouins whether of Arabia or Africa had
not changed at all in that respect between the 13th and the 20th
centuries." (142)

7. Bohn, 420–21. There is an editorial note on this passage: "The Lord de Joinville has here
confounded, as elsewhere, the Bedouins with the Assassins. Jacques de Vitry says positively they
were Arabians, that their residence was near Aleppo and Crack, in Arabia, and that the Assassins
inhabited a canton of the province of Phoemia, enclosed by mountains near Tortosa. However
this may be, every writer agrees that the Bedouins were a wandering and vagabond people." We
may let the point pass, as both Lawrence and Aldington assume they are Bedouins.

What Aldington takes from Joinville is a contemptuous impression of Bedouin rapacity, cowardice, and ugliness. What Lawrence takes helps form and support one of the most sacred of his dreams; surely the reference in *Seven Pillars* to fighting without benefit of armor is directly attributable to and derived from Joinville. "[They were] larding me with titles, which always seemed to me a cowardice—like body-armour in a duel" writes Lawrence. (The milder and later wording is, "Such imputed dignities, like body armour in a duel, were no doubt useful; but uncomfortable, and mean, too" [354].) The Bedouin, according to Joinville, did not put on armor for religious reasons—the day of one's death being preordained, the wearing of armor would be useless at best, impious at worst. Whether Lawrence omits the religious dimension deliberately or whether, in the course of years, the reference was gradually transmuted in his mind cannot be confidently decided. But he retained the connection between lack of armor and lack of fear of death. The connection is made even more clearly in the second report Joinville makes of the Bedouin belief (the repetition also helps the report to stick in the reader's mind): "Another point is, that no man can die before his pre-determined day. This the Bedouins so firmly believe, that they never go in armour to battle; for, if they did, they would think they were acting contrary to the dogmas of their faith. When they sware at their children, they usually say, 'Mayest thou be cursed like him who arms himself for fear of death,' which, they think, every one should be ashamed of" (Bohn, 473).

Perhaps the best-known chronicler of chivalry is Jean Froissart, a contemporary of Chaucer and "still the name that stands for chivalrous adventure in the minds of all the readers of history," in the words of W. P. Ker, in his long introduction to the six-volume translation by Lord Berners. (We know that Lawrence possessed a copy.) Froissart "is accepted without question as the author from whom the portraiture of that age is to be sought" (Ker, 1:ix). Ker finds Froissart a realistic author in that he does not idealize war, battles, and the men who fight in them: "He shows no preference for the kind of fighting which is most like tournaments. Joinville praises a battle in which there is nothing but clean strokes in the mellay, no interference of bolts or arrows; but Froissart knows many different kinds of fighting, and does not disparage any of them for the sake of that which was of course the noblest" (1:lxxi). Life in Froissart's pages, writes Ker, is not theatrical or unreal; our chronicler is "no more ostentatious with his banners and pennons waving in the wind than the Books of Moses are [with their equivalents]" (1:lxix). Ker maintains that "It would be easier to prove Froissart a writer of sad stories than a chronicler of the false splendours of chivalry, if one were to set down with his book before one to find illustrative passages by turning over his pages" (1:lxx).

False or not, the splendors of chivalry do keep cropping up. Present in both Froissart and Lawrence is a sense of the joy of war, and this joy is connected for both with chivalric display. "[T]hey came thyder," writes Froissart of the French forces under King Philip, "in goodly order with baners displayed, that hit was great beautie to beholde their puyssant array" (Ker, 1:325). "It was great beautie to behold shynynyge agaynst the sonne, baners, penons, and clere bassenettes, and so great nombre of people, that the eye of man coude nat nombre them: their speares semed a great thicke wode" (Ker, 3:448). The same feelings inspire certain passages in *Seven Pillars*; Lawrence too feels "the greatness, the catch at heart, of an army moving into battle" (233). Before Crécy (1346), the English king reviews his three battles: "The thirde batayle had the kyng: he had sevyn hundred men of armes and two thousand archers: than the kyng lept on a hobby, with a whyte rodde in his hand, one of his marshals on the one hande and the other on the other hand; he rode fro renke to renke, desyringe every man to take hede that day to his right and honour" (Ker, 1:295). The following, from *Seven Pillars*, is very similar. Lawrence too depicts heraldic splendor, with the hope of martial honor at the beginning of an adventure (the Arab army is advancing on Wejh). Lawrence has, if not a king, a prince, and he casts himself as one of the marshals.

> The starting signal went, but only for us and the Ageyl. The other units of the army, standing each man by his couched camel, lined up beside our road, and, as Faisal came near, saluted him in silence. He called back cheerfully, "Peace upon you," and each head sheikh returned the phrase. When we had passed they mounted, taking the time from their chiefs, and so the forces behind us swelled till there was a line of men and camels winding along the narrow pass towards the watershed for as far back as the eye reached.
>
> Feisal's greetings had been the only sounds before we reached the crest of the rise . . . but there ibn Dakhil . . . dropped back a pace or

two, marshalled our following into a broad column of ordered ranks, and made the drums strike up. Everyone burst out singing a full-throated song in honour of Emir Feisal and his family.

The march became rather splendid and barbaric. First rode Feisal in white, then Sharraf at his right in red head-cloth and henna-dyed tunic and cloak, myself on his left in white and scarlet, behind us three banners of faded crimson silk with gilt spikes, behind them the drummers playing a march, and behind them again the wild mass of twelve hundred bouncing camels of the bodyguard, packed as closely as they could move, the men in every variety of coloured clothes and the camels nearly as brilliant in their trappings. We filled the valley to its banks with our flashing stream. (102–3)

Froissart writes of a world in which honor is of first importance. It is, so to speak, the intangible, invisible counterpart to, and justification of, the chivalric display of the kings and knights. Lawrence can approximate—or even, in a "splendid and barbaric" way, outdo—Froissart's descriptions of banners waving in the wind and gorgeously dressed warriors; he is as preoccupied by the moral content of the code that dictates the warriors' actions as is the medieval chronicler. But though he can imitate and describe the outward show, he cannot reproduce the behavior of a Froissartian knight. The Black Prince is honorable; the majority of Lawrence's Arabs are honorable; Lawrence has irrevocably pawned his own honor; to be more precise, he makes an anachronistic attempt at an honorable integrity of life that is doomed to failure in the postmedieval world.

In the courtly and martial world of Froissart, life is relatively simple. One's life, or freedom, or goods, or one's very kingdom, may be taken away from one. But one's honor will remain intact even in defeat, if one has followed the code. Froissart's famous account of the Black Prince's words to the French King after Poitiers make this point.

But thou he sayd to the kyng, Sir, for Goddessake make non yvell or hevy chere, though God this day dyde nat consent to folowe your wyll: for sir, surely the kynge my father shall bere you as moche honour and amyte as he may do, and shall acorde with you so reasonably that ye shall ever be frendes toguyder after; and sir, methynke ye ought to rejoyse, though the journey be nat as ye wolde have had it, for this day ye have wonne the hygh renome of prowes and have past this day in valyantnesse all other of your partie: sir, I say natte this to mocke you, for all that be on our partie that sawe every mannes dedes, ar playnly acorded by true sentence to gyve you the price and chapelette. (lxix)

One modern historian has written that the same Black Prince's slaughter of the inhabitants of Limoges—usually considered a stain on his character—was also motivated by the Prince's regard for his honor. Froissart, in another celebrated passage (Ker, 2:355–57), shows great pity for the men, women, and children who met their end there. But John Barnie considers that after the Bishop of Limoges had handed the city over to the French, the Black Prince had no option but to show his contempt for the treachery of his former friend. "The citizens suffered as much as the commanders, at the Prince's express command, because honour is collective as well as personal. The treachery of [the bishop] was also their treachery" (78–79). Similarly, when the prince rashly offered the captured du Guesclin (the "famous Constable" whose daughter's memorial brass Lawrence had so admired in Lehon) a ransom of 100,000 francs, thinking the sum too great to be payable, he had to keep his word when the constable did in fact come up with the money. The prince "had no alternative but to stand by his offer if he wished to maintain his reputation for chivalry. Politically and militarily it was an act of the greatest folly. In chivalric terms it was the only logical course open to the prince since honour and reputation are more important than temporary military advantage" (Barnie, 80).

Let us return to La Sale to encapsulate our discussion of honor. Lawrence had certainly read La Sale's best-known work, *Le Petit Jehan*; he very probably had also read a lesser work, *Le Réconfort de Madame du Fresne*, published by J. Nève in 1903 in his book on La Sale.[8] The most important part of *Le Réconfort*, written as a consolatory work for a lady who had lost her first child, is the first of two stories about brave mothers. The Black Prince plays a major role in this tale as well, but here he is unambiguously the villain. He has besieged the fortress of Brest so forcefully that its commander, the

---

8. 101–55. See also Auerbach, *Mimesis,* 232.

Seigneur du Chastel, is obliged to conclude an agreement with the prince to
the effect that he will surrender the fortress at a specified date if no help
arrives before then. As hostage he gives his only son, a boy of thirteen. Four
days before the agreed period expires, a ship arrives at the port with
provisions.

> There is great rejoicing, and the commander sends a herald to the
> Prince with the request that he return the hostage, since help has
> arrived. . . . The Prince, angry at seeing the long-coveted prize, of
> which he had thought himself sure, escape him, refuses to consider
> the arrival of provisions as help in the sense of the agreement, and
> demands that the fortress be surrendered on the specified day,
> otherwise the hostage will be forfeited. (Auerbach, 233)

The remainder of the story may be quickly told. The Black Prince persists in
his threat. The seigneur, giving way privately to despair, is only enabled to
do what must be done by the wisdom of his wife, who realizes that if she
loses her husband to his grief, she loses everything.

> Vous ne avez que ung honneur lequel après Dieu, sur femme, sur
> enffans et sur toutes choses devez plus amer. Et sy ne avez que ung
> filz. Or advisez duquel vous avez la plus grande perte. Et vrayement,
> Monseigneur, il y a grant choiz. Nous sommes assez en aaige pour en
> avoir, se à Dieu plaist; mais vostre honneur une foiz perdu, lasse,
> jamais plus ne le recouvrerz. Et quant mon conseil vous tendrez, les
> gens diront de vous, mort ou vif que soiez: C'est le preudomme et
> très loyal chevallier. Et pour ce, Monseigneur, sy très humblement
> que je scay, vous supplie, fetes comme moy et en lui plus ne penssés
> que se ne l'euissiez jamais eu; ains vous reconffortez, et remerciez
> Dieu de tout, qui le vous a donné pour votre honneur rachetter.
> (quoted in Auerbach, 235)

> [You have but one honor which, after God, you must love more than
> wife, child, and all things. And likewise you have but one son.
> Consider now which would be the greater loss to you. And truly, my
> lord, here is a great choice. We are still of an age to have sons, if it

pleases God. But your honor, once lost, alas, you can never recover. And if you follow my counsel, people will say of you, whether you are dead or alive: That is a man of honor and a very loyal knight. And therefore, my lord, as humbly as I know how, I beg you, do as I do, and think no more of him than if you had never had him. But take courage and thank God for everything, for He has given him to you to redeem your honor.] (Auerbach, 237–38)

In a movingly reported scene the boy is executed. The seigneur eventually obtains revenge by conspicuously hanging twelve high-ranking enemy captives, despite their offers of large ransoms. Others have their right eyes pierced and their right hands and right ears cut off, and are told to thank "vostre seigneur Herodes . . . des autres yeulx, oreilles et poings senestres que je vous laisse, pour ce que il donna le corps mort et innocent de mon filz a Chastel mon herault" ["your master Herod . . . for your left eyes, ears, and hands, which I let you keep because he gave the dead and innocent body of my son to Chastel, my herald."] (Auerbach, 240–41)

Auerbach's comments on this story are most interesting.

> I wish to point out especially how striking a thing it is to a modern reader that a political and military occurrence, which belongs to a historical context well known to us, is viewed exclusively as a problem in the ethos of class. Nothing is ever said about the actual importance of the fortress, about the unfortunate consequences which its fall would have for the cause of France and her king. On the contrary, the entire concern is with the knightly honor of the Seigneur du Chastel, with a pledged word and its interpretation, with the fealty of a vassal, with an oath, with personal responsibility. . . . The impression all this makes is as if the political and military direction of the war were still completely unrationalized, as if any effective control of operations did not exist, so that the measures taken depend largely upon the personal relations, the emotional reactions, and the concepts of knightly honor of the commanders who happen to be facing each other in any particular encounter. (243–44)

This is not exactly the situation in Lawrence's war. In *Seven Pillars*, much *is* said about "the importance of the fortress," or Lawrence's equivalent thereof; much *is* said about "the unfortunate consequences" that "its fall would have for the cause of France and her king," or rather England and her king. But Lawrence does consistently show an interest—indeed, an obsession—with what could be called his "knightly honor . . . with a pledged word and its interpretation . . . with an oath, with personal responsibility." Oft-quoted remarks from *Seven Pillars* must be quoted once more.

> The Cabinet raised the Arabs to fight for us by definite promises of self-government afterwards. Arabs believe in persons, not in institutions. They saw in me a free agent of the British Government, and demanded from me an endorsement of its written promises. So I had to join the conspiracy, and, for what my word was worth, assured the men of their reward. In our two years' partnership under fire they grew accustomed to believing me and to think my Government, like myself, sincere. In this hope they performed some fine things, but, of course, instead of being proud of what we did together, I was continually and bitterly ashamed.
>
> It was evident from the beginning that if we won the war those promises would be dead paper, and had I been an honest adviser of the Arabs I would have advised them to go home and not risk their lives fighting for such stuff. . . . I risked the fraud, on my conviction that Arab help was necessary to our cheap and speedy victory in the East, and that better we win and break our word than lose. (5)

Time and again Lawrence returns to the problem. On the one hand, Faisal, faced with "the sacrifice, or at least the postponement of immediate advantage to the Arabs . . . rose, as ever, to a proposition of honour" (133); on the other hand

> If I did not hesitate to risk my life, why fuss to dirty it? Yet life and honour seemed in different categories, not able to be sold one for another: and for honour, had I not lost that a year ago when I assured the Arabs that England kept her plighted word?

> Or was honour like the Sybil's leaves, the more that was lost the
> more precious the little left? Its part equal to the whole? (436)

There is more here than the distaste of a decent man for the compromises
and duplicities of international politics. Lawrence has imported into twentieth-century geopolitics an anachronistic concept of *personal* honor, for he
believes himself to be surrounded by an anachronistic people who share that
concept ("Arabs believe in persons, not in institutions"). At least, the more
simple and noble share it, but the twentieth century makes itself felt even in
Arabia: "[I] must put on record my conviction that England is out of the Arab
affair with clean hands [after the postwar Colonial Office settlements]. Some
of our Arab advocates (the most vociferous joined our ranks after the
Armistice) have rejected my judgment on this point. Like a tedious Pensioner
I showed them my wounds (over sixty I have, each scar evidence of a pain
incurred in Arab service) as proof I had worked sincerely on their side. They
found me out-of-date: and I was happy to withdraw from a political milieu
which had never been congenial" (*Letters*, 345–46).

G. Wilson Knight hits the point exactly when he writes of Lawrence: "He
aspired to that chivalric unity which was split by the Renaissance into Church
and State, so that soul and nation were henceforth opposed and man tugged
between Christ and politics in a world of warring. Lawrence is central to our
present confusions: that is why he fascinates" (315). And Elie Kedourie
misunderstands when he accuses Lawrence of "[promoting] a pernicious
confusion between public and private, [and looking] to politics for a spiritual
satisfaction which it cannot possibly provide, [investing] it with an impossibly
transcendental significance" (275). He could hardly be more wrong in
accusing Lawrence of writing a corrupt and corrupting book—"corrupting in
a manner particularly familiar to the modern age, when political causes have
come to be endowed with transcendental significance, to warrant the greatest
sacrifice and justify the most heinous crimes" (273). There could not be a
greater difference between the revolutionary (or counterrevolutionary) prepared to commit any enormity in pursuit of his ends, and Lawrence (and the
Seigneur du Chastel, and the Black Prince), who see themselves as ideally,
and often practically, subject to a code greater than themselves and the ends
they seek. Lawrence's ideas of honor are literary-medieval. It is part of his
tragedy that Froissart translates only imperfectly to Arabia in our century.

V·I·I·I

SEVEN PILLARS
AND
NEOMEDIEVAL ROMANCE

LAWRENCE has read accounts—scores or hundreds of accounts, in the form of chronicle, saga, *chanson de geste* or romance—of heroic deeds performed in a past that is "distant and tinselled" (459). He was impelled from bourgeois Oxford and the personal conflicts it represented toward a region where his gifts might have scope and where his longing for what had stirred his imagination could be satisfied without obvious self-deceit. He finds himself, by a mixture of luck and effort, in a region where, and at a time when, the wars of Saladin (or Richard, or almost any medieval hero the reader cares to name) could, in some sense, be fought again. He finds, furthermore, on returning home at the end of the war, that, although he has seen and suffered much that outrages any idea that war and colorful chivalry can coexist, he is very popular with a public that desperately wants to believe they can. This hero-worship delights the vanity and sense of being unique that had helped make England an unsatisfactory home in the first place, while again reinforcing and validating the idealistic dreams damaged but not destroyed by the experiences of the war. The result of all this, when fueled by an intense desire for literary achievement and fame, is *Seven Pillars of Wisdom*, which was written, as Paul Zweig has pointed out, "against the never-mentioned background of his immense fame" (230). Lawrence needs this fame too badly for both personal and political reasons to deny it (at the time of the writing of the early drafts his Arab friends may be sacrificed to the interests of France, and every weapon must be used). So *Seven Pillars* and letters to biographers echo appropriate phrases from Saladin and others. But Lawrence is also far too honest a man to represent his campaign as something that he cannot viscerally feel it was; hence, transmuted references from the *Moallakat* and quoted phrases from works that mock chivalry. After the publication of *Seven Pillars* (considered by its author a failure), Lawrence tends to feel, especially in moments of depression, that to pursue true chivalry is to pursue a chimera; that, in fact, all ethical systems are irremediably contingent.

But even before coming to this disheartening conclusion, Lawrence can depict even his doubts and searchings in a quasi-medieval form; if the virtues of the *chanson de geste* imply adherence to a public ideal, those of the romance tend to concentrate on the strivings and possible failings of the individual. Lawrence's first months in Arabia are months of fascinated induction, during which he hopes to identify himself with the beliefs and practices of the martial and chivalrous Arabs. As time passes, and he is overwhelmed by the horrors of the war, Lawrence dissociates himself more and more from the alien people, and also from the effort to believe in any transcendental philosophy—especially that which had caused him to make such a great physical and emotional investment in the Arabs and their revolt.

To be more specific, there is an important sense, in which *Seven Pillars of Wisdom* is a *Chanson de Roland* manquée. Nationalism has replaced religious faith as the all-important idea to be fought for; the Turks have replaced the "pagans" as the unfailingly evil enemy, from whom no good can ever be expected. The first point is made quite explicitly early in the book, as Lawrence travels to his first portentous meeting with Faisal. "My thoughts as we went were how this was the pilgrim road, down which, for uncounted generations, the people of the north had come to visit the Holy City, bearing with them gifts of faith for the shrine; and it seemed that the Arab revolt might be in a sense a return pilgrimage, to take back to the north, to Syria, an ideal for an ideal, a belief in liberty for their past belief in a revelation" (51–52). (In *Oriental Assembly*, Lawrence writes that "In our fathers' days . . . the men were Moslems first, or Christians, or infidels of some sort. Later on, if there was any reason for it, they might be Turks or Arabs, but about this they were not too certain: the important thing was the faith. We cannot sneer at them. Only too recently, in the manuscript and crossbow days, we were like them" [75]. The Middle East is nearer to the Middle Ages than we are.) The second point is made passim: from beginning to end of *Seven Pillars* not a good word is said about the Turks. They are stupid (e.g., 34, 101, 146, 172,

221), an unworthy enemy, barbarous ([1922], 167), and even "hopeless" (377, 481). If Lawrence does not say "Turques unt tort e Arabes unt dreit" he is not very far from it. Ideally, Lawrence would become a sort of Arab and support, by the strength and efficacy of his arm, the right side. At first there seem to be indications that this may happen: "Some Harb came up, driving a large herd of brood camels, and began to water them. . . . We watched them, without intercourse; for these were Masruh, and we [were] Beni Salem" (54). (Lawrence is here in disguise, and all is new and strange.) "Tafas . . . bought flour, of which with water he kneaded a dough cake. . . . When the cake was warmed he drew it out of the fire, and clapped it to shake off the dust; then we shared it together" (57). And, best of all, is the actual meeting with Faisal, with its color, its "silver-hilted sword" and "dagger," its gloriously antique exoticism and promise, its inspiring Saladin-figure ("The conjunction of Semites, an idea, and an armed prophet held illimitable possibilities," [106–7]).

Tafas said something to a slave who stood there with silver-hilted sword in hand. He led me to an inner court, on whose further side, framed between the uprights of a black doorway, stood a white figure waiting tensely for me. I felt at first glance that this was the man I had come to Arabia to seek—the leader who would bring the Arab Revolt to full glory. Feisal looked very tall and pillar-like, very slender, in his long white silk robes and his brown head-cloth bound with a brilliant scarlet and gold cord. His eyelids were dropped; and his black beard and colourless face were like a mask against the strange, still watchfulness of his body. His hands were crossed in front of him on his dagger.

I greeted him. He made way for me into the room, and sat down on his carpet near the door. As my eyes grew accustomed to the shade, they saw that the little room held many silent figures, looking at me or at Feisal steadily. He remained staring down at his hands, which were twisting slowly about his dagger. At last he inquired softly how I had found the journey. I spoke of the heat, and he asked how long from Rabegh, commenting that I had ridden fast for the season.

The conversation of Lawrence and Faisal is fraught with a half-understood promise, a not quite grasped significance.

> "And do you like our place here in Wadi Safra?"
> "Well; but it is far from Damascus."
> The word had fallen like a sword in their midst. There was a quiver. Then everybody present stiffened where he sat, and held his breath for a silent minute. Some, perhaps, were dreaming of far off success: others may have thought it a reflection on their late defeat. Feisal at length lifted his eyes, smiling at me, and said, "Praise be to God, there are Turks nearer us than that." We all smiled at him; and I rose and excused myself for the moment. (62)

"There are Turks nearer us than that" is an echo of the *Chanson de Roland*. Two "pagans" are talking.

> "Li amiralz est riches e puisant,
> En France irat Carlemagne querant,
> Rendre le quidet u mort o recreant."
> Dist Bramimunde: "Mar en irat itant!
> Plus pres d'ici purrez truver les Francs.
>
> (lines 2731–35)

> ["The Emir is mighty and powerful,
> He shall seek out Charlemagne in France,
> He intends to kill him or force him to concede defeat."
> Bramimonde said: "He'll rue the day he goes so far!
> You will find the Franks nearer here."]
>
> (Brault translation)

But already there have been hints of trouble to come. Lawrence is an Englishman who, unlike one British officer, cannot share his own people's unexamined ideas of right and wrong: "I had called Arab clothes uncomfortable merely. To him they were wrong" (41). Falling between two stools, he can share neither the easy prejudices of his compatriots, nor the unselfconscious practices of the Arabs. Attempting to see the Arabs as latter-day imitators of an idealized Saladin, he is yet obliged to record their lapses.

> The valley was a weird sight. The Arabs, gone raving mad, were rushing about at top speed bareheaded and half-naked, screaming, shooting into the air, clawing one another nail and fist, while they burst open trucks and staggered back and forward with immense bales, which they ripped by the rail-side, and tossed through, smashing what they did not want. The train had been packed with refugees and sick men, volunteers for boat-service on the Euphrates, and families of Turkish officers returning to Damascus. (289–90)

> A minute later, with a howl, the Beduin were upon the maddest looting of their history. Two hundred rifles, eighty thousand rounds of ammunition; many bombs, much food and clothing were in the station, and everybody smashed and profited. (416)

Attempting to see himself as an inhabitant of the Old World, he is obliged eventually to admit the existence of a great divide between himself and the semifeudal Arabs, because he is modern and moderate, and they are not. "I was tired to death of these Arabs; petty incarnate Semites who attained depths and heights beyond our reach, though not beyond our sight. They realized our absolute in their unrestrained capacity for good and evil; and for two years I had profitably shammed to be their companion" (470–71). Attempting to see himself as an anachronistic knight-errant, he is eventually shattered by the accumulated pains of heat, cold, thirst, hunger; by the terrible Deraa incident; by the unknightly necessity of lying to the Arabs about the postwar intentions of the colonialist powers ("Old Nuri Shaalan, wrinkling his wise nose, returned to me with his file of documents, asking in puzzlement which of them all he might believe. As before I glibly repeated, 'The last in date,' and the Emir's sense of the honour of his word made him see the humour" [444]); above all, perhaps, by the fact that T. E. Lawrence has not got what it takes to be a Coeur de Lion, much less a Roland. He is unable to convince himself that anything can justify bloodshed. As Kirkbride wrote, "T. E. L. had a horror of bloodshed and it is because of that that he tends to pile on the agony in the passages of *Seven Pillars of Wisdom* dealing with death and wounds—not because he liked seeing others suffer" (quoted in Mack, 239). The most sensational shedding of blood in *Seven Pillars* is followed by a confession that distances Lawrence from his heroes.

> When the smoke cleared, two [camels] were kicking in agony on the ground. A faceless man, spraying blood from a fringe of red flesh about his neck, stumbled screaming towards our rocks. He crashed blindly over one and another, tripping and scrambling with arms outstretched, maddened by pain. In a moment he lay quiet, and *we who had scattered from him* ventured near: but he was dead.
>
> . . . .
>
> We were certainly caught. My Arabs crouched in their place, meaning to fight like cornered animals, and kill at least some of the enemy before they themselves died. Such tactics displeased me. When combats came to the physical, bare hand against hand, I was finished. The disgust of being touched revolted me more than the thought of death and defeat: perhaps . . . because I so reverenced my wits and despised my body that I would not be beholden to the second for the life of the first. (424, my emphasis)

This is not admittedly the fighting of the *Chanson*, or the alliterative *Morte Arthure* (which also describes fighting and wounds, with an obvious relish) or Malory. But it is similar enough to make it clear that Lawrence is not entirely cast in the medieval mold.

Lawrence was inevitably a child of his century and did not possess a transcendent faith that would make meting out violent death easier or laudable. He cannot take the attitude of Matthew of Edessa, one of the Armenian chroniclers of the Crusades he had read at Oxford: "Maudoud fit tomber sur eux le châtiment de la vengeance céleste avec un tel rigueur que l'Euphrate roula des flots de sang" (Dulaurier, 1:94). Even the young Lawrence's response to the exemplary Chartres Cathedral is inevitably marked by a postmedieval stamp. "Certainly Chartres is the sight of a lifetime, a place truly in which to worship God. The middle ages were truer that way than ourselves, in spite of their narrowness and hardness and ignorance of the truth as we complacently put it: the truth doesn't matter a straw, if men only believe what they say or are willing to show that they do believe something"

(*HL*, 81. See also Chapter 2, this book). This Ruskin-inspired view would hardly be accepted by, for example, the *Chanson*'s Archbishop Turpin, who would not consider the worship of a god other than the Christian one an equally legitimate expression of the impetus towards the Divine. Lawrence, furthermore, had a nihilist streak, which manifests itself as early as the Carchemish days. C. Leonard Woolley remembers, "But another time I might find practically no work being done all, because Lawrence was sitting with the men, discussing some point of village custom or clearing up a question of local dialects; and if I groused at all he would grin and ask what anything mattered" (*BHF*, 87). The adult and experienced Lawrence consciously contrasted himself with his respected mentor C. M. Doughty, who "had a fixed point in his universe, and from one fixed point a moralist will . . . build up the whole scheme of creation."[1] He contrasted himself with Herbert Read, who, in reviewing *Seven Pillars*, wrote that "Great books are written in moods of spiritual light and intellectual certainty, and out of any other mood there only emerges an imperfect work of art. . . . About the epic hero there is an essential undoubting directness. . . . [H]e is self-possessed, self-reliant, arrogant and unintelligent. Colonel Lawrence was none of these things. . . . [I]t is no disparagement to say that out of such stuff no hero is made."[2]

Seven Pillars can be regarded in the light cast by medieval and neomedieval romance. It possesses attributes cited as characteristic of romance by John Stevens in his *Medieval Romance: Themes and Approaches*. Stevens refers to various "idealisms" of the genre, the first of which is the sense of a vocation: a "mysterious challenge or call." Lawrence feels and claims that the Arab revolt is in some sense his own special child, requiring from him self-discipline and self-dedication. He has prepared for the role he is to play; for many years he went "up and down the Semitic East before the war, learning the manners of the villages and tribesmen and citizens of Syria and Mesopotamia" (29). When the dreamed-of moment comes, Lawrence is a mover in the revolt's beginning (37) and conceives a specific goal for it (42). After the discovery of Faisal he thinks that "My duty was now to take the shortest road to Egypt with the news: and the knowledge gained that evening in the palm wood grew and blossomed in my mind into a thousand branches, laden with

---

1. British Library Add. MS 45903. Letter of 4 May 1927 to Charlotte F. Shaw.
2. Read, 36, 38–39. Lawrence's response to this review may be found in *Letters*, 547–51.

fruit and shady leaves, beneath which I sat and half-listened and saw visions"
(67). Lawrence deliberately hardens himself, "tempering my already trained
body for greater endeavour" (127). Ronald Storrs, "the most brilliant Englishman in the Near East" is yet criticized because he will not "deny himself the
world, and . . . prepare his mind and body with the sternness of an athlete
for a great fight" (31).

Second, Stevens notes that the romance often presents the heroine as
distant, mysterious, desirable, inaccessible and beautiful. The goal of Arab
freedom is consistently so presented, for capricious, difficult-to-woo freedom
is the nearest thing to a heroine in *Seven Pillars*. In the last paragraph of the
scene describing Lawrence's first meeting with Faisal (which is a version,
mutatis mutandis, of the motif of the first sight of the beloved) the name
"Damascus" causes a "quiver" to pass through the room while men "dream"
of "far off success" (62).

The third motif is the essential isolation of the hero and his experience.
Lawrence, the English "stranger, the godless fraud inspiring an alien nationality" (438) feels himself "the disillusioned, the sceptic, who envied [the
Arabs] their cheap belief [in the value of their efforts and sacrifices]" (439),
suffering "homesickness . . . at my outcast life among these Arabs" (435).
This leads easily into the sense of "baffled involvement in a mystery," which
Stevens elucidates by quoting Henry James's preface to *The American*: "the
very effect most to be invoked, [is] that of a generous nature engaged with
forces, with difficulties and dangers, that it but half understands." Lawrence
writes of

> the rankling fraudulence which had to be my mind's habit: that
> pretence to lead the national uprising of another race, the daily
> posturing in alien dress, preaching in alien speech: with behind it a
> sense that the "promises" on which the Arabs worked were worth
> what their armed strength would be when the moment of fulfillment
> came. We had deluded ourselves that perhaps peace might find the
> Arabs able, unhelped and untaught, to defend themselves with paper
> tools. Meanwhile we glozed our fraud by conducting their necessary
> war purely and cheaply. But now this gloss had gone from me.
> Chargeable against my conceit were the causeless, ineffectual deaths

of Hesa. My will had gone and I feared to be alone, lest the winds of circumstance, or power, or lust, blow my empty soul away. (399)

  What Stevens calls the "claim of the ideal" is strongly made in *Seven Pillars* as Lawrence tries to maintain his early identification with the highest values represented by the revolt. "Looking for stories to make [Faisal] laugh showed me the funny side of my accidents and corrected for the time the almost insane tension of too-constant striving after an ideal" ([1922], 197).

  So *Seven Pillars* shares certain generic motifs and atmospheres of medieval and postmedieval romance, as Lawrence struggles to describe his extraordinary experiences undergone in circumstances liberated from ordinary restraints. These experiences are more easily made vivid and apprehensible in terms of Malory and Morris than of writers whose characters' dilemmas are anchored in the daily life of the modern world.

  Malory's *Morte d'Arthur* is twice mentioned in *Seven Pillars*. The second occasion is particularly interesting: once again Lawrence is taking refuge in chivalric dreams when reality proves discouraging ("In my saddle-bags was a *Morte d'Arthur*. It relieved my disgust" [385]). *Seven Pillars* owes a number of its archaisms to Malory: *stilly* is probably from the *Morte*.

Malory: and therewithal Sir Palomides arose stilly (VIII, 31)[3]

Lawrence: One by one they sat down stilly on the rugs. (420)

The word questing in the following paragraph is a memory of Malory's "questing beast" (I, 19).

[T]here rose a strange, long wailing round the towers outside. Ibn Bani seized me by the arm and held to me, shuddering. I whispered to him, "What is it?" and he gasped that the dogs of the Beni Hillal, the mythical builders of the fort, quested the six towers each night for their dead masters. (345–46)

---

3. Lawrence carried around with him in the desert the Everyman edition. References are to Caxton's books and chapters within them.

The "questing beast," it will be remembered, was "the strangest beast that ever Arthur saw or heard of. . . . [T]he noise was in the beast's belly like unto the questing of thirty couple hounds." The Laurentian scene takes place in the fort of Azrak. The influence of the old walls leads Lawrence to use *Seneschal* for the only time in *Seven Pillars* ([343], "guest-master" or, once, "comptroller" elsewhere); and to feel that "Past and future flowed over us like an eddying river. We dreamed ourselves into the spirit of the place; sieges and feasting, raids, murders, love-singing in the night" (346–47).

Lawrence's use of *men of worship* (and its variants) is, of course, from Malory.

> (Malory) "Sir Palomides did passing well and mightily; but he turned against the party that he came in withal, and that caused him to lose a great part of his worships, for it seemed that Palomides is passing envious." (X, 81)
> "And for to give all other men of worship courage, I myself will assay to handle your son." (XIX, 10)

> (Lawrence) In the little-peopled desert every worshipful man knew every other. (321)
> I . . . was able . . . to thrust myself with dignity among such men of worship. ([1922], 252)

Unfortunately but predictably, the most memorable reference is pessimistic in its implication. Lawrence realizes that the "epic mode was alien to me as to my generation. Memory gave me no clue to the heroic, so that I could not feel such men as Auda in myself. He seemed fantastic as the hills of Rumm, old as Mallory [*sic*]" (439).

It has been claimed, however, that the greatest single contribution to Arthurian romance is not the works of Malory, but the *Historia Regum Britanniae* of Geoffrey of Monmouth.[4] Geoffrey, born about 1100, issued his

---

4. There is no "proof" that Lawrence read Geoffrey, in the sense that he is not referred to in any Lawrence letters to which I have had access; neither do there seem to be any revealing anecdotes. But Geoffrey is of first importance in the development of Arthurian romance. It is inconceivable that so dedicated a medievalist as Lawrence would not know him.

History about thirty-six years later. Flagrantly inaccurate according to the criteria of modern history inculcated in Lawrence at Oxford—criteria that his experiences of war and diplomacy, among other things, eventually led him to reject—the *History* was highly influential in spreading the fame of the British King Arthur as the rival in glory and military and social achievement of the Greeks' Alexander and the French Charlemagne. Transformed from the shadowy commander of British forces fighting the Saxons at Mount Badon around 490 to the conqueror of the same Saxons, along with a great deal of northern Europe, Geoffrey's Arthur is a splendid figure. But attitudes toward the *History* even among Geoffrey's near contemporaries ranged from delight at his enchanting adventures to grave suspicion of his historical fraudulence. The latter is best exemplified by a story recounted by Geraldus Cambrensis: a man plagued by evil spirits could pick out false passages in books. When St. John's Gospel was placed on his breast, the spirits vanished; when the History was put there they returned, "more horrible and numerous than before" (Barber, 41–42).

In our century as well there is disagreement about Geoffrey's aims and his status as a historian. In the *Cambridge History of English Literature*, we read that

> he imitates the practices and assumed the pose of an authentic chronicler with the deliberate purpose of mystifying his readers. For Geoffrey's *History* is, on the last analysis, a prose romance, and, in its Arthurian portions in particular, a palpable excursion in fiction. . . . Read in the light of the general literary history of its time, and of its immediate and immense popularity, Geoffrey's *History* can be adequately explained only as the response of a British writer, keenly observant of the literary tendencies of the day, to the growing demand for romance. (W. Lewis Jones, 1:169)

On the other hand, R. W. Southern, in a presidential address of the Royal Historical Society, has a different assessment. Southern declares that "the first duty of a historian is to produce works of art," and goes on to explain:

> By this I do not primarily mean works that are finely written, but works that are emotionally and intellectually satisfying, that combine

> a clear unity of conception with a vivacity of detail, and portray people
> whose actions are intelligible within the framework of their circum-
> stances and character. It is thus that one might describe the aims of a
> Balzac or a Tolstoy: I say therefore that a historian should aim at
> satisfying the same emotional and intellectual needs as a novelist or
> poet. (175)

This conception of historical writing was admired by classical historians, who
aspired to write "works of art that are rich in colour, distinctive in diction,
and perfect in shape." Truth was important, but "historical truth did not
exclude a generous freedom to select, arrange, and fill out events to produce
dramatic and intellectually satisfying confrontations." Early medieval scholars
understood their models when they "filled their works with appropriate
speeches and documents of their own composition" (Southern, 178). The
medieval contribution to thought about the problems of historical change
was minimal; nonetheless, as Southern reminds us, history was perceived as
a branch of the art of rhetoric, and the "presentation of great and noble
events in language appropriate to the subject-matter, and the moulding of
this subject matter into artistically contrived patterns" was seen as a highly
desirable aim (180).

This philosophy of history helps produce accounts of actions and events
that would be the despair of "a modern historian in search of a fact" (187).
Einhard, a biographer of Charlemagne, scarcely mentions Roncevaux; he
wished to evoke an image of imperial greatness and "It is a striking fact that
men who wrote in the ancient rhetorical tradition seem to have been unable
to admit any blemishes in the image they wished to convey" (184). Southern
cites the author of a life of Cnut's queen, the *Encomium Emmae*. This author
wishes to praise the woman who "could interpret England to her alien
husband" (186) and who allegedly brought peace and prosperity to a land
that had previously known only hatred and strife. But the compromises he
must make, however, with what our century would regard as historical fact
"are very shocking to a modern scholarly conscience" (186). But the writer
in question does grasp the essential characteristics of the people he treats.

If the first lesson taught to medieval historians by classical ones, Southern
continues, was how to write history rhetorically, then the second was that
"the destiny of nations is the noblest of all historical themes" (188). Geoffrey

of Monmouth is not only the encourager of romanticism and fantasy: he also writes "the history of an ancient and noble people, descended in blood from Troy, the source of all worldly nobility, buffeted by fortune, guided by visions and heavenly visitations, and led to settle in a distant land" (193). There are two differences, however, between Geoffrey and other historians who write from the same inspiration and to the same model. First, Geoffrey's account is far fuller than that of any predecessor. He is "overflowing with detail; he makes us conscious all the time of the confusion and unpredictability of real events. He gives his distant characters an independent, almost a plausible, life of their own" (194). Second, he tells a tragic story of decline and destruction.

In previous chapters we have seen that Lawrence's view of himself and of the Arabs is based on seven old poems, that his potrayal of an Arab leader is literary-medieval in inspiration, and that his concept of personal honor is anachronistically more appropriate to the Middle Ages than the twentieth century. We are now to see that he was not born in Wales for nothing. Thomas of Tremadoc writes a history that is like that of Einhard, like the *Encomium Emmae*, and like, above all, Geoffrey of Monmouth. Jeffrey Meyers is mistaken in saying that Lawrence "creates a unique literary form, a blend of imaginative and historical writing" (139). The model for *Seven Pillars*'s implicit view that truth is not to be sought in the examination of documents; that the imagination, working on the bones of historical "fact" can create a comely figure from whose lips we hear truth; that a history should be "rich in colour, distinctive in diction, and perfect in shape," and that it should "aim at satisfying the same emotional and intellectual needs as a novelist or poet" had existed for nearly eight hundred years. There can be no doubt that Lawrence knew the *History* in particular and other works in the same tradition in general. When he came to write his own account of "great and noble events in appropriate language," when he came to set down that phase he had witnessed of "the history of an ancient and noble people," he turned his back on the modern history school at Oxford, which taught him as little to write history as to organize a raiding party. As Lawrence wrote in one of his letters,

> Remember that the manner is greater than the (?) matter, so far as modern history is concerned. One of the ominous signs of the time is that the public can no longer read history. The historian is retired

into a shell to study the whole truth; which means that he learns to attach insensate importance to documents. The documents are liars. No man ever yet tried to write down the entire truth of any action in which he has been engaged. All narrative is parti pris. And to prefer an ancient written statement to the guiding of your instinct through the maze of related facts, is to encounter either banality or unreadableness. We know too much, and use too much knowledge. (*Letters*, 559)

To George Bernard Shaw, who asked of *The Mint*, "record of fact" or "work of art?" Lawrence replied, "Neither, I fancy. When I had writing ambitions, they were to combine these two things. *The Seven Pillars* was an effort to make history an imaginative thing. It was my second try at dramatizing reality" (*Letters*, 603). To his great confidante Charlotte F. Shaw, he writes critically of one author that "She was hobbled by truth all through, & so never took wing."[5] An uncharacteristic anger and contempt manifests itself when he writes to the same correspondent of a projected film about his exploits: "They wanted to make it historically accurate. So you'd glue peacock feathers to a canvas showing a peacock, I suppose. That wish for accuracy, in a thing that has really happened, is vicious: a sign of something worse than stupidity."[6]

Lawrence once commented to Lowell Thomas, "History isn't made up of truth anyway, so why worry?" (*BHF*, 214). Indeed, Lawrence's knowledge of the power of that which is different from and greater than "truth," whether it be myth, legend or merely "rumour" is early displayed. After the publication in the *Jesus College Magazine* of his "The Kaer of Ibn Wardani," he wrote home that "the palace is famous all over North Syria, and my description of it is more like the rumour than the reality" (*HL*, 248).

The inner needs that drove Lawrence to become world-famous as "of Arabia" enabled him too to understand Geoffrey's legendary history of the Britons, and to write his own imaginative history. Lawrence is well aware that the lies of the creative artist are truer than the truth of the half-seeing ordinary man. He knows the power of legend in literature and politics both,

---

5. British Library Add. MS 45904. Letter of 19 January 1930 to Charlotte F. Shaw.
6. British Library Add. MS 45903. Letter of 25 February 1928 to Charlotte F. Shaw.

and makes use of it, as military leader and as historian of military and political action. "Arabs told me Newcombe would not sleep except head on rails, and that Hornby would worry the metals with his teeth when gun-cotton failed. These were legends, but behind them lay a sense of their joint insatiate savagery in destroying till there was no more to destroy" (*Seven Pillars*, 185). More important, "A second buttress of a polity of Arab motive was the dim glory of the early Khalifate, whose memory endured among the people through centuries of Turkish misgovernment. The accident that these traditions savoured rather of the Arabian Nights than of sheer history main-tained the Arab rank and file in their conviction that their past was more splendid than the present of the Ottoman Turk" (263). In fact, Lawrence deliberately and even unscrupulously uses legend for his own political ends. Knowing that "men were always fond to believe a romantic tale" (450), he lies to HQ about Auda's treasonable correspondence with the enemy:

> We rang up Cairo and announced that the situation at Guweira was thoroughly good, and no treachery abroad. This may have been hardly true; but since Egypt kept us alive by stinting herself, we must reduce impolitic truth to keep her confident and ourselves a legend. The crowd wanted book-heroes, and would not understand how more human old Auda was because, after battle and murder, his heart yearned towards the defeated enemy now subject, at his free choice, to be spared or killed: and therefore never so lovely. (255–56)

The effect of Faisal's army is all the greater for its being "a whispered legandary thing . . . led by renowned or formidable names" (503).

Writing on the two matters of Arthur, the historical and the fabulous, Gillian Beer considers "the demarcation between [them] . . . not easy to establish, and the romance thrives in the shifting borderland between legend and fact. The Arthurian cycle offered a combination of history and myth which was particularly acceptable to a society intent upon mythologizing itself" (22). The Arab awakening, Lawrence said, "made a new nation; restored a lost influence, gave twenty millions of Semites the foundations on which to build an inspired dream-palace of their national thoughts" (cf. *Seven Pillars*, 4). All nations like to mythologize their origins or renaissances. The historian Dudo, becoming aware that the Normans were "on the point of becoming the most influential Christian nation in Europe" wrote (c. 995) a history of their dukes, drawing them as "heroes and martyrs, mainly concerned with the purity of their own lives and the endowment of the church, [contradicting] almost every known fact in the lives of these men" (Southern, 192). Such a history states that a new force in the world is to be taken into account; it attempts to explain "the phenomenon of the conversion of a blood-thirsty crew into a Christian state, and a crowd of pirates into an ordered society" (Southern, 192). We shall understand *Seven Pillars* better if we regard it as the work of the Dudo of the Arabs.

I·X

LAWRENCE
AND
RUSKINIAN MEDIEVALISM

WORLD War I was a mechanized war, with uniformed men, armored tenders and airplanes. Before discussing the covert mockery of chivalry that finds its way into *Seven Pillars*, we shall examine Ruskin's influence upon it and *The Mint*; indeed, we shall see how Lawrence's entire biography is reflected in the best-known chapter of *The Stones of Venice*, "The Nature of Gothic."

During the 1906 bicycling tour in France Lawrence had bought and read with interest and approval Ruskin's glorification of Gothic architecture (*HL*, 21, 24, 25). Jeffrey Meyers has convincingly claimed that *Seven Pillars* shows the influence of Ruskin's *The Seven Lamps of Architecture*, in title, in theme and structural principle, and in phraseology (46–47, 63, 78). But that "The Nature of Gothic" had an influence on Lawrence's two most important works has never been acknowledged. Unlikely as it may seem at first, Ruskin's lines about the superior human and artistic value of the Gothic style deal with matters Lawrence found of obsessional, lifelong interest. First, the young aesthete gained from Ruskin "some conception of the right way in which to study architecture, and how to draw the truest lessons from it" (*HL*, 24). Second, the author of *Seven Pillars* saw in Ruskin's distinction between "servile ornament" and "the mediaeval, or especially Christian, system of ornament" a parallel to—probably an inspiration for—his own differentiation between the natures and roles of regular armies and Arab guerrillas. Third, the recorder of the dehumanizing training meted out to R.A.F. recruits found himself a victim of those who demanded "servile ornament" (189). The more content and usefully employed airman of part 3 of *The Mint* echoed, as we shall see, other Ruskin sentiments.

Ruskin's distinction between pre-Christian Greek, Ninevite, and Egyptian attitudes to architectural ornament and "the medieval or especially Christian system" lies in the latter's recognition "in small things as well as great, of the individual value of every soul" (Cook and Wedderburn, 10:189–90). The Greek master-workman, writes Ruskin, could not tolerate imperfection; "therefore, what ornament he appointed to be done by those beneath him was composed of mere geometical forms, balls, ridges, and perfectly symmetrical foliage, which could be executed with absolute precision by line and rule" (Cook and Wedderburn, 189). The Assyrian and Egyptian master-workmen practice a less extreme version of the same approach: lower workmen were given tasks that they could execute only imperfectly, but were trained so that they would not fall beneath a certain set standard. "The workman was in both cases a slave" (189). Renaissance ornament is the product of the opposite mistake, "the executor of every minor portion being required to exhibit skill and possess knowledge as great as that which is possessed by the master of the design" (189).

The Gothic school, however, is content to admit human, hence artistic, imperfection.

> That admission of lost power and fallen nature, which the Greek or Ninevite felt to be intensely painful, and, as far as might be, altogether refused, the Christian makes daily and hourly. . . . It is, perhaps, the principal admirableness of the Gothic schools of architecture, that they thus receive the results of the labour of inferior minds; and out of fragments full of imperfection, and betraying that imperfection in every touch, indulgently raise up a stately and unaccusable whole. (190)

In the nature of even the simplest workman is to be found "some tardy imagination, torpid capacity of emotion, or tottering steps of thought" (191). The master-workman must either acknowledge those fallible capacities, even potentialities (i.e., must accept imperfect work) or demand rote-work from human machines.

You must either make a tool of the creature or a man of him. You cannot make both. Men were not intended to work with the accuracy of tools, to be precise and perfect in all their actions. If you will have that precision out of them, and make their fingers measure degrees like cog-wheels, and their arms strike curves like compasses, you must unhumanise them. All the energy of their spirits must be given to make cogs and compasses of themselves. All their attention and strength must go to the accomplishment of the mean act. The eye of the soul must be bent upon the finger point, and the soul's force must fill all the invisible nerves that guide it . . . that it may not err from its steely precision. . . . Let him but begin to imagine, to think, to try to do anything worth doing; and the engine-turned precision is lost at once. (192)

Lawrence's war is a guerrilla war, and the effectiveness of the Arabs against their enemy depends not on formal discipline or esprit de corps, but on the initiative, courage, and dash of self-reliant, individual warriors. "[T]he Arabs were, as individuals, magnificent fighters. Used in single-man-battles, as I used them, each was equal to three Turks."[1] Lawrence combined the chivalric admiration for single combat with Ruskin's ideas on Gothic architecture, for "in irregular war, of two men together, one was being wasted. Our ideal should be to make our battle a series of single combats, our ranks a happy alliance of agile commanders-in-chief" (*Seven Pillars*, 265–66). *Seven Pillars of Wisdom* is the account of a "rebellion [that] was more like peace than like war," of a struggle between the regular army of the Turks, plantlike, "immobile, firm-rooted, nourished through long stems to the head" (*Seven Pillars*, 145) and Arab irregulars, "an influence, an idea, a thing intangible, invulnerable, without front or back, drifting about like a gas . . . a vapour, blowing where we listed" (145).

In *Seven Pillars* Lawrence represents himself at one point as lying in a tent disabled by illness and using the novel, enforced leisure to reflect on the aims and methods of the Arab uprising. Its aims, he decides, are "geographical, to extrude the Turk from all Arabic-speaking lands in Asia" (144). They are not, *pace* authorities like Foch, Clausewitz, and Goltz, to annihilate the

---

1. British Library Add. MS 45903. Letter of 14 April 1927 to Charlotte F. Shaw.

enemy or even to break his courage. In fact, Lawrence decides that the war in the Hejaz is already won: the Arabs control nine hundred and ninety-nine thousandths of it, the Turks only the tiny portion they stand on. "A regular soldier might be helpless without a target, owning only what he sat on, and subjugating only what, by order, he could poke his rifle at" (145).

The words "by order" are deliberate. Lawrence is again insisting on the difference between his guerrillas, who fight well when they think, and enlisted soldiers, whether they be Turk, British, Australian, or Indian (although even the regulars in the Arab Army share the guerrillas' virtues):

> In the Arab Army there was no power of punishment whatever: this vital difference showed itself in all our troops. They had no formality of discipline; there was no subordination. Service was active; attack always imminent: and, like the Army of Italy, men recognized the duty of defeating the enemy. For the rest they were not soldiers, but pilgrims, intent always to go the little farther.
>
> I was not discontented with this state of things, for it had seemed to me that discipline, or at least formal discipline, was a mark of peace: a character or stamp by which to mark off soldiers from complete men, and obliterate the humanity of the individual.
>
> . . . It was a process of the mass, an element of the impersonal crowd, inapplicable to one man, since it involved obedience, a duality of will. It was not to impress upon men that their will must actively second the officer's, for then there would have been, as in the Arab Army and among irregulars, that momentary pause for thought transmission, or digestion; for the nerves to resolve the relaying private will into active consequence. On the contrary, each regular Army sedulously rooted out this significant pause from its companies on parade. The drill instructors tried to make obedience an instinct, a mental reflex, following as instantly on the command as though the motor power of the individual wills had been invested together in the same system. (405–6)

In the explicitly Christian reference to the Arab fighters being "pilgrims, intent always to go the little farther" Lawrence remembers Ruskin's claim that it is Christianity that enables the Gothic master-builders to acknowledge the full humanity of the underworkers. (He remembers the same claim when he writes of the Arabs, whether actively or passively hostile to their oppressors, "Our kingdoms lay in each man's mind" [145].) The rest of the paragraph predicts the course of Lawrence's life after the war; that is, it predicts how "The Nature of Gothic" will be transmuted in the account of service life that is *The Mint*.

Seven Pillars (subtitled *A Triumph*) is the record of how a once-great people freed itself. The "humanity" of the Arab irregulars is not "obliterated": it is allowed to express itself in the struggle for freedom, a struggle that is "an Arab war waged and led by Arabs for an Arab aim in Arabia" (3). Fighting guerrilla-fashion enables the Arabs to bring their full humanity into play. It is the antithesis of the self-reification that is the lot of other soldiers.

> We had not discipline in the sense in which it was restrictive, submergent of individuality, the Lowest Common Denominator of men. In peace-armies discipline meant the hunt, not of an average but of an absolute; the hundred per cent standard in which the ninety-nine were played down to the level of the weakest man on parade. The aim was to render the unit a unit, the man a type; in order that their effort might be calculable, and the collective output even in grain and bulk. The deeper the discipline, the lower was the individual excellence; also the more sure the performance.
>
> By this substitution of a sure job for a possible masterpiece, military science made a deliberate sacrifice of capacity in order to reduce the uncertain element, the bionomic factor, in enlisted humanity.
>
> . . . The moral strain of isolated fighting made "simple" war very hard upon the soldier, exacting from him special initiative, endurance, enthusiasm. Irregular war was far more intellectual than a bayonet charge, far more exhausting than service in the comfortable imitative obedience of an ordered army. Guerrillas must be allowed liberal work room: in irregular war, of two men together, one was being wasted. Our ideal should be to make our battle a series of single combats, our ranks a happy alliance of agile commanders-in-chief. (265–66)

This obviously refers back to the Ruskinian chapter 23. Lawrence does not want the Arab fighting forces to become like a plant, "immobile, firm-rooted, nourished through long stems to the head." He rejects modern concepts of war (in which "the fighting man was the product of the multiplied exertions of a long hierarchy, from workshop to supply unit, which kept him active in the field"), opting for "a series of single combats," his men being "self-contained." Above all, he wants his warriors to use that which other armies "sedulously root out": thought and initiative.

In substituting a "sure job for a possible masterpiece" (a word normally applied to art, including cathedrals) military authorities sin against man's capacities. Ruskin writes that

> while in all things that we see or do, we are to desire perfection, and strive for it, we are nevertheless not to set the meaner thing, in its narrow accomplishment, above the nobler thing, in its mighty progress; not to esteem smooth minuteness above shattered majesty; not to prefer mean victory to honourable defeat; not to lower the level of our aim, that we may the more surely enjoy the complacency of success. (Cook and Wedderburn, 191)

As we shall see when we come to examine *The Mint*, Lawrence the man masochistically reified himself after the war; Lawrence the writer always did his best. *Seven Pillars* is the product of great pains: "if I'd aimed low I could have hit my target as squarely as Beerbohm or Belloc hits it: but their works are only a horrid example, and I'm much happier to have gone high and flopped than not to have tried, or to have tried half-measures" (*Letters*, 361).

Ruskin's phrase "shattered majesty" is echoed in the dedicatory poem to *Seven Pillars*.

> Men prayed me that I set our work, the inviolate house,
> as a memory of you.
> But for fit monument I shattered it, unfinished: and now
> The little things creep out to patch themselves hovels
> in the marred shadow
> Of your gift.
> (lines 16–21)

The first stanza of this poem contains an architectural comparison. Freedom is called the "seven pillared worthy house;" and behind both "The Nature of Gothic" and "To S.A." lies the idea of a superb building representing a spiritual achievement, a deliberately smashed or ignoble building representing failure, honorable or dishonorable.

Ruskin's influence permeates *Seven Pillars*. The contrast between Gothic freedom and Greek–Ninevite–Egyptian slavery had become an ineradicable part of the young Lawrence's consciousness. The contrast between idealistic, striving man and man as dehumanized thing parallels, to simplify somewhat, the contrast between the pre-Deraa and the post-Deraa Lawrences. A sentence like "A man who could fight well by himself made generally a bad soldier, and these champions [i.e., Faisal's tribesmen] seemed to me no material for our drilling" (73) brilliantly brings together in the last word the insult to the human spirit that is the routine production of "geometrical forms, balls, ridges and perfectly symmetrical foliage" and the insult to the human spirit constituted by parade-ground gyrations.

Service in all regular armies but that of the Arabs is seen in *Seven Pillars* as an abnegation of selfhood, a denial of life.

> [T]hese . . . were really soldiers, a novelty after two years' irregularity. And it came upon me freshly how the secret of uniform was to make a crowd solid, dignified, impersonal: to give it the singleness and tautness of an upstanding man. This death's livery which walled its bearers from ordinary life, was sign that they had contracted themselves into a service not the less abject for that its beginning was voluntary.
>
> . . . .
>
> Convicts had violence put upon them. Slaves might be free, if they could, in intention. But the soldier assigned his owner the twenty-four hours' use of his body; and sole conduct of his mind and passions. A convict had license to hate the rule which confined him, and all humanity outside, if he were greedy in hate; but the sulking soldier was a bad soldier; indeed, no soldier. His affections must be hired pieces on the chess-board of the king. (514)

A regular soldier wears "death's livery." Lawrence's men "all wore my livery" (242), that is, the heraldic, vivid livery of life. Lawrence is engaged in a struggle for "freedom, a pleasure to be tasted only by a man alive" (144), waged by men who know what they are doing and why. Like the Gothic master-workman, he makes one flame of his subordinates' individual sparks. "My personal duty was command, and the commander, like the master architect, was responsible for all" (145).

Finally, it may be observed that one of the most famous paragraphs of *Seven Pillars* is inspired by "The Nature of Gothic."

> All men dream: but not equally. Those who dream by night in the dusty recesses of their minds wake in the day to find that it was vanity: but the dreamers of the day are dangerous men, for they may act their dream with open eyes to make it possible. This I did. I meant to make a new nation, to restore a lost influence, to give twenty millions of Semites the foundations on which to build an inspired dream-palace of their national thoughts. So high an aim called out the inherent nobility of their minds, and made them play a generous part in events. (*Seven Pillars*, 4)

Compare Ruskin:

> It is that strange *disquietude* of the Gothic spirit that is its greatness; that restlessness of the dreaming mind, that wanders hither among the niches, and flickers feverishly around the pinnacle and frets and fades in labyrinthine knots and shadows along wall and roof, and yet is not satisfied, nor shall be satisfied. (Cook and Wedderburn, 214)

Both passages speak of dreaming in a dark corner of a splendid building of the mind. Lawrence writes "dream by night in the dusty recesses of their minds" and then speaks of "an inspired dream-palace," a phrase that harks back to the first and last stanzas of the dedicatory poem ("the seven pillared worthy house . . . the inviolate house"). Ruskin has "that restlessness of the dreaming mind . . . niches . . . flickers feverishly around the pinnacles and frets and fades in labyrinthine knots and shadows along wall and roof." Both passages deal with idealistic aspiration, although Lawrence's effective dream is dreamed in the sunlight.

Faisal's men may have been "no material for our drilling" but after the soiling experiences of the war Lawrence subjected himself to the mint, to be hammered into shape like a coin. *The Mint* is partly the story of how fifty individuals become a flight. At the best, like Assyrian and Egyptian workmen, they are given a standard and not allowed to fall beneath it: "Here we will be (we are) punished for any mistake, for any falling short of standard; or of requirement, or fancied requirement" (*The Mint*, 183–84). Men become if not tools then at least things: "This movement [i.e., the wind moving the airmen's uniforms] singularly destroyed the illusion we were set to give, of blue cylinders standing most stiffly, hardly breathing, eyes level and straight ahead. . . . We were dressed ham-bones all tightly sewn up in bags of unvarying serge" (225–26)

Some airmen would attempt to deny that they are always responsive, never active. "They try, by making their impulse supplement the directing impulse, to retain a fig of voluntariness. They 'will' right turn when the sergeant says right turn, and so on. A pitiful soul-salve, that, in my judgment, and a corruption of discipline. The good soldier is inconsequential as a child" (155).

The ambiguous status of "flight"—ambiguous because some corporate life is gained, although all individual life is lost—is achieved after weeks of "sleeping and shitting and eating together" (111).

> Our hut used to arrive at an opinion by discussion, by contradicting the early word that the first fool rushed out. Later this turned into instinct. We have come, unknowing, to a corporate life. Today we think, decide, act on parade without a word said. Men are becoming troops when like one body they are sluggish (to a bad instructor), mulish (when angered), willing (to an open-hearted man). We have attained a flight-entity which is outside our individualities. The self-reliance each has singly lost is not lost to us all. As a flight we're stiff-necked and spirited as though the excellencies of Sailor and Snaggle had been buttered thinly over all the fifty. The person has died that to the company might be born a soul. (191)

But if individuality is taken from men to make them a flight, it is given back after the training period: "At Depot we had soldiered so long and so harshly that soldiering had become second nature: sterility quickly beds down into habit, by use. Now at Cadet College I was to learn to be an airman, by unlearning that corporate effort which had been the sole spirituality of the square" (218–19). Drill is then relegated to its proper place, as punishment.

Lawrence is no longer capable of the leadership and striving of the war period. When he led the Arabs he was like the man who, in Ruskin's words, creates "the picture or statue . . . the work of one only, in most cases more highly gifted than his fellows" (Cook and Wedderburn, 213–14). Now he is like a humbler worker on a cathedral, one who helps do "the work of the whole race" (Cook and Wedderburn, 213).

"Our profession is to help conquer the air. We are vowed to this enterprise (a corporate effort in which success will visit the joined hands of a million obscure) to win the freehold of the upper element in as full measure as man's licence on land, or a sailor's liberty at sea" (*The Mint*, 95–96). Elsewhere Lawrence wrote that the individual genius raids, but that the common people occupy and possess.

·X·

FURTHER QUESTIONINGS
OF THE CHIVALRIC ETHOS

IT is in *The Mint* that we find Lawrence's most explicit questioning of the chivalric ethos. Here, as he was at the introduction of an armored car's "trim crew" to Azraq, Lawrence is wary of phlegmatic northerners:

> Perhaps, in days of chivalry, even the north took the parade of arms lovingly, and throbbed at the feel of swords, the sight of banners. Perhaps: though I've chased through medieval literature after the days of chivalry, and found their revivals, and legends or reminiscences or ridicule of them, but never the real thing. Today these modes are right out of tune with the social system, whose firm-seatedness makes one doubt if an Englishman's blood can ever have flowed hotly enough for him to swallow a tomfoolery divorced from alcohol. (189)

This passage takes us back to *Seven Pillars*, the writing of which was an attempt to add to the shelf of "titanic" works Lawrence admired. One of these "big books" was *Don Quixote* (*Letters*, 467, 548). The absurd adventures of the deluded would-be knight-errant (who is not quite so anachronistic as the "Arabian knight") satirize romances inspired by the chivalry Lawrence now fears never really existed, at least in the North. Heraldry, chivalry's daughter, does not escape Cervantes' attention. Don Quixote has mistaken two flocks of sheep for opposing armies and now identifies the famous warriors he thinks he sees before him.

"But cast thy Eyes on this Side, *Sancho*, and at the Head of t'other
Army see the ever victorious *Timonel* of *Carcaiona*, Prince of *New
Bascay*, whose Armour is quarter'd *Azure, Vert, Or*, and *Argent*, and
who bears in his shield a Cat *Or*, in a Field *Gules*, with these four
letters, *MIAU*, for a motto, being the beginning of his Mistress's Name,
the beautiful *Miaulina*, Daughter to *Alpheniquen* Duke of *Algarva*. . . .
He whom you see pricking that py'd Courser's Flanks with his arm'd
Heels, is the mighty Duke of *Nervia, Espartafilado* of the Wood,
bearing in his Shield a Field of pure Azure, power'd with *Asparagus*
(*Esparrago*) with this motto in Castilian, *Rastrea mi suerte; Thus trails,
or drags my Fortune.*" (Cervantes, 115)

Cervantes' commentator sympathizes with the Spaniard's scorn, and glosses
Esparrago, thus:

The Gingle between the Duke's Name *Espartafilado* and Esparrago
(his Arms) is a Ridicule upon the foolish Quibbles so frequent in
Heraldry. . . . The *trailing* of his Fortune may allude to the Word
Esparto, a sort of Rush they make ropes with. Or perhaps he was
without a Mistress, to which the Sparagrass may allude: For, in Spain
they have a Proverb, *Solo comes el Esparrago*: As solitary as Sparagrass,
because every one of 'em springs up by itself." (115)

Canting arms (arms that make a punning reference to a name, usually the
name of their bearer) are the object of Cervantes' scorn here. (The motto,
really an adjunct to the coat of arms itself, may also cant.) Lawrence was
familiar with the concept: he had been educated in a city the arms of which
show an ox crossing a ford; and he had rubbed the brass of, to give only one
example, Sir Roger de Setvans (1306) at Chartham, Kent, whose surcoat and
ailettes[1] show seven winnowing fans (*sept vans*) and his shield three similar
fans. The young Lawrence's consistent misspelling, Septvans, with a medial *p*,
in the letter about Lehon, for example, is a forgetful product of his knowledge
of the knight's coat of arms and its inspiration.

1. *Ailettes* "were small shields fastened at right angles to the shoulders, to lessen the force of
a sweeping blow" (Clayton, 13).

Mockery of canting arms implies more than mere impatience with recondite puns. This type of arms evolved in an age of general illiteracy, but it is easy to see how a knight could identify more readily with a coat of arms that embodied his name than one that did not. (Heraldry's beginnings were purely utilitarian, based in the need to make one's identity plain in the period of the closed helm. Nonetheless, the honor accorded a knight and that accorded his coat of arms soon, by natural extension, became one and the same.) To attack canting arms is implicitly to attack a whole series of correspondences. If canting arms are "foolish Quibbles" then individual acts of bravery may be fortuitous, lacking significance, and not the product of awareness of a transcendental code and the necessity of living up to it. Chivalry itself (if it ever existed) may be the result of a method of waging war that had its day and then became obsolete, not an earthly reflection of what is forever pleasing to God. (That Lawrence knew that acts of bravery or cowardice *are* sometimes fortuitous may be inferred from his letters to Ernest Thurtle, the M.P. who tried to have abolished the death sentence for cowardice in the face of the enemy.)

Lawrence knew that he lived in the age of the relative outlook. He contrasted himself with C. M. Doughty, the author of *Arabia Deserta* (1888). Doughty, along with Blunt, was one of his great inspirations to travel and adventure in the Middle East. Lawrence writes of his mentor with a sort of wondering, wistful incredulity.

> Surely that unshakeable conviction of his own rightness is a proof of deep roots? Doughty really believed in his superiority to the Arabs. It was this pride which made him meek in oppression. He really believed that he held a knowledge of the truth, and that they were ignorant. He really believed that the English were better than the Arabs: that this thing was better than that thing: in fact, he did really believe in someting. That's what I call an absolute. Doughty, somewhere, if only in the supremacy of Spenser, had a fixed point in his universe, & from a fixed point a moralist will, like a palaeontologist, build up the whole scheme of creation.[2]

2. British Library Add. MS 45903. Letter of 16 June 1927 to Charlotte F. Shaw.

He goes on to compare his and Doughty's written works in the light of these epistemological differences. But if we substitute "life" for "book" we find that Lawrence is explaining his entire career: "Search my book through, & you will hardly find an assertion which is not immediately qualified: and certainly not an assertion which is not eventually qualified. It's due to an absence of the fixed point from which Doughty radiated."[3] Lawrence also contrasted himself with Herbert Read, who, in reviewing *Seven Pillars*, said that "Great books are written in moods of spiritual light and intellectual certainty"[4] and "About the epic hero there is an essential undoubting directness: his aim is single and unswerving; he questions neither himself, his aims, nor his destiny. He may share his glory with his chosen band, his comitatus, but essentially he is self-possessed, self-reliant, arrogant and unintelligent" (Read, 38–39). Lawrence responded: "I would maintain against him that these works never produced an imaginative work the size of a mouse from any of the people sterile enough to feel certain. . . . I do not like his categorical specification of a hero. . . . [W]ho in God's name laid this down? Is the hero to be a changeless thing in the world?"

Lawrence was writing his book at the same time as struggling with a sense of guilt at the blood he had shed and the defilement of Deraa; at this same time he was also being portrayed as a popular hero. He could see no fixed point from which to view himself. On the one hand the code of chivalry had become fossilized as the code of the gentleman, according to which he was often praised. "He is," wrote the sixth Earl Winterton, formerly of Eton and New College, Oxford, "a very inspiring gentleman adventurer."[5] One war correspondent referred to "this gallant gentleman" (quoted in Mack, 490, n. 16). Lawrence realized, however, that he was also looked at askance. "Allenby," he wrote to Mrs. Shaw, "is a very large downright and splendid person, and the being publicly yoked with a counter-jumping opportunist like me must often gall him deeply. You and G. B. S. live so much with poets and politicians and artists that human oddness attracts you, almost as much as it repels. Whereas with the senior officers of the British Army conduct is a

3. Ibid.
4. The review is quoted and discussed in *Letters*, 547–51.
5. Diary entry for 26 August 1918. Quoted in Brodrick, 178.

very serious matter."[6] Straightforward and plain-dealing British officers often found Lawrence's self-consciousness, impertinence, and deviousness intolerable. Such people would never dream of writing false reports of their actions or condoning the massacre of prisoners (Lawrence has been accused of both, of course), but they lived by a code the contingency of which they would not, or could not, see. Lawrence, alone and talented, had been so brave, or so foolish, as to invest his sense of worth in chivalry as a living philosophy (creative, and therefore dangerous and undependable), rather than in the ossified social code of the gentleman (safely dead and backed up by the well-bred herd). He had made himself vulnerable to the stupidity or blood-lust of the least of his followers.

Lawrence knew that he was not the only twentieth-century medievalist to be aware of the conflict between relative and absolute, between the eternal and the time-based. James Branch Cabell is the American author of a number of stories set in a medieval Poictesme. The name of this region is an amalgam of Poitiers and Angoulême, but it would be as sensible to search for it on the map as to seek Shakespeare's Bohemia. Cabell's name is little heard nowadays. The 1920s are no longer called "The James Branch Cabell Period."[7] Leslie A. Fiedler too harshly writes: "Not only has it become impossible to think of him as a 'great writer,' but even as a minor one of real interest" (138). Although British and American publishers have reissued some of his novels as "fantasy," presumably in the hope of attracting the audience that made works like *Lord of the Rings* such a success, Cabell is almost unknown today.

It was not so when Lawrence was working on *Seven Pillars*. Cabell became famous and esteemed early in the 1920s largely due to the suppression, trial, and exoneration of *Jurgen: A Comedy of Justice* (1919), some of the comedy of which was found (as he knew it would be) unacceptably phallic. Double-entendres about Jurgen's sword, lance, and staff notwithstanding, James Branch Cabell was an author with a serious interest in chivalry and gallantry; indeed, these philosophies provided him with the titles of two of his books.

---

6. British Library Add. MS 45903. Letter of 3 April 1929 to Charlotte F. Shaw.
7. As they once were by Peter Monro Jack in the *New Republic*. Quoted in Davis, *James Branch Cabell*, preface.

Even so, *Chivalry*'s author could give a cynical explanation for the popularity of the ethos.

> The cornerstone of Chivalry I take to be the idea of vicarship: for the chivalrous person is, in his own eyes at least, the child of God, and goes about this world as his Father's representative in an alien country. It was very adroitly to human pride, through an assumption of man's responsibility in his tiniest action, that Chivalry made its appeal; and exhorted every man to keep faith, not merely with the arbitrary will of a strong god, but with himself. There is no cause for wonder that the appeal was irresistible, when to each man it thus admitted that he himself was the one thing seriously to be considered. . . . So man became a chivalrous animal; and about this notion of divine vicarship builded his elaborate mediaeval code, to which, in essentials, a great number of persons adhere even nowadays. (quoted in Van Doren, 15–16)

Lawrence had read *Jurgen* and admired it (*Letters*, 423). The book is an ironic retelling of the solar myth of regained youth, but begins with a reference to the Faust legend. The eponymous hero, a poet, a pawnbroker of forty-and-something, a man who has perforce made a series of half-reluctant compromises with life, speaks casually and wittily in favor of the Prince of Darkness to a monk who has just tripped over a stone in the road and curses the devil who put it there. In gratitude, a "black gentleman" met immediately afterwards by Jurgen removes from the pawnbroker's life the source of much of its care, namely Dame Lisa, his wife, "a high-spirited woman, with no especial gift for silence" (*Jurgen*, 9). Jurgen, under social pressure to do the manly thing and get her back, advances into a cave and thus begins the series of adventures that ends precisely one year later, with wife restored, middle-aged body restored (after an interview with a certain Mother Sereda, Jurgen had got back his twenty-one-year-old body), and his uncomprehending resignation much reinforced.

Although toward the end of the book Jurgen spends some time in Hell as an emperor and in Heaven as a pope, his three main adventures are in regions called Glathion, Cocaigne, and Leukê, which represent three "great historical systems of value or ways of life" (Davis, 92). Leukê represents the

Hellenic tradition; Cocaigne, the pagan side of the medieval tradition. But we have most to do with the first, for Glathion represents the ethos of Christian chivalry.

Jurgen, by now the possessor of a young body and an experienced heart, arrives at Glathion as the escort of Guenevere, betrothed to Arthur of the Britons, whom he has rescued from an evil king. It is Jurgen's habit to try to follow the customs of whatever country he finds himself in. Surrounded now by "men who considered that all you possessed was loaned to you to devote to the service of your God, your King, and every woman who crossed your path" (*Jurgen*, 101), he tries to be chivalrous. Outwardly he succeeds. As the owner of an enchanted sword, "resistless Caliburn," he finds "the despatching of thieves and giants and dragons . . . hardly sportsmanlike (102–3). As the rescuer of "a princess, the fairest and most perfect of mortal women . . . [whom] very shortly he was to stand by and see married to another" he finds himself in "a situation to delight the chivalrous court of Glathion, for every requirement of romance was exactly fulfilled" (94). But Jurgen is troubled because he cannot feel the appropriate emotions, or have confidence in the common beliefs. Of Guenevere he reflects that "She is a princess. . . . She is quite beautiful. She is young, and whatever her father's opinion, she is reasonably intelligent, as women go. Nobody could ask more. Why, then, am I not out of my head about her? . . . Come, Jurgen, man! is there no heart in this spry young body you have regained? Come, let us have a little honest rapture and excitement over this promising situation!" (98). Jurgen spends his time not unpleasantly, seducing Guenevere (and, incidentally, finding her much like other women when the barriers are down) but he cannot even write a sirvente to her without thinking that "when I proclaim that my adored mistress's hair reminds me of gold I am quite consciously lying. It looks like yellow hair, and nothing else: nor would I willingly venture within ten feet of any woman whose head sprouted with wires, of whatever metal. . . . If we poets could actually behold the monsters we rhyme of, we would scream and run" (95).

Jurgen is made uncomfortable by his inability to believe in the wisdom of an omnipotent and benevolent Creator. "To talk of serving God sounded as sonorously and as inspiritingly as a drum: yes, and a drum had nothing but air in it" (101). (Jurgen has also cynically noted the behavior of "the gallant [i.e., amorous] Bishop of Merion.") Serving the King is not an idea to be

taken seriously, for "there in plain view was [King Gogyrvan Gawr], for
anyone who so elected, to regard and grow enthusiastic over: Gogyrvan
might be shrewd enough, but to Jurgen he suggested very little of the Lord's
anointed. To the contrary, he reminded you of Jurgen's brother-in-law, the
grocer, without being graced by the tradesman's friendly interest in [his]
customers. Gogyrvan Gawr was a person whom Jurgen simply could not
imagine any intelligent Deity selecting as steward" (102). The chivalric
conception of courtly love cannot be taken seriously: "And finally, when it
came to serving women, what sort of service did women most cordially
appreciate? Jurgen had his answer pat enough, but it was an answer not
suitable for utterance in mixed company" (102). Everywhere is self-deceit. In
the week of tourneys and feasting preceding Guenevere's being taken to
London for marriage, "dukes and earls and barons and many famous knights"
contend for honor "and a trumpery chaplet of pearls" (109).

 Jurgen, then, outwardly conforms to the customs. But

> all the while he fretted because he could just dimly perceive that ideal
> which was served in Glathion, and the beauty of this ideal, but could
> not possibly believe in it. Here was, again, a loveliness perceived in
> twilight, a beauty not clearly visioned.
>
> . . . .
>
> So Jurgen abode among these persons to whom life was a high-
> hearted journeying homeward. God the Father awaited you there,
> ready to punish at need, but eager to forgive, after the manner of all
> fathers: that one became a little soiled in travelling, and sometimes
> blundered into the wrong lane, was a matter which fathers under-
> stood. (103)

 Cabell, Jurgen, and Lawrence all believe they have asked for bread and
been given a stone. It is impossible not to fail one's vision and high-colored
ambitions after adolescence, despite one's longing for a world in which they
could be honored. Lawrence read the Glathion chapters of Cabell's *Comedy
of Justice* with an understanding granted to few. Disillusion, however, only
acquires its poignancy by contrast with the ideals, hopes, and happiness that
preceded it. The pages describing the now middle-aged Jurgen's meetings

with the love of his youth are those particularly remembered by Lawrence when writing *Seven Pillars*.

The first stage of Jurgen's search for his wife is a visit to "the garden between dawn and sunrise," where "each man that ever lived has sojourned for a little while, with no company save his illusions" (20), before going on to become a respectable alderman, merchant, or bishop, an admired captain or king, a pawnbroker, a temporary and calmly contemptuous diplomat, or the dogged retainer of the armed forces' lowest rank. Jurgen, middle-aged and pot-bellied, sees "in the first glow of dawn" a "host" of people who are "young and glad and very lovely and quite heart-breakingly confident . . . foreknowing life to be a puny antagonist from whom one might take very easily anything which one desired" (20). Only one of the girls there walks alone, the boy who loved her being dead. Jurgen realizes that he is talking to Dorothy la Désirée, the local lord's daughter, whom for one idyllic summer he had loved and been loved by. Dorothy is still four months short of eighteen, still in love with the young Jurgen, and still scornful of the wealthy count—"and he is twenty-eight, and looks every day of it!" (20)—proposed as a husband for her. In bittersweet anguish Jurgen remembers the boy "who loved a girl, with such love as it puzzles me to think of now." He remembers their belief that the social gulf between them did not matter, as "the boy firmly intended to become a duke or emperor or something of that sort, so the transient discrepancy did not worry them"; he remembers "a blinding glory of green woods and lawns and moonlit nights and dance music and unreasonable laughter. . . . her hair and eyes, and the curving and the feel of her red mouth." Finally he remembers his desolation and defensive cynicism, his loss of faith in life when, after his departure for the wars, Dorothy did marry the count. Even now "it is a cordial to the tired and battered heart which nowadays pumps blood for me, to think that for a little while, for a whole summer, these two were as brave and comely and clean a pair of sweethearts as the world has known" (25; repeated, 32–33).

Lawrence remembered the mood of the garden between dawn and sunrise, the recognition of what is both endlessly precious and irrevocably lost. He had, after all, also had Jurgen's experience, as the dedicatory poem to *Seven Pillars* and widely available biographical information reminds us. Lawrence had shared work, holidays, and clothes with Dahoum. He had wrestled with him and used him as a model for a carved naked figure. He had looked after

Dahoum during a nearly fatal illness, and been looked after by him when ill himself. The area was scandalized by the closeness of the relationship. Dahoum died of typhus during the war. Lawrence, barred from the place and bereft of the person, looked back on prewar Carchemish as a lost paradise, "the jolliest place I've ever seen," "a miracle"; where he lived "a perfect life," "the best life I've ever lived," and even "A marvellous, unreal, pictured pageant of a life" (*RGLH*, 1:50; 1:51; 1:81; 2:84; 1:50). "Carchemish," he told Mrs. Shaw, "was a wonderful place and time: as golden as Haroun el Raschid's in Tennyson."[8] (The reference is to "Recollections of the Arabian Nights," to "A goodly place, a goodly time, / For it was in the golden prime / Of good Haroun Alraschid.") Lawrence too could remember, from the dry, if bearable, desert of postwar loss his own version of the "blinding glory of green woods and lawns and moonlit lights and dance music and unreasonable laughter": soporific heat, perhaps, and Arabic lessons and holiday adventures and unreasonable laughter (we may surely keep the unreasonable laughter).[9] Not only did he remember it: he also dramatized it in *Seven Pillars* in the relationship between his servants Farraj and Daud, "my heavenly twins" (241). Time and again these two disrupt the peace of their elders: by kidnapping and dyeing in various gaudy colors a prized camel, by crying snake when there are no snakes and by sitting silent as one does slither toward their master. Lawrence and the rest do not know how to deal with them.

> [T]he only punishment possible to our hands in this vagrant life was corporal, which had been tried upon the pair so often and so uselessly that I was sick of it. . . . Their sins were elvish gaiety, the thoughtless-ness of unbalanced youth, the being happy when we were not; and for such follies to hurt them mercilessly like criminals till their self-control melted and their manhood was lost under the animal distress of their bodies, seemed to me degrading, almost an impiety towards

8. British Library Add. MS 45903. Letter of 12 August 1927 to Charlotte F. Shaw.

9. Perhaps it would be impertinent to wonder whether the second half of my quotation, or an equivalent, was remembered. Tabachnick is probably as close as we will get in saying that "Lawrence was above all a Puritan and only a latent homosexual who had an idealized love relationship with Dahoum, which did involve some degree of the sense of touch, but not much" (*T. E. Lawrence*, 155 n. 15).

two sunlit beings, on whom the shadow of the world had not yet fallen—the most gallant, the most enviable, I knew. (242, my emphasis)[10]

The imagery of sun and shadow is a memory of the garden between dawn and sunrise, where the lovers are seen "in the first glow of dawn." The young Jurgen and the young Dorothy are twice described as "as brave and comely and clean a pair of sweethearts as the world has known." Farraj and Daud are "the most gallant, the most enviable [beings], I knew." Nostalgia is common to Cabell's early pages and Lawrence's half-paragraph. Once again Lawrence has homosexualized heterosexual love;[11] once again his source is quasi-medieval. It is noteworthy that he could take less than seriously a previously mentioned evocation of early lost love; I refer to his treatment of the opening lines of Imr-el-kais's and Tarafa's odes. There the love was left heterosexual and slightly mocked; here it is rendered homosexual (or perhaps merely homophile) and taken seriously, for obvious personal and biographical reasons.

Another quotation from *Jurgen* is no less pessimistic. The pawnbroker has now been given back his youth and is reliving a certain Wednesday night from the never-to-be-forgotten summer. He swears that this time he will not repeat his mistakes. Jurgen, hoping to spare himself and others "the ruinous years which lay ahead" (52) kills the count who in fact married Dorothy la Désirée. Jurgen's words to his victim are, "it is highly necessary you die tonight, in order that my soul may not perish too many years before my body" (54).

These words Lawrence remembered. Sherif Nasir of *Seven Pillars* is one version of the perfect warrior. "He was the opener of roads, the forerunner of Feisal's movement, the man who had fired his first shot in Medina, and who was to fire our last shot at Muslimieh beyond Aleppo on the day that Turkey asked for an armistice, and from beginning to end all that could be

---

10. A photograph of two Arab youths on p. 46 of Graves's *Lawrence of Arabia and His World* purports to show "Farraj and Daud." The source of the photograph is given as "Mr. and Mrs. T. W. Beaumont" (121). Perhaps if called upon to do so Beaumont could also supply a photograph of Lancelot and Guenevere.

11. As he did with W. S. Blunt's description of love during the brief desert springtime. See Chapter 4.

told of him was good" (118). (Notice the rhythmical movement of the sentence, caused by the two *ands*. The last phrase is certainly a borrowing from some chivalric or neochivalric romance or chronicle [see Appendix].) But Nasir, with his sophisticated Medina background, is the Arab most like Lawrence. He stands out in the glorious court and military life of Arab warriors and aristocrats. He lives in an alien world. "[H]e was body-weary after months of vanguard service, and mind-weary too, with the passing of youth's careless years. He feared his maturity as it grew upon him, with its ripe thought, its skill, its finished art; yet which lacked the poetry of boyhood to make living a full end of life. Physically he was young yet: but his changeful and mortal soul was aging quicker than his body—going to die before it, like most of ours" (176). "In most men," Lawrence later writes, "the soul grew aged long before the body" (325).

Toward the end of his adventures Jurgen meets Guenevere again, offered her as his wife by the nearest thing to an omnipotent God that the cosmos contains, the ineffectual and harassed Koschei. Jurgen is moved to tears, anguished as only the garden between dawn and sunrise had previously anguished him.

> "Madam Guenevere, when man recognised himself to be Heaven's vicar upon earth, it was to serve and to glorify and to protect you and your radiant sisterhood that man consecrated his existence. You were beautiful, and you were frail; you were half goddess and half bric-à-brac. Ohimé, I recognise the call of chivalry, and my heart-strings resound: yet for innumerable reasons, I hesitate to take you for my wife, and to concede myself your appointed protector, responsible as such to Heaven. For one matter, I am not altogether sure that I am Heaven's vicar here upon earth. Certainly the God of Heaven [an imagined creation of man's—but not a being with any power—whom Jurgen had met during his stay in Heaven] said nothing to me about it, and I cannot but suspect that Omniscience would have selected some more competent representative." (335–36)

Jurgen here repeats to Guenevere his description of how life lost its savor and meaning after Dorothy's marriage. The loss of one's first innocent love and that of the ability to believe in benevolent omniscience are linked; he thus makes the point that he elsewhere has put into so many words: "Chivalry is for young people" (328). Jurgen and Lawrence have experienced life, and find they can no longer be heart-whole, accepting, unafraid. The mere process of living "dulls and kills whatever in us is rebellious and fine and unreasonable" (346). It is Jurgen (but it might be Lawrence too) who cries, "Oh, I have failed my vision! . . . I have failed and I know very well that every man must fail: and yet my shame is no less bitter. For I am transmuted by time's handling! . . . I have not retained the faith, nor the desire, nor the vision" (347–48, 357–58).

The story of Jurgen the pawnbroker, plagued by a "doubtfulness of himself . . . closer to him than his skin" (25), rendered hesitant because he has "no faith in anything, not even in nothingness" (297), meant a great deal to the ranker who had once had exalted ideas. If Lawrence's memories of the *Moallakat* tend, on the whole, to represent the upward and aspiring half of the parabola, then those of the *Comedy of Justice* represent the downward fall.

Lawrence was often able to lose himself in idealistic effort and ambition when writing *Seven Pillars*, but otherwise true heroism seemed nebulous and faraway. This discouraged view is reflected in a letter written after a trip to Glastonbury in 1924 to see a musical version of Thomas Hardy's *The Famous Tragedy of the Queen of Cornwall*. Glastonbury is identified by Geraldus Cambrensis with Avalon; it is where the tomb of Arthur and Guenevere was found in the reign of Henry II. "Its tremendous past makes one walk expectant in the streets, so that the smallest sign is a wonder: only why (except to try us) is all the wonder of the abbey sunk to a perfectly-preserved kitchen?" The principal actors did not impress; Tristram especially gave offence. "[H]e was fat faced, & shiny-faced, with a long turned-up nose, & glittering lecherous eyes. His mouth slobbered, & when he hugged, or was hugged by the pair of Iseults the satisfaction on his face was too horrible for words. Of course it may have been true, & Tristram far from being heroic may have been just a stout greasy snarer of women."[12] That last sentence gives us some indication of Lawrence's final submission.

Heraldry has appeared from time to time in this study. Lawrence's occasional postwar references to the subject are not without interest. He replied

---

12. British Library Add. MS 45903. Letter of 30 August 1924 to Charlotte F. Shaw.

to a correspondent who asked him for the derivation of *fylfot cross* with "One takes these names for granted. Of course the Weekly suggested derivation is bosh. It does not fill feet [i.e., of manuscripts]. Besides it was ecclesiastical ornament in the late XII Century before English was used by clerks. They must look again. I suggest a foreign word, anglicized in the later Middle Ages: but I am 30 years stale in archaeology and bookless here" (*Letters*, 747). Lawrence's bookless state led him to miss the point: there may have been fylfot crosses in church ornament in the late twelfth century but the only authority for the word denoting the sign it does (a sort of swastika; the letter Lawrence is answering dates from 1932) is MS Landsdowne 874, which was produced before 1500 and "The context in which the word there occurs seems to favor the supposition that it is simply *fill-foot* meaning a pattern or device for 'filling the foot' of a painted window" (*OED*). He told another correspondent that the SS collar (a ceremonial chain with the letter *S* worked into its pattern) might have its origin in the phrase "Spiritus Sanctus."[13] There are more than half a dozen suggestions for the collar's origin (Purey-Cust, 30–33), but the most likely is that it was connected with Henry IV's badge, "and may have been adopted as the initial of his personal motto, *Sovereygne*" (Brooke-Little, 192). Lastly he once observed vis-à-vis his illegitimacy, "Bars sinister are rather jolly ornaments" (Knightley and Simpson, 16). Let us ignore this common solecism (a bar, being a horizontal band, can be neither sinister [descending from bearer's top left] nor dexter [descending from bearer's top right]), either as the product of a moment's forgetfulness, or as the result of a reluctance to introduce technicalities into a letter to one not knowledgeable in heraldry. Lawrence never pushed the subject of heraldry to the back of his mind, although it must have recalled to him his youth, and the nonfunctional high-minded attitude of his favorite Tennyson's "Balin and Balan."

To conclude this chapter a few words should be said about Lawrence's last work: his translation of the *Odyssey* (1932). It represents another acknowledgment of disillusion and defeat. The young and egotistic Lawrence saw adventure and honor where it probably was not; the older and egotistic Lawrence could not find it where it probably was. Homer, according to

---

13. British Library Add. MS 45903. Letter of 30 August 1924 to Charlotte F. Shaw.

Lawrence, is another Lawrence. He is found decadent and mannered, living so far from the original source of epic that the water is now muddy and slow.

> Crafty, exquisite, homogeneous—whatever great art may be, these are not its attributes. . . .
> Epic belongs to early man, and this Homer lived too long after the heroic age to feel assured and large.
>
> . . . .
>
> He, like William Morris, was drawn by his age to legend, where he found men living untramelled under the God-possessed skies. ("Translator's Note," *Odyssey*, 380)

Lawrence too had felt that "The epic mode was alien to me, as to my generation" (439). He had criticized *Seven Pillars* for its "old-maidish neatness and fastidiousness about the style" (*Letters*, 380).

Lawrence's *Odyssey* is another version of *Seven Pillars*; Homer had even "sprinkled tags of epic across his pages" ("Translator's Note," *Odyssey*, n.p.). It is another attempt to come to terms with, perhaps recapture, the old enchanted past. He rejected William Morris's version: "He does not help me: for I want to keep the medieval city-state feeling out of it. The thing is Greek island, I feel sure."[14] But his opinion that the work he was translating was "an *archaistic* tale: one whose modern bones keep on showing through the Wardour St. fleshings"[15] led him to indulge (that is the only word) in medievalism. Here, in a translation, his scope is inevitably limited. He is restricted largely to word-choice and manipulation of syntax in the matter of self-expression. Lawrence made a conscious decision to employ the less obvious word: "Wherever choice offered between a poor and a rich word richness had it to raise the colour" ("Translator's Note," n.p.). The rich words often have some medieval reference; they sometimes overlap with the medieval, or medievalizing vocabulary of *Seven Pillars*. It is sad that Lawrence feels "Wardour-Street" English is appropriate to Homer's "Wardour-Street" Greek; such sentiments are more than implicit criticism of the language, and genuineness, of *Seven Pillars*.

14. British Library Add. MS 45904. Letter of 30 October 1928 to Charlotte F. Shaw.
15. British Library Add. MS 45904. Letter of 17 July 1928 to Charlotte F. Shaw.

"Chapman's Homer" (the joke is Lawrence's, a reference to his father's real name) provides a richly emotional and intellectual vocabulary. Regret and estrangement are interwoven with once-evocative words and scraps of knowledge, as in its author's casual postwar allusions to heraldry. Lawrence's *Odyssey* is a world of "criers and pages" (3), of "squires" and "beldams" (253, 268, 302), where "champions and councillors . . . sally out" (106). People wear "wimples" and "baldrics," and take (mercifully, not "crave") the "boon" of sleep (10, 168). Admittedly, some of this vocabulary is almost unavoidable. "Criers and pages" is, not surprisingly, rendered by Morris (whose verse translation outmedievalizes even his disciple's) as "heralds and lads of service fain" (*The Odyssey of Homer*, Book 1, line 5). But even Richmond Lattimore, who has produced the best of modern translations, writes "heralds and hard-working henchmen" (30).

The most revealing paragraph of Lawrence's translation is Teiresias' speech to Odysseus in Book 11 (154–55). It is worth quoting at length.

> [I]n your house you shall find trouble awaiting you, even overbearing men who devour your substance on pretext of courting your worshipful wife and chaffering about her marriage dues. Yet at your coming shall you visit their violence upon them, fatally. After you have killed these suitors, either by cunning within the house or publicly with the stark sword, then go forth under your shapely oar till you come to a people who know not the sea and eat their victuals unsavoured with its salt: a people ignorant of purple-prowed ships and of the smoothed and shaven oars which are the wings of a ship's flying. I give you this token of them, a sign so plain that you cannot miss it: you have arrived when another wayfarer shall cross you and say that on your doughty shoulder you bear the scatterer of haulms, a winnowing-fan. Then pitch in the earth your polished oar and sacrifice goodly beasts to King Poseidon, a ram and a bull and a ramping boar. Afterward turn back; and at home offer hecatombs to the Immortal Gods who possess the broad planes of heaven: to all of them in order, as is most seemly. At the last, amidst a happy folk, shall your own death come to you, softly, far from the salt sea, and make an end of one utterly weary of slipping downward into old age. All these things that I relate are true.

Lawrence has four characteristic medievalisms. The first is his use of "chaffer-ing," which appears in *Seven Pillars*[16] and is probably borrowed from Morris in the first place. Morris does not use it in his translation; he has "proffering the gifts of the bride" (194–95) for Lawrence's "chaffering about her marriage dues." Lattimore has "offering gifts to win [your godlike wife]" (171). (Although Morris and Lattimore both have "godlike" for Odysseus's wife, Lawrence has the Malorian "worshipful.") The second is the phrase *winnow-ing-fan*, the device of the canting Setvans's arms. Both Morris and Lattimore use it, but Lawrence's version is fuller and more vigorous. He has not forgotten "Septvans" and the cycling trips in France in search of a winnowing-fan to use as a wastepaper basket in Oxford.

> (Lawrence) say that on your doughty shoulder you bear the scatterer of haulms, a winnowing-fan.

> (Morris) Who saith that thy noble shoulder is bearing a winnowing-fan. (194)

> (Lattimore) and says you can carry a winnowing-fan on your bright shoulder. (171)

Third, Lawrence chastens and medievalizes the rutting of animals.

> (Morris) A ram and a bull to wit, and a boar the mate of a sow. (194)

> (Lattimore) one ram and one bull, and a mounter of sows, a boar pig. (171)

Lawrence has "a ram and a bull and a ramping boar." Finally, he reproduces a phrase from Morris's poem "The Defence of Guenevere." Morris has "So day by day it grew, as if one should / Slip slowly down some path." Vyvyan Richards recalls a letter Lawrence wrote to him, which contained the passage: "to talk of settling down to live in a small way anywhere else but here was

---

16. "Not being a tribe, [the Ageyl] had no blood enemies, but passed freely in the desert: the carrying trade and chaffer of the interior lay in their hands" (109).

beating the air; and so gradually I slipped down until a few months ago, when I found myself an ordinary archaeologist."[17]

It is significant that Lawrence's sentiments about the peacefulness of old age are different from those of Morris and Lattimore. Lawrence writes, "and make an end of one utterly weary of slipping downward into old age" (155). Morris has the (dreadful!) "thereby shalt thou fade out / By eld smooth-creeping wasted" (195). And Lattimore writes, "it will end you / in the ebbing time of a sleek old age" (171).

One cannot but feel that in the *Odyssey* Lawrence's medievalism appears to least advantage.

17. Vyvyan Richards, 56. The phrase also occurs in *Seven Pillars:* "We slipped down behind them to end Tallal's suspense" (505). Another quotation from Morris appears in both a letter to Richards and *Seven Pillars.* The letter has "My bodyguard of fifty Arab tribesmen, picked riders from the young men of the desert, are more splendid than a tulip garden" (*Letters,* 246). *Seven Pillars* has "Fellows were very proud of being in my bodyguard, which developed a profession-alism almost flamboyant. They dressed like a bed of tulips" (369). From *News from Nowhere:* "The majority . . . were young women clad . . . not mostly in silk, but in light wool most gaily embroidered; the men being all clad in white flannel embroidered in bright colours. The meadow looked like a gigantic tulip-bed because of them" (189–90). The inhabitants of Morris's romance have escaped a soulless England into a satisfactory future; Lawrence has gone to the past.

X·I

LAWRENCE
THE
ASCETIC

IN 1968 the *Sunday Times* published four articles about Lawrence, one of which (23 June) made public for the first time that from at the latest 1923 (when Lawrence enlisted in the Tank Corps) he had had himself beaten by a young Scotsman called John Bruce. Bruce had been persuaded to perform the beatings by an elaborate fiction about a powerful uncle allegedly displeased by Lawrence's actions; eventually he disclosed his part in Lawrence's life because of poverty, age, and illness. The two journalists who wrote the articles, Phillip Knightley and Colin Simpson, used them as a basis for a book that appeared the following year, *The Secret Lives of Lawrence of Arabia*. After this first disclosure of Lawrence's flagellatory activities (apart from one oblique reference to be mentioned later) since his death thirty-three years earlier, evidence, claims, and counterclaims began to appear more frequently. The most substantial contribution was the next. In 1976, with the cooperation of the Lawrence family (especially Arnold Lawrence, T. E.'s younger brother), who wished "to set this aspect of T. E.'s life in an appropriate perspective (Mack, 523, n. 42), John E. Mack, a professional psychiatrist, provided a more detailed account of the relationship between Lawrence and Bruce and their activities (apparently there were others who performed the same function as Bruce, although we know little of them) (415–31). Mack also reports the evidence of another service friend of Lawrence's and of material left at Clouds Hill after his sudden death, this material consisting in part of letters written purportedly to the uncle (actually instigated and received by Lawrence) in which arrangements are made and

Lawrence's reactions to the beatings reported. In 1977 Desmond Stewart added to the now-burgeoning story, claiming that Lawrence had "attended flagellation parties in Chelsea conducted by an underworld figure called Bluebeard" (275). When Bluebeard's imminent divorce proceedings threatened to broadcast unsavory details, Lawrence is reported to have written to the Home Secretary asking for the foreigner's expulsion and a ban on the German magazine in which the details would appear. This information was supplied to Stewart by "one of the few students of Lawrence's life who have been given access to certain otherwise embargoed papers in the Bodleian Museum [sic]" (332, n. 15). The Bluebeard story was promptly quashed; in 1977, H. Montgomery Hyde "made a prolonged and thorough search of the many hundreds of letters comprising the material in question and failed to find any trace of the . . . letter" (261, n. 16), which was said to have disappeared some time after the "student of Lawrence's life" (actually Colin Simpson) had provided Stewart with an account of its contents. There the matter rests for the moment, although Thomas J. O'Donnell's later critical study, *The Confessions of T. E. Lawrence*, makes something of Lawrence's "masochism."

The oblique hint of Lawrence's activities already referred to had been made much earlier than the *Sunday Times* disclosures. Indeed, within two years of Lawrence's death, A. W. Lawrence wrote in the "Editor's Postscript" to the collection of reminiscences about his brother *T. E. Lawrence By His Friends* that "his subjection of the body was achieved by methods advocated by the saints whose lives he had read" (*BHF*, 592). With hindsight it seems remarkable that the secret was kept so long, for Lawrence manifested a chronic interest in flagellation. In a postwar essay on James Elroy Flecker he remembers conversations of 1911 and 1912 with the poet and dramatist, who was "[c]arelessly flung beneath a tree talking of women's slippers, and of whippings, of revising *Hassan*" (T. E. Lawrence, *Men in Print*, 22). In 1933, after reading the galley proofs of Robert Graves's *I, Claudius*, Lawrence asked its author, "[W]ere the vine-shoots of the Roman N.C.O.'s really the rods that kill? I envisaged them as light cane-like minor punishments" (*RGLH*, 1:174). Graves's reply was "The vine-shoots of the centurions *were* used by the mutineers to beat them to death with. 'Shoots' is a mistranslation. I would not like to be beaten with a vine stem. They are as tough & pliant as rawhide almost" (A. W. Lawrence, *Letters to T. E. Lawrence*, 110).

Even excluding the notorious Deraa incident, *Seven Pillars* itself contains descriptions of beatings. The reader of *Seven Pillars* will recollect that Farraj and Daud first came to Lawrence's attention when Daud pleads with the Englishman for intercession to prevent his companion's being beaten for burning a tent "in a frolic"; Lawrence has the punishment divided between the two boys (183). Lawrence himself orders them to be given "a swinging half-dozen each" (210) after they have played one trick too many on him. Yusuf, the governor of Aqaba, beats the same two boys with a palm-rib when they dye a favorite camel gaudy colors: they "walk mile after mile," feeling "a new form of saddle-soreness, called 'Yusufiyeh' " (308–9). All this is light-hearted. The punishments are completely ineffectual, but Lawrence is reluctant "to hurt them mercilessly like criminals till their self-control melted and their manhood was lost under the animal distress of their bodies" (242). Lawrence writes more seriously of his bodyguard's attitude to the "savagery" with which they were ruled and of what he sees as the Oriental attitude to "the relation of master and man" (369). The "steward's whip" might "print red rivers of pain about [servants'] sides," but, the "spirits" of master and man being equal, those in the subordinate role showed "a gladness of abasement, a freedom of consent to yield to their master the last service and degree of their flesh and blood" (369). Lawrence's morbid interest in pain here manifests itself, as does, even more so, what he later called "moral masochism"; that is, his obsession with willing subordination and humiliation joyfully embraced, a subject to which we shall return. "With the sorrow of living so great, the sorrow of punishment had to be pitiless. . . . When there was reason and desire to punish we wrote our lesson with gun or whip immediately in the sullen flesh of the sufferer, and the case was beyond appeal. The desert did not afford the refined slow penalties of courts and gaols" (9). Finally, Lawrence stops the whipping of one of his bodyguard, as the "shrill whip-strokes were too cruel for my taught imagination" (385). This incident occurs after Deraa, of course.

In addition to this specific interest in beatings, Lawrence showed a lifelong obsession with asceticism in general; and a lifelong contempt for the body and the claims it made upon him. Story after story recounts his efforts to deny those claims, either by deliberately and consistently denying himself the comforts most men seek, or by taking advantage of any chance opportunity offered for self-mortification, whether in war or in peace. For example,

Lawrence's successor in Transjordan, H. St. John Philby, blithely unaware of the implications of what he is saying, reports the aftermath of an investigation into a shooting incident conducted by the two men.

> Lawrence . . . and I started back for Amman at 9.30 [p.m.] in the engine. The rain which had been with us off and on all day now settled down to a steady drizzle, and made things extremely miserable as the engine travelled in reverse down the track. . . . It was 1.30 a.m. by the time we reached [Amman station], whence Lawrence and I had an hour's walk over a muddy pool-dotted road before we reached home. I managed to get Peake's servant out of bed to give me something to eat, and then I slept soundly, forgetting the woes of a long and tiring day. I was drenched through though I had had a comparatively snug seat close to the boiler . . . but Lawrence, who had insisted on riding the whole journey on the foot-plate of the engine, completely exposed to the icy rain, had had the worst of it, and was really worn out by the time we got home. (Philby, 104)

Perhaps Lawrence's preoccupation with the earthly transience of the body started early. As a boy he possessed a coffin-shaped box, almost six feet long, two feet high, and two feet wide: "His mother complained, 'That boy of mine's sleeping there every night now' " (Mack, 24). One of the brass-rubbings in his room showed a corpse being eaten by worms. "Every night when he went to bed, 'he'd think of this chap dying, eaten by worms' " (Mack 24). This must have been a rubbing of the brass of Ralph Hamsterley, to be found in Oddington, Oxfordshire, only seven miles from the Lawrence home. Hamsterley is recorded as a "rector, fellow of Merton Coll., Oxford"; the brass, which was engraved c. 1510, shows "a skeleton in shroud eaten by worms, scroll with verses 'vermibus hic doctor,' etc., and foot inscription."[1] One need not make too much of this boyish ghoulishness, but it is worth noting when added to everything we know about the elder Lawrence. Clouds Hill is reported as containing a monk's chest decorated by Lawrence, at what stage of his life we do not know (*Clouds Hill*, 7). But long before he took to

1. Stephenson, 410. Hamsterley's brass is the only possibility. An illustration of a rubbing of this brass is to be found in Norris, *Brass Rubbing*, 61, fig. 72.

flagellation to mortify the flesh (an activity he could hardly talk about), perhaps even before he began the punishing bicycle rides in France and certainly before the straining Middle East walk of 1909, there was one basic human activity dear to most from which Lawrence could conspicuously keep himself aloof, thus gratifying his vanity while making a deeply felt claim about what we should really be like. Lawrence chose to make a point about eating, or rather not eating. Perhaps the first person the point was made to (outside Lawrence's family; he avoided family meals) was Vyvyan Richards, an Oxford friend who shared some of his medieval interests. Richards later wrote,

> To go without food for days together, replenishing fully, like a Bedouin, when chance offered: to sleep as little as was absolutely necessary: to train his nerve and muscle for defence or attack: to shun wasteful narcotics and so on—all this was no more than a good workman keeping his kit of tools keen and ready. In Oxford he observed Christmas Day as the fast day it should be (he pretended), alone in his garden room out of protest, not against uncanonical practices, but against the absurdity of all feasting. (52)

A later biographer, Desmond Stewart, thinks that this must refer to Christmas 1908, soon after Lawrence (says Stewart) learned of his illegitimacy (37). If Stewart is right then he is providing more evidence to support the feeling that a core of sexual guilt accounts for much of the renunciation.

Robert Graves, writing when Lawrence's quite genuine feats of physical endurance had made his opinions of more general interest, also has something to say about Lawrence's eating habits (or rather Lawrence has it to say himself; the italicized words were supplied almost verbatim by Lawrence and simply copied out by Graves [*RGLH*, 1:72]).

> He avoids eating with other people. Regular mealtimes are not to his likeing. *He hates waiting more than two minutes for a meal or spending more than five minutes on a meal. That is why he lives mainly on bread and butter. And he likes water better than any other drink.* It is his opinion that feeding is a very intimate performance and *should be done in a small room behind locked doors.* He eats,

when he does eat, which is seldom, in a casual abstracted way. He
came to visit me one breakfast time on his racing motorbicycle: he
had come about two hundred miles *in five hours*. He would eat no
breakfast. I asked him later what the food was like in the camp. "I
seldom eat it: it's good enough. I am now a storeman in the Quarter-
master's stores, so I don't need much." "When did you last have a
meal?" I asked. "On Wednesday." Since when apparently he had [had]
some chocolate, an orange and a cup of tea. This was Saturday. Then
I think I put some apples near him, and after a while he reached for
one. Fruit is his only self-indulgence. . . . *It is his occasional habit to
knock off proper feeding for three days—rarely five—just to make
sure that he can do it without feeling worried or strained. One's sense
of good things gets very keen by this fasting, he finds, and it is good
practice for hard times.* (Graves, *Lawrence and the Arabs*, 43–44)

Lawrence also arrived at a mealtime when working with his third biographer. "He came while we were at dinner. Urged him to take something, but
he wouldn't—said he didn't mind in the least watching us eat if we did not
mind. Gave him the satisfaction of feeling what a lot of bother—of eating—
he was escaping. He had never found it a pleasure" (*RGLH*, 2:210). Another
revealing comment is "He summed us all up in one expression. 'There are
the real and the unreal,' he said; 'the real eat anything, while the unreal
require chicken followed by a Napolean brandy' " (*BHF*, 544). If it is said that
both philanderers and puritans have a morbid consciousness of sex, then
Lawrence seems to spend as much time talking about food as any gourmand.

His purpose is twofold: to help create the myth and to speak out the truth
as he sees it. But he has given us a clue, in one of the more extreme
comments already quoted, about the inspiration for his remarks, and therefore about the attitude he finds sympathetic and the type of life he would
imitate.

[St.] Anthony [of Egypt] went back as usual to his own cell and
intensified his ascetic practices. Day by day he sighed as he meditated
on the heavenly mansions, longing for them and seeing the short-
lived existence of man. When he was about to eat and sleep and
provide for the other needs of the body, shame overcame him as he

thought of the spiritual nature of the soul. Often when about to partake of food with many other monks, the thought of spiritual food came upon him and he would beg to be excused and went a long way from them, thinking that he should be ashamed to be seen eating by others. He did eat, of course, by himself, because his body needed it; and frequently too with the brethren—embarrassed because of them, yet speaking freely because of the help his words gave them.[2]

I often knew [Isidore the elder] to weep at table, and upon asking the reason for the tears, I received this reply: "I am ashamed to partake of irrational food; I am a rational being and I ought to be in a paradise of pleasure because of the power given to us by Christ." (Palladius, 32)

"When the monks are eating, let them cover their heads with their cowls, so that a brother may not perceive his neighbor chewing." (Palladius, 93)

Lawrence's view that "feeding is a very intimate performance and should be done in a small room behind locked doors"; that it is as shamefully physical an act as the voiding of food, with which comparison is obviously being made (Lawrence had in fact first written "in a closet, behind locked doors"); and Anthony's, and Isidore's, and one other's "shame" are the same emotion in the same circumstances. A 1913 remark, "To escape the humiliation of loading in food, would bring one very near the angels" (HL, 258), makes even more clear Lawrence's identification with the self-denial of the monks of Nitria.

Lawrence makes few overt references to this region, but there can be no doubt that he was familiar with the story of the first Christian monks, those of the fourth century inhabiting the Egyptian deserts of Nitria ("about thirty-seven miles distant from Alexandria, and named after the neighbouring town

2. St. Athanasius, 57–58. Meyer draws attention to the first sentence of Porphyry's *Life of Plotinus:* "Plotinus the philosopher who lived in our day, seemed to be ashamed of living in a body" (118 n. 161). So did Lawrence, of course: "They talked of food and illness, games and pleasures with me, who felt that to recognize our possession of bodies was degradation enough, without enlarging upon their failings and attributes. I would feel shame for myself at seeing them wallow in the physical which could be only a glorification of man's cross. Indeed, the truth was I did not like the 'myself' I could see and hear" (453).

in which nitre is collected" [Waddell, 52]); Cellia, nine miles further into the desert and offering a starker and more isolated life; and Scete, fifty miles further into the desert than Nitria, and with no track leading to it (Waddell, 60). The two most important contemporary sources for this, the beginnings of monasticism, are St. Athanasius's *Life of St. Anthony* and Palladius's *Lausiac History*, so named after its dedicatee, Lausius, royal chamberlain to Emperor Theodosius II. St. Athanasius wrote his biography of the model and inspirer of Christian monasticism about A.D. 357; Palladius's work dates from approximately sixty years later (Palladius, 3). Lawrence was also familiar with the *Acta Sanctorum* (Bollandists), a collection of saints' lives. He would sometimes take a volume up to the mound at Carchemish from the impressive library formed by the archeologists there.

"Go into the desert for a few years," said Lawrence to a friend, "and you will return a prophet. If you stay there too long, you will never speak again." L. B. Namier, to whom these words were addressed, goes on to say that "Had [Lawrence] been born on the fringe of a desert, he would have become a prophet; had he lived in the Christian Middle Ages, he would have become a saint. He had the instincts and negations of both, without their faith" (*BHF*, 226–27). Lawrence implicitly admitted to Namier that he had a "craving for mortification" (*BHF*, 227). His "few years" in the desert gave him the opportunity, his "instincts and negations" the wish, to mortify his flesh and work wonders. We have already seen Lawrence's preoccupation with the temptation represented by food. His scorn of the physical here had the effect of enabling him to function efficiently as a desert leader. Both St. Anthony and the British general who described Lawrence's role in the Arab revolt as "a spiritual even more than a physical exploit" (*BHF*, 149) would have understood the remarks in *Seven Pillars* occasioned by the paucity and vileness of desert fare immediately after the capture of Aqaba. Lawrence describes the dreamlike atmosphere at this moment of triumph, when his usual habit of "imagining for myself a spirit-reality" beyond his men's features proved useless, as "to-day each man owned his desire so utterly that he was fulfilled in it, and became meaningless."

> Green dates loaded the palms overhead. Their taste, raw, was nearly as nasty as the want they were to allay. Cooking left them still deplorable; so we and our prisoners sadly faced a dilemma of constant

hunger, or of violent diurnal pains more proper to gluttony than to our expedient eating. The assiduous food-habit of a lifetime had trained the English body to the pitch of producing a punctual nervous excitation in the upper belly at the fixed hour of each meal: and we sometimes gave the honoured name of hunger to this sign that our gut had cubic space for more stuff. Arab hunger was the cry of a long-empty labouring body fainting with weakness. They lived on a fraction of our bulk-food, and their systems made exhaustive use of what they got. A nomad army did not dung the earth richly with by-products. (245–46)

Note that the earthy product of the earthly process of eating receives its mention.

"For years before the war," Lawrence tells us,

I had made myself trim by constant carelessness. I had learned to eat much at one time; then to go two, three, or four days without food; and after to overeat. I made it a rule to avoid rules in food; and by a course of exceptions accustomed myself to no custom at all.

So, originally, I was efficient in the desert, felt neither hunger nor surfeit, and was not distracted by thought of food. On the march I could go dry between wells, and, like the Arabs, could drink greatly to-day for the thirst of yesterday and to-morrow. (370)

We get a passing insight into Lawrence's self-mortification as part of a pattern of life, leading to greater spiritual self-control, when we read in the reminiscences of a fellow-soldier that

He was a most economical companion, needing very little water for his personal requirements; no matter how badly we prepared our food, he relished it. In the Wadi Hamdh, when the progress of our car was reduced to about one mile per hour on account of thick thorn bushes and large boulders, and in a very unpleasantly hot temperature—we measured it once, 131° in shade—his temper remained imperturbable as ever. (*BHF*, 159–60)

But the human body needs sleep as well as food. The abbot Arsenius is quoted as saying that "It sufficeth a monk if he sleep for one hour: that is, if he be a fighter." It was written of Arsenius, "All the night through . . . he waked, and when toward morning he craved for very nature to sleep, he would say to sleep, 'Come, thou ill servant,' and would snatch a little sleep, sitting: and straightway would rise up" (Waddell, 69). Arsenius would have approved of Lawrence's prowess in the matter: "In the same way, though sleep remained for me the richest pleasure in the world, I supplied its place by the uneasy swaying in the saddle of a night-march, or failed of it for night after laborious night without undue fatigue. Such liberties came from years of control (contempt of use might well be the lesson of our manhood), and they fitted me peculiarly for our work" (370–71). Lawrence goes on to say that although he lacked the "conception of antithetical mind and matter," considering himself a "nihilist," his experience showed him that physical break is due to defectiveness of spirit, not body. "Collapse rose always from a moral weakness eating into the body, which of itself, without traitors from within, had no power over the will. To men whose spirits were filled with desire there was no flesh" (371; second sentence only in 1922 edition, 203). One particularly successful tribe had been "supreme, riders of the spirit before whom material bars shattered and fell away" ([1922], 212). Anthony and Arsenius on the one hand, and Lawrence on the other inhabit different universes in some senses, and certainly use different terms, but they share several ideas. Both parties believe that human activity exists "only in unending effort towards unattainable imagined light" (*Seven Pillars*, 439) and that the sufferings of the body in that progress are unimportant, indeed, beneficial in that they make easier the task of the spirit (or soul).

What is to be feared is the endangering of one's soul, its being taken over by some aspect of the world. Lawrence the disillusioned warrior eventually left the world for the monastery of an armed force's powerless lowest rank not only because of the discoveries he made at Deraa (of which more shortly), but also because of the almost inevitably staining nature of power and command. The gravest sins are not those of physical self-indulgence; the gravest sins are spiritual, and anger is sufficient to imperil the soul, as another story of Waddell's makes clear: "One of the brethren, that had been insulted by another, came to the abbot Sisois and told him the scorn that had been put upon him, and said, 'I am set to revenge myself, Father.' " Sisois persuades

the offended brother of the God-denying error of his ways; the brother "fell
at the old man's feet seeking pardon, and promised that he would contend
no more with the man against whom he was angered" (Waddell, 140–41).
Similarly, Isidore (whom we have already met as an impressive abstainer
from food) is "so mightily" feared by "the devils" because "[f]rom the time
that I was made a monk, I have striven not to suffer anger to mount as far as
my throat" (71). Similarly, "The abbot Ammonas said that he had spent
fourteen years in Scete, entreating the Lord day and night that He would give
him power to master anger" (87). The incidental misunderstandings and
petty insults of daily life and their fruit are one thing; but the anger of a
charismatic military leader who disposes of the lives of others is a danger to
his men's and his enemies' bodies in this world and to his own soul in the
next. One of Waddell's anonymous old men describes what happened to
Lawrence in Wadi Hesa, "the gorge of great width and depth and difficulty
which cut off Kerak from Tafileh, Moab from Edom" (*Seven Pillars*, 376).

> An old man said, "If any enjoin somewhat upon his brother in the
> fear of God and in humility, that word which was spoken for God's
> sake compels the brother to obey, and to do what was enjoined upon
> him. But if any anxious to rule hath chosen to command his brother
> not according to the fear of God but for the sake of his own authority
> and his own will, He who seeth the secrets of the heart will not suffer
> him to hear, lest he should do what was commanded him; for that
> which is done for God's sake is manifestly a work of God: and that
> which was ordained for pride's sake is manifestly the authority of
> men. Whatsoever things are from God, have their spring in humble-
> ness: but such things as spring from authority and anger and strife,
> these are of the Enemy." (Waddell, 145)

"Authority and anger and strife": Lawrence frankly arraigns himself when
reporting the Hesa incident, and does so with an explicitness lacking in his
account of the notorious Tafas massacre.

He feels that the incompetence of his enemy has presented him with an
opportunity for administering conventional punishment that he is unable to
forego.

I was in a furious rage. The Turks should never, by the rules of sane generalship, have ventured back to Tafileh at all. It was simple greed, a dog-in-the-manger attitude unworthy of a serious enemy, just the sort of hopeless thing a Turk would do. . . . [I]t was an icy morning, and I had been up all night and was Teutonic enough to decide that they should pay for my changed mind and plan.

They must be few in number, judging by the speed of their advance. We had every advantage, of time, of terrain, of number, of weather, and could checkmate them easily: but to my *wrath* that was not enough. We would play their kind of game on our pygmy scale; deliver them a pitched battle such as they wanted; *kill them all*. . . .

This was villainous, for with arithmetic and geography for allies we might have spared the *suffering factor of humanity*; and to make a conscious joke of victory was wanton. We could have won by refusing battle, foxed them by manoeuvring our centre as on twenty such occasions before and since; yet *bad temper and conceit* united for this time to make me *not content to know my power, but determined to give public advertisement of it to the enemy and to everyone.* (377, my emphasis)

The battle is duly fought and won. Lawrence realizes that the defeated enemy will fare badly: "It was going to be a massacre and I should have been crying-sorry for the enemy; but after the angers and exertions of the battle my mind was too tired to care to go down into the awful place [i.e., the intricacies of Wadi Hesa] and spend the night saving them" (382). He realizes that his own side has fared worse than was necessary: "By my decision to fight, I had killed twenty or thirty of our six hundred men, and the wounded would be perhaps three times as many. . . . This evening there was no glory left, but the terror of the broken flesh, which had been our own men, carried past us to their homes" (382). In the 1922 *Seven Pillars* Lawrence writes of his "lasting shame." Even in the more detached 1976 edition he considers that "Chargeable against my conceit were the causeless, ineffectual deaths of Hesa. My will had gone and I feared to be alone, lest the winds of circumstances, or power, or lust, blow my empty soul away" (399).

After doing his best at Versailles to fulfill what he considers obligations, he retreats and deliberately leads a powerless and in some ways degraded life.

Remarks made in a letter to a former colleague in Arabia are illuminating: "As you say, in such a surrender [i.e., to serving something outside oneself] lies a happiness . . . but this seems to me an immoral feeling, like an overdraft on our account of life. We should not be happy: and I think I've dodged that sin successfully! The Tank Corps is a hefty penance for too rich and full a youth!" (*BHF*, 157). The last comment has a perfect parallel in another saying of the abbot Arsenius. "He said again that not more than once a year did he change the water for steeping the palm-leaves, but only added to it. And he would make a plait of those palm-leaves and stitch it until the sixth hour. The fathers asked him once why he did not change the palm-water, because it stank. And he said to them, 'For the incense and the fragrance of the perfumes that I used in the world, needs must I use this stench now" (Waddell, 69). "We should not be happy" has an only slightly less striking parallel in the utterance of another monk (its mood is characteristic of many in Waddell's collection): "Theophilus, bishop of good memory, came to him and the bishop said to him, 'What further hast thou found on this road, Father?' And the old man said, 'To blame and reproach myself without ceasing.' And the bishop said to him, 'There is no other road to follow, only this' " (Waddell, 118–19).

Lawrence's letter uses the same metaphor as a paragraph of *Seven Pillars*, which, not coincidentally, refers to Nitria and the movement inspired by St. Anthony.

> We Westerners of this complex age, monks in our bodies' cells, who searched for something to fill us beyond speech and sense, were, by the mere effort of the search, shut from it forever. Yet it came to children like these unthinking Ageyl, content to receive without return, even from one another. We racked ourselves with inherited remorse for the flesh-indulgence of our gross birth, striving to pay for it through a lifetime of misery; meeting happiness, life's overdraft, by a compensating hell, and striking a ledger-balance of good or evil against a day of judgement. (404)

The slaughter at Hesa and elsewhere no doubt caused Lawrence guilt. But what caused him more guilt, as the above extract makes clear, was the shame of physical sexual relations, and heterosexual relations only. Lawrence has just been writing that women in the East are denied equality of consideration: "Whence arose . . . partnerships of man and man, to supply human nature with more than the contact of flesh with flesh." His dismissive, uncomprehending, or hate-filled comments about sex are almost as numerous as his comments about food. One more observation—his response to D. H. Lawrence's last novel—will suffice to give the tone of many: "I'm deeply puzzled and hurt by this *Lady Chatterley* of his. Surely the sex business isn't worth all this damned fuss? I've met only a handful of people who really cared a biscuit for it" (*Letters*, 652). A. W. Lawrence writes of his elder brother that "against sex in particular he rebelled unceasingly. His hatred of sex was an irrational instinct which went far beyond reason's limits, as he himself recognized" (*BHF*, 591). When T. E. found himself in the Tank Corps, in the same hut as twenty of the unemployable, then the disgust at sexuality boils over in a series of famous letters to Lionel Curtis.

> I lie in bed night after night with this cat-calling carnality seething up and down the hut, fed by streams of fresh matter from twenty lecherous mouths. . . . *We are all guilty alike, you know.* You wouldn't exist, I wouldn't exist without this carnality. Everything with flesh in its mixture is the achievement of a moment when the lusty thought of Hut 12 has passed to action and conceived: and isn't it true that the fault of birth rests somewhat on the child? I believe it's we who led our parents on to bear us, and it's our unborn children who make our flesh itch.
>
> . . . .
>
> It's terrible to hold myself voluntarily here: and yet I want to stay here till it no longer hurts me. . . . Do you think there have been many lay monks of my persuasion? One used to think that such frames of mind would have perished with the age of religion: and yet here they rise up, purely secular. It's a lurid flash into the Nitrian desert: seems to strip the sainthood from Anthony. How about Teresa? (*Letters*, 414, 416. My emphasis)

Certainly Lawrence's attitudes to sex do resemble a sort of dechristianized version of those of Nitria. And the steps he took to conquer physicality in general and sexual desire in particular were, in his brother's words, those

"advocated by the saints whose lives he had read." We read of the deacon
Evagrius that "The demon of fornication bothered him so oppressively, as he
himself told us, that he stood naked throughout the night in a well. It was
winter at the time and his flesh froze" (Palladius, 113). We remember Philby's
story of Lawrence: that he "insisted on riding . . . on the foot-plate of the
engine, completely exposed to the icy rain." During the war Lawrence willy-
nilly was in the position of the old monk who could say, "Since the time that
I became a monk I have never given myself my fill of bread, nor of water,
nor of sleep, and tormenting myself with appetite for these things whereby
we are fed, I was not suffered to feel the strings of lust" (Waddell, 80). But
the safe regularity of life imposed by service routine—the forced regularity
for which he joined—made him again conscious of sexual desires. We are
told that Lawrence was in the habit of scourging himself at the outset of the
Arabian campaign. "His explanation of this was that he believed that he
would one day be called upon to suffer some terrible torture and was
training himself to be able to withstand whatever pain might be inflicted
upon him."[3] At the nagging of a morbid compulsion, he took up the habit
again after the peace settlements, his aim now being the subjugation of his
sexuality, expiation for the past rather than self-hardening for the future. "He
hated the thought of sex," elaborated A. W. Lawrence in a television interview.
"He had read any amount of medieval literature about characters, some of
them saints, some of them not, some ordinary people, who'd quelled sexual
longings by beating, and that's what he did" ("Lawrence and Arabia").

At Deraa Lawrence had experienced both physical pain and sexual pleasure
("I remembered the corpral kicking with his nailed boot to get me up. . . . I
remembered smiling idly at him, for a delicious warmth, probably sexual,
was swelling through me" [351]). The experiencing of such pleasure in
circumstances so defiling disgusted Lawrence; his surrender to physical pain
in such a matter seemed to go against the whole current of his life, an offense
never to be redeemed. As he wrote to Mrs. Shaw, "For fear of being hurt, or
rather to earn five minutes respite from a pain which drove me mad, I gave
away the only possession we are born with—our bodily integrity."[4] To create
a descending spiral of shame requiring punishment, the nature of which

3. Nutting, 244. Nutting gives no reference for this somewhat unlikely story.
4. British Library Add. MS 45903. Letter of 26 March 1924 to Charlotte F. Shaw.

punishment again in some sense induces humiliation and shame, Lawrence found himself subject to a morbid desire for a repetition of the beating. In a passage omitted from the 1976 edition of *Seven Pillars*, he wrote,

> I was feeling very ill, as though some part of me had gone dead that night in Deraa, leaving me maimed, imperfect, half myself. It could not have been the defilement, for no one ever held the body in less honour than I did myself. Probably it had been the breaking of the spirit by that frenzied nerve-shattering pain which had degraded me to beast level when it made me grovel to it, and which had journeyed with me since, a fascination and terror and morbid desire, lascivious and vicious, perhaps, but like the striving of a moth towards its flame."
> ([1922], 193)

Whether Lawrence now suspected an invalidating perversion of the flesh where previously he had seen a triumph of the spirit we do not know. Neither do we know whether, had he been given the chance to read them, certain lines from T. S. Eliot's "Little Gidding" would have meant more to him than to most.

> And last, the rending pain of re-enactment
>   Of all that you have done, and been; the shame
>   Of motives late revealed, and the awareness
> Of things ill done and done to other's harm
>   Which once you took for exercise of virtue.
>   Then fools' approval stings and honor stains.
>   (lines 138–43)

"Once," wrote the post-Deraa Lawrence, "I fancied I was very near the angels, and the coming so abruptly to earth was a jar—and a very wholesome jar. Angels, I think, we imagine. Beasts, I think, we are" (*Letters*, 554).

Others *have* seen such a perversion, though, and have gone on to see in the demand that the post-Deraa beatings be so administered as to produce a seminal emission absolute proof. "Lawrence, in the R.A.F., employed a fellow ranker, under a ludicrous high-minded pretext, to administer regular flagellation on his bare buttocks, for sexual excitement. This shed a new and interesting light on the Atonement for the Arabs [i.e., postwar denial of wealth and position], as also on some other episodes in his life, and on his brother's statement that he sought to imitate the pious austerities of the desert saints. Perhaps it also sheds a new light on the desert saints."[5] Some evidence to support this view is given by an authority on asceticism. J. Ribet is very aware of the possible abuses of penitential flagellation.

> Le souvenir de la flagellation du Sauveur n'a pas peu contribué sans doute à accréditer ce genre de pénitence. Cependant on ne le voit apparaître qu'au moyen age. A cette époque, les flagellants, qui dégénérèrent en hérétiques, se frâppaient souvent les uns les autres en public.
>
> . . . .
>
> La flagellation se fait régulièrement sur le dos. Il paraît que prati-quée sur les épaules, elle présente des dangers pour la santé. Il en est qui l'exercent à la partie dorsale inférieure et au haut des jambes, au siège, en un mot. Ce mode est signalé comme périlleux pour la chasteté. Selon Benoit XIV, cela ne peut être que l'exception, et ceux qui ressentiraient de tels effets n'auraient qu'à s'abstenir ou à prendre une autre partie du corps. La flagellation aux mollets n'offre pas cet inconvénient; si elle n'en a pas d'autres, elle a celui d'être fort doloureuse. (432–33)

[The memory of the flagellation of Our Savior has doubtless helped not a little to justify this form of penitence. However, flagellation only began in the Middle Ages. At this time flagellants, who came to be regarded as heretics, would often beat each other in public.

. . . .

Flagellation is usually practiced on the back. Apparently, it presents danger to health if inflicted upon the shoulders. There are people who practice it on the lower dorsal area and at the top of the legs: on the backside, in a word. This method has been reported as dangerous to chastity. But according to Benedict XIV this can only be so in exceptional cases; and those who do feel themselves in danger have

5. Roper, 36. A. W. Lawrence did not specify the desert saints.

only to abstain or to choose another area of the body. Flogging on the calves of the leg does not have this disadvantage. If it has no others, it has that of being extremely painful.] (My translation)

Be that as it may, Lawrence would have used his knowledge of the medieval practice to some degree to legitimize his activities and perhaps suggest their form. It is impossible to cite any one flagellatory saint's life that Lawrence can be shown to have read (St. Anthony does not count in that his biographer makes no mention of his employing the practice). As he read Joinville, however, he knew of the manner in which "the pious king received the discipline."

He had three cords bound together about eighteen inches long and in each of these cords four or five knots. And every Friday throughout the year, and in Lent, on Mondays and Wednesdays, he searched thoroughly in every corner of his room to see that no person remained there, and then he closed the door and remained shut in with Brother Geoffrey of Beaulieu, his confessor of the Order of Preachers; there they were a long time together. And it was believed and said among the chamberlains, who were out of the room, that the Blessed King then confessed himself to the said brother, and the said brother disciplined him with the aforementioned cords.[6]

Perhaps Lawrence was familiar with Garnier de Pont-Sainte-Maxence's account of how St. Thomas Becket mortified his flesh.

D'aspre haire aveit braies, de peil de chievre gros,
D'un altre haire aveit trestut sun cors enclos,
E les braz e les chutes e le ventre e le dos.
La vermine i esteit a torkes e a tors,
Qui ne laissout aveir a sa char nul repos.
      Encor faiseit il plus al cors mal endurer:
Chascune nuit faiseit sa char discipliner,

---

6. Gougard, 192. Gougard writes: "The part of the body exposed to receive the blows was generally the back" (193). He is referring to the practice in monasteries.

As curgies trenchanz e batre e descirer.
Robert de Meretune en sot le veir cunter,
Qui saint' obedïence n'en osout trespasser.
   Robert de Meretune sis chapelains esteit.
Mult li esteit privez; en sa chambre giseit.
Mais quant vint a la mort, e vit le grant destreit,
Dunc a primes gehi; car af'ïé l'aveit
Qu'en trestut sun vivant sun estre ne dirreit.
   Quant Robert ert culchiez, e deüst reposer,
Tantes afflictuins, ço dist, perneit li ber,
Bien le tierz de la nuit ne voleit il cesser;
Dunc veneit a Robert e sil faiseit lever,
Baillout lui les curgies a lui discipliner.
   Quant tant l'aveit batu qu'il esteit tut lassez
E de pitié conpunz, d'angoisse tresuez,
Getout jus les curgies os tuz les chiefs nuez.
"Chaitif, faiseit il dunc, pur quei fui unches nez?
De tuz les chaitifs sui li plus mal eurez."
   Mais quant li chapelains s'esteit alez culchier,
Sainz Thomas nel volet encor a tant laissier:
Il meimes perneit sun cors a depescier,
A l'une de ses mains sa char a detrengler.[7]

[He wore trousers of coarse hair of thick goat fur,
With another hair garment he had covered his whole body,
His arms and his elbows, his belly and his back.
Vermin was everywhere.
Which gave his flesh no repose.
   And he made his body endure even more ills:
Each night he could cause his flesh to be disciplined,
To be beaten and torn with sharp whips.
Robert de Merton told the truth about it
Who dared not offend against holy obedience.

7. Pont-Sainte-Maxence, 121–22, lines 3936–65. I thank Professor Gerard J. Brault of the Department of French, The Pennsylvania State University, for the English translation.

Robert de Merton was his chaplain.
He was very close to him and slept in his chamber.
But when Thomas died, and he Robert witnessed the affliction,
He immediately revealed the secret; for he had promised
that he would not speak of it while Thomas was alive.
When Robert was in bed and supposed to be resting,
The saint would be deep in prayer,
A full third of the night he did not want to stop;
And he would come to Robert and make him get up,
Thomas would give the whip to him and asked to be disciplined.
When Robert had beaten him so that he was all tired out
He felt pity for him sweating with anguish,
He was moved to pity and threw down the whips with their knotted ends.
"Scoundrel, why was I ever born?" Robert would say.
"Of all the unfortunate people I am the most miserable."
But the chaplain had gone to bed again,
Even then Saint Thomas did not want to stop;
And he himself began to punish his own body,
He would tear his own flesh with one hand.]

He had, undoubtedly, been familiar with works like it, which presented themselves to his mind as he lay in Hut 12, disgusted at the carnality around him and wishing again, perhaps for ambiguous reasons, to have his flesh "torn."

Paucity of publicly available evidence and the subterranean nature itself of the matter under discussion will, perhaps, always make an evaluation of Lawrence's self-imposed beatings less satisfactory than one would like. But what is again obvious is Lawrence's application of the attitudes and procedures of an earlier century to life in the present. Not for the first time, Lawrence is applying to his modern life a belief that has its origin and justification in another age. And, not for the first time, it is in the clash between the old philosophy and that philosophy's now anachronistic surroundings that the real significance (certainly the real interest) lies. Lawrence interests us today because of his part in the Arab revolt and the book he wrote. Both would have been different, might not even have come into being, but for his medieval leanings and the character traits that are their source.

He would certainly interest us much less if the overlap between the thirteenth century and his twentieth had been complete.

Lawrence's one brief reference to Freud (in a letter to Lionel Curtis [Letters, 414]) does not make much clearer which century dominated his view of the beatings. For one thing, Lawrence did not absorb the public school tradition of birchings because he never went to one; instead, he studied as a day-pupil at the Oxford High School. Yet he missed that ritual only to be whipped with regularity, as a much younger boy, by his mother, who administered the household discipline evaded by a passive father. The rod or staff that comforted him later seems to have had other origins than those that affected many of his upper-class contemporaries. One sympathetic writer about Lawrence's masochism has claimed that it need not be an invalidating aberration. Like Trevor-Roper, G. Wilson Knight suspects a hidden sexual gratification in "our greatest exemplars of martyrdom and sacrifice," but he considers that "there is probably no final distinction between noble sacrifice and what is known as 'sexual perversion.'" Lawrence's image of the moth and flame (see page 184 above) writes Wilson Knight, corresponds to Browning's use of it for Caponsacchi's nobly *desired* self-immolation in *The Ring and the Book*: " 'the very immolation made the bliss;' it was 'as if the intense centre of the flame' should turn out to be a 'heaven' to the 'fly' who seeks it; the 'ecstasy' has a 'thrill' that can 'out-throb pain.' "[8] This may be acceptable to us, but would not have occurred to Lawrence's probable models. The first chapter of *Seven Pillars* juxtaposes most ambiguously self-abnegation and the "ideal."

> As time went by our need to fight for the ideal increased to an unquestioning possession, riding with spur and rein over our doubts. Willy-nilly it became a faith. We had sold ourselves into its slavery, manacled ourselves together in its chain-gang, bowed ourselves to serve its holiness with all our good and ill content. The mentality of ordinary human slaves is terrible—they have lost the world—and we had surrendered, not body alone, but soul to the overmastering greed of victory. By our own act we were drained of morality, of volition, of responsibility, like dead leaves in the wind. (8)

8. G. Wilson Knight, 325. Knight is quoted from *The Ring and the Book*, VI, 953–73.

Indeed, the self-abnegation (normally an action or attitude we praise) is suspiciously near to self-reification, an abstention from the human being's necessity to choose, and the healthy give-and-take of most sexual relationships. The war hero ("I was . . . charged by duty to lead the Arabs forward. . . . If I could not assume their character, I could at least conceal my own") and the masochist ("Several [of them—or of us]; thirsting to punish appetites they could not wholly prevent, took a savage pride in degrading the body, and offered themselves fiercely in any habit which promised physical pain or filth") are perilously close. Lawrence is surely more aware (or honest with himself) than some of the Nitrian or later flagellants were.

Lawrence's difficulties and paradoxical triumphs, here and elsewhere, arise chiefly from the lack of an all-embracing and all-explaining philosophy. E. M. Forster, in the notes he wrote when preparing an edition of Lawrence's letters, produced his subject's biography *en petit*.

> From eighteen onwards he extended his holiday range to France— circled there more and more widely until, at Aigues-Mortes, he was stopped by the Mediterranean. By the time he was twenty he had picked up medieval military architecture, and seen every twelfth century castle of importance in England, Wales, France. The notion of a Crusade, of a body of men leaving one country to do noble deeds in another, possessed him, and I think never left him, though the locality of the country varied: at one time it was Arabia, later it was the air. Had he been a Christian, his medieval equipment would have been complete and thought-proof: he would have possessed a positive faith and been happier: he would have been the "parfait gentil knight," the defender of orthodoxy, instead of the troubled and troublous genius who fascinated his generation and failed to fit into it. He would have been much smaller.[9]

Unfortunately, the man who "had the mind of a medieval monk," whose "values were quite different from ours . . . and of ambition or dreams in the usual worldly sense he had none" (Edwards, 344) did have a disabling lack of confidence (or faith) in any future world, an unmedieval sexual sophisti-

9. Bodleian Library Res. MSS b55. Quoted in Mack, 55.

cation, and an increasingly overwhelming horror at what he saw and experienced. Lawrence could not entirely deal with the Deraa incident and other offenses of the flesh in an unrelenting annihilation of that flesh. Flagellation both expiated guilt and produced more.

CONCLUSION

"YOU are," wrote Lawrence to Vyvyan Richards, concerning Richards's response to the 1922 *Seven Pillars*, "*intoxicated with the splendour of the story.* That's as it should be. The story I have to tell is one of the most splendid ever given a man for writing" (T. E. Lawrence, *Fifty Letters*, 8).

Behind these words is the joy of someone who has found his long-sought subject and the confirmation of a long-held feeling of singularity and superiority. Lawrence's adventure had been lived before it had been written, and it could not have been lived had not the land of his dreams existed, more or less. The outsider of Oxford, the eccentric of Carchemish, the misfit of Cairo, had justified his innate belief in the uniqueness of his destiny. *Seven Pillars of Wisdom* is the product of a long-standing ambition to create a work of art, the material for this work having been provided by its author's chivalric adventures in an antique land. The impetus toward these adventures arose from chivalric reading, reading pursued with such thoroughness because it flattered and reinforced certain idealistic elements in the young Lawrence's character. (Lawrence is one of those people for whom, finally, there is no distinction between life and literature.) *Seven Pillars* is the product of an identifiable phase in the life of its creator. Had it been written earlier or later, it would not be the work we possess now. Just as a fleeting glimpse of a smiling face may show us one abstracted half-second's emotion from the growth and fading of amusement or pleasure, one ever so slightly changing part of the movement and life of human response, so *Seven Pillars* shows us the state of Lawrence's being in the few years following the end of the war. I have already compared the arc of aspiration and the decline of disillusion to a parabola. *Seven Pillars* represents the summit of the parabola, equidistant in emotion if not exactly in years both from the joy of innocent medievalizing discovery, begun independently abroad when "I was 17, which is the age at which I suddenly discovered myself," remembered by Lawrence even in 1927 as "a dream of delight" (*Letters*, 553); and from the desolating thoroughness with which he turned his back on his younger self: "People are a nuisance. They will not understand that I have no intention of continuing the acquaintances I had before 1914. That part of the business is finished. I am a different person now" (*HL*, 373).

But *Seven Pillars* not only re-creates the moment at which the smile, so to speak, was fading from Lawrence's face: it also captures the moment at which it began fading finally from the face of the Middle East. Englishmen before Lawrence had seen the region as one where chivalry still survived. But does a certain sort of dissatisfied romantic project onto a less-developed people, for subconsciously selfish reasons, the virtues he admires? Or is he able, because of that cast of mind and personality that made him a dissatisfied romantic in the first place, to perceive what is in fact there, even if his compatriots, blinded by a mixture of fear and prejudice, fail to see it? These questions cannot be fully answered. But Lawrence was not the first or the last to see the practice of chivalry as an especially Arab habit. It is worthwhile to set him between two other Arabophile Englishmen who have done the same thing. This will give us some external, incidental, justification for the validity of Lawrence's dreams, and help us to examine for the last time in these pages why he retreated from them.

Lawrence had read, without admiring, the works of Richard Burton. Burton, different from Lawrence in so many ways (his response to Doughty's tribulations—the Doughty whom Lawrence always treated with such gentle reverence—was to write angrily and uncomprehendingly of an *Englishman* being "compelled to stand the buffet from knaves that smell of sweat"),[1] nonetheless wrote of the *Moallakat* in terms almost undistinguishable from those of Blunt (2:92–93). He goes on to claim that "From ancient periods of the Arab's history we find him practising knight-errantry, the wildest form of chivalry" (2:95). He quotes with approval certain sayings of Antar: "This valiant man . . . hath defended the honour of women," "Mercy, my lord, is the noblest quality of the noble," and, above all, "Birth is the boast of the *fainéant*; noble is the youth who beareth every ill, who clotheth himself in mail during the noontide heat, and who wandereth through the outer darkness of night" (2:95) (Burton writes too of the Albanians that "They have yet another point

1. Quoted in Assad, 96. This rhythmical phrase is probably the most pleasing that Burton, not an elegant writer, ever produced.

of superiority over us; they cultivate the individuality of the soldier, whilst we strive to make him a mere automaton. In the days of European chivalry, battles were a system of well-fought duels" [1:268]). Lawrence found Blunt a far more congenial man and writer than Burton, but the two share many beliefs.

Let us turn from a nineteenth-century writer to a twentieth-century one. Glubb Pasha lived and fought with the Arabs at a time when one would expect the philosophy of Antar to be completely superseded. But not so: this spine-tingling anecdote dates from 1948.

> [The young boy] had one of those frank, open faces which can sometimes be seen among the tribes. He gave me a dirty piece of paper, inscribed in pencil in a shaky hand. It was from Aid ibn Rubaiyan, the shaikh of a section of the Dahamshah, themselves a branch of the great bedouin tribe of Aneiza. The letter was to introduce the boy, who wished to be a soldier. Then Aid added these lines:
>
> "We long for you to return to us. The *effendis* only want money. But we who want glory want you back."
>
> The letter had come five hundred miles across the waterless desert, from the water-holes of Shabicha. For a moment I could see that glaring dusty hollow, the rows of ragged black tents, the flies and the dust, the herds of great camels, the desert horizon with its range after range of pale blue hills. In the middle stood Aid's big tent, the coffee pots, the threadbare carpets, and Aid himself leaning over the shoulder of the only man in the camp who could write and saying: "Tell him we want him back because we love honour, not money."[2]

Godfrey Lias considers that old-fashioned chivalric ideas die a very hard death among the Jordanians at least, modern ways of waging war notwith-

---

2. Glubb, *A Soldier With the Arabs*, 178. Glubb glosses *effendi* as "the word used for Mister. In this instance the reference is to civilian officials" (178). Ironically Lawrence's and Glubb's work implied the growing power of the *effendis*, despite their love for "honor." Glubb never lost his high opinion of the men he had once led. After nearly thirty years of exile—for exile it must have seemed—he still remembered that "They had a tremendous sense of chivalry. . . . They were very honourable men. Simple and straightforward." Quoted in Tim Heald, "The Old Commander Recalls His Legion," *Daily Telegraph* (London), 31 March 1984.

standing. The old life of the men of the Arab Legion, he writes, "taught them to sing to their armoured cars as they went into battle, to engage aeroplanes as well as men in single combat from the ground, to live and die as heroically and happily as in the days of the first Khalifs of Islam and of Saladin . . . and of Ivanhoe and Richard Lionheart" (10). He tells the story of Sheikh Zaal ibn Mutlaq, who, during the Second World War, shot at flight after flight of bombers as "The air around him was filled with fragments and the ground was churned and furrowed with bullets." On his failure to bring an aircraft down he exclaimed, "*Al harb al yom ma biha leddha*" ("War today is without joy").[3]

Lawrence is not the only modern author, not the only combatant of 1914–18, to represent his battle as being in the tradition of medieval encounters. But he is probably the only modern author to do so convincingly. David Jones's *In Parenthesis* (1937) attempts the same thing. This work, a mixture of prose and poetry, crammed even more densely than *Seven Pillars* with allusions to chivalric and other writings, and also to myth and ritual, relates the experience of a British unit from December 1915 and embarkation to July 1916 and decimation in battle. Jones is concerned with establishing an at least partial identification of the Tommies of the Great War with the heroes

---

3. But some are differently attuned. For Richard Meinerzhagen (a friend, or acquaintance, of Lawrence, mentioned in *Seven Pillars*) what links Burton, Lawrence, Glubb and others is not a response to chivalry: "It is remarkable how many British eccentrics are attracted to Arabia or is it that a certain type becomes an eccentric after contact with the Arab? From the earliest days— Gordon, Lady Elphinstone, Doughty, Burton—down to the host of modern eccentrics such as Lawrence, Philby, Glubb. I suppose a slightly unbalanced mind and a craving for romance or solitude is attracted by the dirt, squalor, dishonesty, inefficiency, laziness, intolerance and unreliability of the Arab" (*Middle East Diary*, quoted in Jeffrey Meyers, *Wounded Spirit*, 79). One expert on the Middle East and those who have affected its destiny this century reports that Meinerzhagen began as a pro-Zionist suspicious of the Jews and became pro-Jewish and suspicious of the Zionists (H. V. F. Winstone, *Gertrude Bell*, 211). Be that as it may, Meinerzhagen was in no two minds about the Arabs; he claimed once that he borrowed a British soldier's uniform and gun, and killed three Arabs in the fighting for Haifa (Stewart, *T. E. Lawrence*, 191–92). And the fact that Meyers uses this quotation as a preface to a chapter on Doughty (who did indeed witness "dirt, squalor, dishonesty, inefficiency, laziness, intolerance and unreliability" in Arabia) does not make it any the less an ignorant and insulting racial caricature, which should have been more distanced from authorial attitude than it actually is in *The Wounded Spirit*. What, pray, would be the response in Western Europe and North America if an equally insulting characterization of the Jew were prefaced to an academic discussion of a Gentile's literary account of his adventures, or misadventures, among Jews?

of Malory: "I think the day by day in the Waste Land, the sudden violences and long stillnesses, the sharp contours and unformed voids of that mysterious existence, profoundly affected the imaginations of those who suffered it. It was a place of enchantment. It is perhaps best described in Malory, book iv, chapter 15—that landscape spoke 'with a grimly voice' " (D. Jones, x–xi). In addition, he tends to see the perennial experience of the soldier, especially as expressed in the "Boast" of part 4 (79–84), as a permanently valid metaphor for the necessary endurances and inevitable sufferings of human existence. So part 6 begins with a three-and-a-half–line mixture of Malorian quotations (135, 218; part 6, n. 1); and the following is not intended to mock the collocation of modern mechanical war and Malorian chivalry.

> He gave them the latest as he had heard tell of the devising of this battle . . . and in what manner it should be. He said that there was a hell of a stink at Division—so he had heard from the Liaison Officer's groom—as to the ruling of this battle—and the G.S.O.2 who used to be with the 180th that long bloke and a man of great worship was in an awful pee—this groom's brother Charlie what was a proper crawler and had some posh job back there reckoned he heard this torf he forgot his name came out of ther Gen'ral's and say as how it was going to be a first clarst bollocks and murthering of Christen men and reckoned how he'd throw in his mit an' be no party to this so-called frontal-attack never for no threat nor entreaty, for now, he says, blubbin' they reckon, is this noble fellowship wholly mischiefed.[4]

This extract implies a conguency of experience rather than a contrasting. Again, an ordinary soldier speaks: "My fathers were with the Black Prinse of Wales / at the passion of the blind Bohemian king. / They served in these fields, / it is in the histories that you can read it" (D. Jones, 79).

More than one critic has been troubled by Jones's juxtaposition of Flanders and the Waste Land, of a historical twentieth-century war and Arthurian legends and romances. Paul Fussell treats Jones with sympathy and respect, but he finds the gap between King Pellam's Launde, Pellam being the maimed

---

4. D. Jones, 138. Jon Silkin (324) is perhaps unnecessarily puzzled as to what extent the historical material is meant to support or contrast with the modern.

king of the Grail story, and France too great for "Jones' . . . ritual-and-romance machinery" (150) to bridge. *In Parenthesis* is an "Honorable Miscarriage" (Fussell, 144), for

> [t]he reader comes away . . . persuaded that the state of the soldier is universal throughout history. But the problem is, if soldiering is universal, what's wrong with it? And if there is nothing in the special conditions of the Great War to alter cases drastically, what's so terrible about it? Why the shock? But Jones's commitment to his ritual-and-romance machinery impels him to keep hinting that this war is like others. (Fussell, 150)

Jones, like another soldier with Welsh links, is an incorrigible viewer of what surrounds him as material for treatment as part of a literary tradition, that tradition recording and praising a noble ethos.

> [He] has attempted . . . to elevate the new Matter of Flanders and Picardy to the status of the old Matter of Britain. That it refuses to be so elevated, that it resists being subsumed into the heroic myth, is less Jones's fault than the war's. The war will not be understood in traditional terms: the machine gun alone makes it so special and unexampled that it simply can't be talked about as if it were one of the conventional wars of history. Or worse, of literary history. (Fussell, 153)

Jones asks "if Mr. X adjusting his box-respirator can be equated with what the poet envisaged in 'I saw young Harry with his beaver on'" (xiv). For Fussell the answer is no.

But I have labored in vain if I have not persuaded the reader that Lawrence and his Arabs are more convincing as figures in the Matter of Araby. They too know King Pellam's Launde, the "abominable desolation . . . called . . . El Houl"

> and to-day we rode in it without seeing signs of life; no tracks of gazelle, no lizards, no burrowing of rats, not even any birds. We, ourselves, felt tiny in it, and our urgent progress across its immensity

was a stillness or immobility of futile effort. The only sounds were the hollow echoes, like the shutting down of pavements over vaulted places, of rotten stone slab on stone slab when they tilted under our camels' feet; and the low but piercing rustle of the sand, as it crept slowly westward before the hot wind along the worn sandstone, under the harder overhanging caps which gave each reef its eroded, rind-like shape. (*Seven Pillars*, 191)

Here too we have the "long stillnesses, the sharp contours and unformed voids" of the Waste Land as perceived by Jones. One of the "sudden violences" soon strikes the travelers. The evil of El Houl is not chemical, like mustard gas. It is innate to the land. It partly manifests itself in, as Lawrence goes on to tell, the fiery breathless wind called the *khamsin*, the effect of which may be somewhat alleviated by the Arabs' daily wear: "[They] drew their head-cloths tightly across their noses, and pulled the brow-folds forward like vizors with only a narrow, loose-flapping slit of vision." (191) The twentieth-century citizen, taken from his desk or lathe to spend a few admittedly terrible years in France in parentheses ("the war itself was a parenthesis—how glad we thought we were to step outside its brackets at the end of '18" [D. Jones, xv]), does not convince as "young Harry with his beaver on." The Arabs in Arabia pull their head-cloths round their faces "like vizors." And to Lawrence's words we do not object.

But if Lawrence has the advantage of fighting a medieval-style war in a technologically undeveloped world, then Jones has a different, more valuable advantage. Jones is a devout Christian, living in a meaningful, coherent, and finally love-created and love-energized world, a world in which he is not a stranger. For Jones the universe is a place in which one *can* finally put cordial faith, no matter what horrors one may meet in the Waste Land. It is a comprehensible place, where associations and links *can* be made, testimony to the ubiquity of God in His world. "If," wrote Jones in the Preface to *The Anathémata* (1952), "the painter makes visual forms, the content of which is chairs or chair-ishness, what are the chances that those who regard his painting will run to meet him with the notions 'seat,' 'throne,' 'session,' 'cathedra,' 'Scone,' 'on-the-right-hand-of-the-father,' in mind?" (quoted in Fussell, 145). Jones even thinks that the weapons of the First World War can be so humanized. It was easier to see the earlier stages of the war as in the same tradition as wars read about.

> [July 1916] roughly marks a change in the character of our lives in the Infantry on the West Front. From then onward things hardened into a more relentless, mechanical affair, took on a more sinister aspect. The wholesale slaughter of the later years, the conscripted levies filling the gaps in every file of four, knocked the bottom out of the intimate, continuing, domestic life of small contingents of men, within whose structure Roland could find, and, for a reasonable while, enjoy, his Oliver. In the earlier months there was a certain attractive amateurishness, and elbow-room for idiosyncrasy that connected one with a less exacting past. (D. Jones, ix)

But Jones also has faith (the *mot juste*) that whatever is the invention of man is ultimately "creaturely," and therefore capable of ennoblement by association.

> It is not easy in considering a trench-mortar barrage to give praise for the action proper to chemicals—full though it may be of beauty. We feel a rubicon has been passed between striking with a hand weapon as men used to do and loosing poison from the sky as we do ourselves. We doubt the decency of our inventions, and are certainly in terror of their possibilities. That our culture has accelerated every line of advance into the territory of physical science is well appreciated—but not so well understood are the unforeseen, subsidiary effects of this achievement. We stroke cats, pluck flowers, tie ribands, assist at the manual acts of religion, make some kind of love, write poems, paint pictures, are generally at one with that creaturely world inherited from our remote beginnings. Our perception of many things is heightened and clarified. Yet must we do gas-drill, be attuned to many newfangled technicalities, respond to increasingly exacting mechanical devices; some fascinating and compelling, others sinister in the extreme; all requiring a new and strange direction of the mind, a new sensitivity certainly, but at a considerable cost.
>
> We who are of the same world of sense with hairy ass and furry

wolf and who presume to other and more radiant affinities, are finding it difficult, as yet, to recognise these creatures of chemicals as extensions of ourselves, that we may feel for them a native affection, which alone can make them magical for us. It would be interesting to know how we shall ennoble our new media as we have already ennobled and made significant our old—candle-light, fire-light, Cups, Wands and Swords, to choose at random. (xiv)

Logically, Jones is perfectly right. Wounds made by a machine-gun cannot be more agonizing to suffer or ghastly to behold than those made by a sword. If the latter has been ennobled, then why not the former? Indeed, the incomparably more deadly weapons we now possess should also be capable of ennoblement, for they too are the invention of a being created in God's image. But to those who lack Jones's faith even if they share his mythopoeicizing habit of mind, there comes a point when modern war is simply too horrible to take: when any tendency to trust in a supreme being with the attributes of a Father is drowned in blood.

We have already had occasion to note that Lawrence lacks faith, that his characteristic response to the world is a radical mistrust. For Lawrence the world is not coherent and meaningful as it is for the Christian Jones. Time and again Lawrence reveals his profound doubts about the transcendental and absolute, sometimes in very unlikely ways and places. When writing in an archaeological treatise about the lack of written records in northern Sinai and the consequent reliance scholars must place on "the remains of occupation [remarkably] preserved [by climate and isolation] in the country itself," he remarks that "The careless traveller who piles up four stones in a heap by the roadside here erects an eternal monument to himself" (T. E. Lawrence, *The Wilderness of Zin*, 18). The epistemological resonance of this comment is surely rare in such a work.

But Lawrence does yearn for the possibility of belief. He is unsettled at best, tormented at worst, by the absence of a meaningful framework. On one occasion in the desert, "We started on one of those clean dawns which woke up the senses with the sun, while the intellect, tired after the thinking of the night, was yet abed. For an hour or two on such a morning the sounds, scents and colours of the world struck man individually and directly, not filtered through or made typical by thought; they seemed to exist sufficiently by themselves, and the lack of design and of carefulness in creation no longer irritated" (*Seven Pillars*, 409–10). Lawrence would have been happier had he been able to share the religious beliefs of his brother Montagu Robert, who did see "design and . . . carefulness" in creation: toward the end of his life he considered the turning of small branches by a storm into "gleaming ropes of ice" to be evidence of the imminent second coming of Christ (Mack, 15).

In such a decentered world death in battle also loses its significance; the Christian belief that sustained the heroic martyr Roland and, by extension, all beliefs, become almost collective fantasies: "With man-instinctive, anything believed by two or three had a miraculous sanction to which individual ease and life might honestly be sacrificed. To man-rational, wars of nationality were as much a cheat as religious wars, and nothing was worth fighting for: nor could fighting, the act of fighting, hold any meed of intrinsic value. Life was so deliberately private that no circumstances could justify one man in laying violent hands upon another's" (*Seven Pillars*, 438–39). By the time Lawrence comes to write *The Mint*, and to live the self-reified life described therein he has abandoned all attempt at comprehension, the medieval world of faith and the actions faith inspired being represented only by a jeering carving. We are now far indeed from the statuary of Chartres.

> We sat to pray, and the emanations of wet wool and sweat gathered over us. Surely we were steeped in flesh. Before me stood the font, from whose quatrefoil panel into my face leered a mediaeval face, with ringed mouth and protruding tongue. Its lewdness somehow matched our prison-coloured lolling heads: while the padre read a lesson from Saint Paul, prating of the clash of flesh and spirit and of our duty to fight the body's manifold sins. The catalogue of these sins roused us to tick off on grubby fingers what novelties were left us to explore. For the rest we were just uncomprehending. Our ranks were too healthy to catch this diseased antithesis of flesh and spirit. Unquestioned life is a harmony, though then not in the least Christian. (*The Mint*, 67)

APPENDIX:
"ORIENTALISM"
AND THE
UNDISCOVERED SUBTEXTS
IN
SEVEN PILLARS OF WISDOM

"CAN'T [the critics]," asked Lawrence, in a letter to Charlotte F. Shaw, "see the subtlety of [*Seven Pillars*'] construction, all filled with hidden quotation & allusion to half the accepted prose-and-poetry achievements of the English language? Really, I'm coming to believe that I must be considerably skillful, to hide my tricks and contrivances from all those practised eyes!"[1]

The student of *Seven Pillars*, of its author's letters, of Lawrence generally, does not take long to realize that Lawrence's inspiration, whether for action or writing, is often literary. The student reads the "prose-and-poetry achievements," in English and other languages, that he knows or very strongly suspects that Lawrence read, and learns to look out for borrowed or transmuted phrases within the text of *Seven Pillars*, as an entry into the work. He is not surprised to find Lawrence going on to say, in the same letter, that "it was my literary method, in making the MS now in the Bodleian, to take its destroyed original, paragraph by paragraph, & to dwell on each till it contained some one sentence, or cadence, or word only, which gave me pleasure. One per paragraph was the ration: because if each sentence had been pleasurable the thing would have become a surfeit. . . . Now in 90% of

---

1. British Library Add, MS 45903. Letter of 21 April 1927 to Charlotte F. Shaw.

cases this point which gave me pleasure was a quotation more or less disguised."

It would, perhaps, be rather pedestrian ("Teutonic," Lawrence would say) to note that there are 121 chapters in *Seven Pillars*; to work out that an average chapter has eighteen paragraphs; that 90 percent of these 2,178 paragraphs is roughly 1,960; and then gravely to look for nearly two thousand "hidden quotation[s] & allusion[s] to half the accepted prose-and-poetry achievements of the English language." It would, perhaps, be even more plodding to attempt to divide these quotations and allusions into large and more or less useful groups: a notional third from the Classical era, maybe, to take account of Lawrence's reading of the ancients;[2] a notional third from the Middle Ages; and a final third from Modern (i.e., Renaissance and after) literature. It would perhaps but not certainly be unimaginative to try to find an allusion, of one kind or another, in every paragraph of *Seven Pillars*; Lawrence insists, again in the same letter to Mrs. Shaw, that he is not exaggerating: "At this point I began to fear that I was speaking without book. So I opened the infamous Seven, where it wanted to open, which was page 401, and read it. Para i. has an echo (intentional) of a phrase of Gray's, in the Elegy. Para ii's original of the 'gleam' is obvious. Para iii is a crib of Robert Vansittart's Singing Caravan. Para iv is my own. I breathe refreshed."

Page 401 of the 1926 *Seven Pillars* gives us the opening paragraphs of Chapter 76 of modern trade editions, as follows.

> Just at sunset we said good-bye to them, and went off up our valley, feeling miserably disinclined to go on at all. Darkness gathered as we rode over the first ridge and turned west, for the abandoned pilgrim road, whose ruts would be our best guide. We were stumbling down the irregular hill-side, when the men in front suddenly dashed forward. We followed and found them surrounding a terrified pedlar, with two wives and two donkeys laden with raisins, flour and cloaks. They had been going to Mafrak, the station just behind us. This was awkward; and in the end we told them to camp, and left a Sirhani to

---

2. It has been suggested that there is a book to be written on *The Classicism of Lawrence of Arabia.* I offer the idea, gratis, to anyone in search of a Ph.D. dissertation topic or other project.

see they did not stir: he was to release them at dawn, and escape over the line to Abu Sawana.

We went plodding across country in the now absolute dark till we saw the gleam of the white furrows of the pilgrim road. It was the same road along which the Arabs had ridden with me on my first night in Arabia out by Rabegh. Since then in twelve months we had fought up it for some twelve hundred kilometres, past Medina and Hedia, Dizad, Mudowwara and Maan. There remained little to its head in Damascus where our armed pilgrimage should end.

But we were apprehensive of to-night: our nerves had been shaken by the flight of Abd el Kader, the solitary traitor of our experience. Had we calculated fairly we should have known that we had a chance in spite of him: yet a dispassionate judgement lay not in our mood, and we thought half-despairingly how the Arab Revolt would never perform its last stage, but would remain one more example of the caravans which started out ardently for a cloud-goal, and died man by man in the wilderness without the tarnish of achievement.

Some shepherd or other scattered these thoughts by firing his rifle at our caravan, seen by him approaching silently and indistinctly in the dark. He missed widely, but began to cry out in extremity of terror and, as he fled, to pour shot after shot into the brown of us. (330)

I have said that the reader of *Seven Pillars* learns to look for more or less hidden references to other texts. But one can fail to notice the three allusions pointed out by Lawrence. Indeed, the first one is a little puzzling even after Lawrence has identified the pre-text, but one assumes that the first two clauses of his first sentence and the first half of his second have their origin in lines 1–5 of "Elegy Written in a Country Church Yard."

> The Curfew tolls the knell of parting day,
> The lowing herd wind slowly o'er the lea,
> The plowman homeward plots his weary way,
> And leaves the world to darkness and to me.
>
> Now fades the glimmering landscape on the sight . . .
> (Starr and Hendrickson, 37)

"Para ii's original of the 'gleam' " is, again, not so obvious as Lawrence finds it, but is presumably Tennyson's "Merlin and the Gleam," especially lines 83–84: "The Gleam, that had waned / to a wintry glimmer / On icy fallow" (Ricks, 1416). Lawrence has "we saw the gleam of the white furrows." Note too that the opening ten words of "Para ii" ("We went plodding across country in the now absolute dark") are a reminiscence of lines 4–5 of the "Elegy." "Para iii," writes Lawrence (he actually means the last thirty words or so), "is a crib of Robert Vansittart's Singing Caravan." A quick look through Lawrence's diplomatic kinsman's versifying suggests no particular stanza or lines as source, but rather aspects of the poem as a whole. In this case, it does not seem worthwhile to try to dig any deeper.

All this raises the question of the strength of the molding force of literature and the validity of specifically "literary" responses to life, often hinted at in these pages. To what extent is Lawrence inventing his Arabs on literary-medieval lines? To what extent is he seeing his Arab warriors through a distorting lens of medieval reading and imagining? And, conversely, to what extent is he reporting what is "objectively" there, but clearer to his perceptive and sensitized gaze than to our duller eyes, perhaps? Edward Said has discussed the concept of "Orientalism," claiming that the dominant West has consistently invented the East in terms flattering, and politically useful, to the stronger perceiver. The baffling, intimidating East has characteristically been approached *textually*; that is, "as something one read about and knew through the writings of recent as well as classical European authorities" (80). Napoleon, for example, decided on his Egyptian campaign for a number of reasons: his military successes in Europe left him, by 1797, only the East to turn to; he wished to embarrass England, and to acquire a Moslem colony; and he "knew" Egypt through the books and myths of Westerners. He had read Marigny's *Historie des Arabes*, "and it is evident from all of his writing and conversation that he was steeped . . . in the memories and glories that were attached to Alexander's Orient generally and to Egypt in particular." So "for Napoleon Egypt was a project that acquired reality in his mind, and later in his preparations for its conquest, through experiences that belong to the realm of ideas and myths culled from texts, not empirical reality" (80). Napoleon and Lawrence have been compared before, but the similarity between them here is obvious. Lawrence too had read (and read, and read) about the East. His views of it and ambitions for it (although these ambitions were not so crudely exploitative as Napoleon's) were formed by literature, by old story and romance. "There was," he writes in the Epilogue to the 1922 *Seven Pillars*, "ambition, the wish to quicken history in the East, as the great adventurers of old had done. . . . The Arabs made a chivalrous appeal to my young instinct, and when still at the High School in Oxford already I thought to re-make them into a nation, client and fellow of the British Empire."

Lawrence's work has itself become part of the literary tradition of the West's attempt to understand and describe—to possess intellectually, Said would say—the East, as the book partly inspired by books helps inspire other books in its turn. It will be remembered that Lawrence half-apologizes in the 1922 *Seven Pillars*, in an explicitly medieval metaphor, for his incorrigible literariness and expresses the hope that later writers may borrow from him.

> As a great reader of books, my own language has been made up by choosing from the black heap of words those which much-loved men have stooped to, and charged with rich meaning, and made our living possession. Everywhere there are such phrases and ideas, not picked out by footnotes and untidy quotation marks, since great lords of thought must be happy to see us tradesmen setting up our booths under their castle-walls and dealing in their struck coinage. At least, I should be happy if anyone found a phrase of mine worth lifting. (12)

Of course our views have been affected by Lawrence. We are like Roland Barthes, who says that he reads other writers through Proust:

> Reading a text cited by Stendhal (but not written by him) I find Proust in one minute detail. The Bishop of Lescars refers to the niece of his vicar-general in a series of affected apostrophes (*My little niece, my little friend, my lovely brunette, ah, delicious little morsel!*) which remind me of the way the two post girls at the Grand Hotel at Balbec, Marie Geneste and Celeste Albaret, address the narrator (*Oh, the little black-haired devil, oh, tricky little devil! Ah, youth! Ah, lovely skin!*)." (35–36)

"Elsewhere," Barthes writes, "in the same way, in Flaubert, it is the blossoming apple trees of Normandy which I read *according* to Proust" (36). Barthes recognizes that

> Proust's work, for myself at least, is *the* reference work, the general *mathesis*, the *mandala* of the entire literary cosmogony—as Mme de Sévigné's letters were for the narrator's grandmother, tales of chivalry for Don Quixote, etc.; this does not mean that I am in any way a Proust "specialist": Proust is what comes to me, not what I summon up; not an "authority," simply a *circular memory*. Which is what the inter-text is: the impossibility of living outside the infinite text— whether this text be Proust or the daily newspaper or the television screen: the book creates the meaning, the meaning creates life. (36)

For Lawrence, *the* reference work, the *mathesis,* the *mandala* of the entire literary cosmogony (that is to say, of the cosmogony *tout court*) is chivalric, neochivalric, and pseudochivalric literature.

SELECTED BIBLIOGRAPHY

WORKS BY T. E. LAWRENCE

Manuscripts

British Library Add. MSS 45903 and 45904 (Letters to Charlotte F. Shaw)

Published Works

Crusader Castles. 2 vols. London: Golden Cockerel, 1936.
The Essential T. E. Lawrence. Edited by David Garnett. London: Cape, 1951.
Fifty Letters: 1920–1935. An Exhibition. Austin, Tex.: Humanities Research Center, 1962.
The Home Letters of T. E. Lawrence and His Brothers. Edited by M. R. Lawrence. Oxford: Blackwell, 1954.
"Introduction" to *Arabia Felix,* by Bertram Thomas. London: Cape, 1932.
The Letters of T. E. Lawrence of Arabia. Edited by David Garnett. London: Cape, 1938.
Men in Print: Essays in Literary Criticism by T. E. Lawrence. Edited by A. W. Lawrence. London: Golden Cockerel, n.d.
Minorities. Edited by J. M. Wilson. Preface by C. Day Lewis. New York: Doubleday, 1972.
The Mint. New York: Norton, 1963.
The Odyssey of Homer. (T. E. Shaw, pseud.) London: Oxford University Press, 1935.
Oriental Assembly. Edited by A. W. Lawrence. London: Williams and Norgate, 1939.
Secret Despatches From Arabia Published by Permission of the Foreign Office. Preface by A. W. Lawrence. London: Golden Cockerel, 1939.
Seven Pillars of Wisdom: A Triumph. Oxford, 1922.
Seven Pillars of Wisdom: A Triumph. London: Cape, 1976.
T. E. Lawrence to His Biographers Robert Graves and Liddell Hart. 2 vols. 2d ed. 1938. Reprint. London: Cassell, 1963.
The Wilderness of Zin. With C. Leonard Woolley. London: Palestine Exploration Fund, 1915.

WORKS ABOUT T. E. LAWRENCE

Aldington, Richard. *Lawrence of Arabia: A Biographical Enquiry*. London: Collins, 1955.

Allen, M. D. "Lawrence's Medievalism." In *The T. E. Lawrence Puzzle*, edited by Stephen E. Tabachnick, 53–70. Athens: University of Georgia Press, 1984.

———. *The Medievalism of T. E. Lawrence ("of Arabia")*. Ph.D. diss. The Pennsylvania State University, 1983.

Benkovitz, Miriam J., ed. *A Passionate Prodigality: Letters to Alan Bird from Richard Aldington*. New York: New York Public Library, 1975.

Clouds Hill: Dorset. London: National Trust, 1980.

E[dwards], J. G. "T. E. Lawrence." *Jesus College Magazine* 4 (June 1935): 4, 343–45.

Forster, E. M. "T. E. Lawrence." In *Abinger Harvest*, 139–44. London: Arnold, 1936.

Graves, Richard Perceval. *Lawrence of Arabia and His World*. London: Thames and Hudson, 1976.

Graves, Robert. *Lawrence and the Arabs*. London: Cape, 1927.

———. *Poetic Craft and Principle*. London: Cassell, 1967.

Hart, B. H. Liddell. "T. E. Lawrence" in *Arabia and After*. London: Cape, 1934.

Hyde, H. Montgomery. *Solitary in the Ranks: Lawrence of Arabia as Airman and Private Soldier*. London: Constable, 1977.

Jones, Thomas. *A Dairy With Letters, 1931–1950*. London: Oxford University Press, 1954.

Kedourie, Elie. "Colonel Lawrence and His Biographers." In *Islam in the Modern World and Other Studies*, 261–75. New York: New Republic Books/Holt, Rinehart & Winston, 1981.

Kirby, H. T. "Lawrence of Arabia—Brass rubber!" *Apollo* 28 (July 1938): 18–19.

Knight, G. Wilson. "T. E. Lawrence." In *Neglected Powers: Essays on Nineteenth and Twentieth Century Literature*, 309–51. London: Routledge and Kegan Paul, 1971.

Knightley, Phillip, and Colin Simpson. *The Secret Lives of Lawrence of Arabia*. London: Nelson, 1969.

Larès, Maurice. *T. E. Lawrence, la France et les Français*. Paris: Imprimerie nationale, 1980.

Lawrence, A. W., ed. *Letters to T. E. Lawrence*. London: Cape, 1962.

———, ed. *T. E. Lawrence By His Friends*. London: Cape, 1937.

Mack, John E. *A Prince of Our Disorder: The Life of T. E. Lawrence*. London: Weidenfeld and Nicolson, 1976.

MacNiven, Ian S., and Harry T. Moore, eds. *Literary Lifelines: The Richard Aldington-Lawrence Durrell Correspondence*. London and Boston: Faber and Faber, 1981.

Meyers, Jeffrey. "Faithful are the Wounds." Review of *Solitary in the Ranks*, by H. M. Hyde, in *Southern Review* 16 (Spring 1980): 506.

———. *The Wounded Spirit: A Study of* Seven Pillars of Wisdom. London: Martin Brian & O'Keeffe, 1973.

Nutting, Anthony. *Lawrence of Arabia: The Man and the Motive*. New York: Bramhall, 1961.

O'Donnell, Thomas J. *The Confessions of T. E. Lawrence: The Romantic Hero's Presentation of Self.* Athens: Ohio University Press, 1979.

Philby, H. St. John. "T. E. Lawrence and His Critics." In *Forty Years in the Wilderness*, 82–109. London: Hale, 1957.

Read, Herbert. "*The Seven Pillars of Wisdom.*" In *The Bibiophile's Almanac for 1928*, 35–41. London: Fleuron, 1928.

Richards, Vyvyan. *Portrait of T. E. Lawrence: The Lawrence of the* Seven Pillars of Wisdom. London: Cape, 1936.

Roper, Hugh Trevor-. "A Humbug Exalted." *New York Times Book Review* (8 November 1977): 1, 34, 36, 38.

Stewart, Desmond. *T. E. Lawrence.* London: Hamish Hamilton, 1977.

Tabachnick, Stephen E. *T. E. Lawrence.* Boston: Twayne, 1978.

———, ed. *The T. E. Lawrence Puzzle.* Athens: University of Georgia Press, 1984.

Tidrick, Kathryn. *Heart-beguiling Araby.* Cambridge: Cambridge University Press, 1981.

Thomas, Lowell. *With Lawrence in Arabia.* London: Hutchinson, 1924.

Trevor-Roper. *See* Roper.

Weintraub, Stanley, and Rodelle Weintraub. *Lawrence of Arabia: The Literary Impulse.* Baton Rouge: Louisiana State University Press, 1975.

TELEVISION PROGRAM

"Lawrence and Arabia." *Omnibus.* B.B.C. 18 April 1986. Produced by Julia Cave.

OTHER WORKS

Adams, Henry. *Mont-Saint-Michel and Chartres.* N.p.: Riverside, 1919.

Aldis, H. G. "Scholars and Antiquaries. II: Antiquaries." In *The Cambridge History of English Literature*, 9:382–400. Edited by A. W. Ward and A. R. Waller, Cambridge: Cambridge University Press, 1912.

Arberry, A. J., ed. *Poems of Al-Mutanabbi.* Cambridge: Cambridge University Press, 1967.

———. *The Seven Odes: The First Chapter in Arabic Literature.* London: Allen and Unwin, 1957.

Ashmolean Museum. *Notes on Brass-Rubbing.* Rev. ed. Oxford: Ashmolean Museum, 1973.

Assad, Thomas J. *Three Victorian Travellers: Burton, Blunt, Doughty.* London: Routledge and Kegan Paul, 1964.

Athanasius, Saint. *The Life of Saint Anthony*. Translated by Robert T. Meyer. Westminster, Md.: Newman, 1950.

Auerbach, Erich. *Mimesis: The Representation of Reality in Western Literature*. Translated by Willard Trask. Princeton, N.J.: Princeton University Press, 1953.

Barber, Richard. *Arthur of Albion: An Introduction to the Arthurian Literature and Legends of England*. London: Barrie and Rockliff, 1961.

Barnie, John. *War in Medieval Society: Social Values and the Hundred Years War, 1337–99*. London: Weidenfeld and Nicolson, 1974.

Barthes, Roland. *The Pleasure of the Text*. Translated by Richard Miller. London: Cape, 1976.

Beer, Gillian. *The Romance*. London: Methuen, 1970.

Behâ ed-Dîn. *What Befell Sultan Yûsuf*. Translated by Palestine Pilgrims' Text Society. No. 13. London: P.P.T.S., 1897.

Bennett, J. A. W., ed. *Essays on Malory*. Oxford: Clarendon Press, 1963.

Blackmore, C. D. "Expedition Jordanian Ride, 10 February to 18 March, 1985, Post-Expedition Report." 24 May 1985.

Blackmore, Charles. *In the Footsteps of Lawrence of Arabia*. London: Harrap, 1986.

Blackwood, Algernon. *The Centaur*. London: Macmillan, 1911.

Bloch, Marc. *Feudal Society*. 2 vols. Translated by L. A. Manyor. London: Routledge and Kegan Paul, 1965.

Blunt, Wilfrid Scawen, and Lady Anne Blunt. *The Seven Golden Odes of Pagan Arabia, Also Known as the Moallakat*. London: Chiswick, 1903.

Bohn, Henry F., trans. *Chronicles of the Crusades*. London: Bohn, 1848.

Bollandists, eds. *Acta Sanctorum*. Antwerp and Brussels, 1643–1867; Paris, 1863–.

Bonet, Honoré. *The Tree of Battles of Honoré Bonet: An English Version with Introduction*. Translated by G. W. Coopland. Liverpool: Liverpool University Press, 1949.

Brault, Gerard J. *The Song of Roland*. 2 vols. University Park and London: The Pennsylvania State University Press, 1978.

Brieger, Peter. *English Art 1216–1307, Oxford History of English Art*. 4th ed. Oxford: Clarendon Press, 1968.

Brodrick, A. H. *Near to Greatness: A Life of Lord Winterton*. London: Hutchinson, 1965.

Brooke-Little. *See* Little.

Burton, Richard F. *Personal Narrative of a Pilgrimage to Al-Madinah and Meccah*, 2 vols. London: Tylston and Edwards, 1893.

Cabell, James Branch. *Jurgen: A Comedy of Justice*. New York: Robert M. McBride, 1919.

Cervantes, Miguel de. *Don Quixote*. Translated by Peter Motteux. Revised by Ozell. London: John Lane, Bodley Head, 1934.

Chandler, Alice. *A Dream of Order: The Medieval Ideal in Nineteenth-Century English Literature*. London: Routledge and Kegan Paul, 1971.

Clark, A. *Survey of the Antiquities of the City of Oxford*. 3 vols. Oxford: Oxford Historical Society, 1889, 1890, 1899.

Clark, Kenneth. *Ruskin Today*. London: Murray, 1964.

Clayton, Muriel. *Victoria and Albert Museum—Catalogue of Rubbings of Brasses and Incised Slabs*. London: Board of Education, 1929.

Coleridge, Sara. *The Right Joyous and Pleasant History of the Feats, Gests, and Prowesses of the Chevalier Bayard, The Good Knight Without Fear and Without Reproach, By the Loyal Servant.* London: George Newnes, Newnes' Pocket Classics, n.d.

Compton-Rickett. *See* Rickett.

Cook, E. T., and Alexander Wedderburn. *The Works of John Ruskin.* Vols. 8 and 10. London: Allen, 1903.

Cust, A. P. Purey-. *The Collar of SS.* Leeds: Jackson, 1910.

Davis, Joe Lee. *James Branch Cabell.* New York: Twayne, 1962.

Dixon, P. W. *The Oxford University Archaeological Society, 1919–1969: An Outline History.* Oxford: 1969.

Dulaurier, E., ed. *Documents arméniens.* 2 vols. Paris: Imprimerie impériale. 1869. (*Recueil des Historiens des Croisades.* Paris: Académie des Inscriptions et Belles-Lettres, 1841–1906).

Encyclopedia Britannica. "Condottieri." In *Micropedia,* 1974 ed.

Fedden, Robin. *Crusader Castles: A Brief Study in the Military Architecture of the Crusades.* London: Art and Technics, 1950.

Ffoulkes, Charles. *Armour and Weapons.* Oxford: Clarendon Press, 1909.

Fiedler, Leslie A. "The Return of James Branch Cabell; or, The Cream of the Cream of the Jest." In *James Branch Cabell: Centennial Essays,* edited by M. Thomas Inge and Edgar E. MacDonald, 131–41. Baton Rouge: Louisiana State University Press, 1983.

Fleming, William. *Arts and Ideas.* New York: Holt, Rinehart & Winston, n.d.

Fussell, Paul. *The Great War and Modern Memory.* New York and London: Oxford University Press, 1977.

Ghali, Wacyf Boutros. *La Tradition chevaleresque des Arabes.* Paris: Plon-Nourrit, 1919.

Girouard, Mark. *The Return to Camelot: Chivalry and the English Gentlemen.* New Haven and London: Yale University Press, 1981.

Glubb, John. "Arab Chivalry." *Journal of the Royal Central Asian Society* 24 (1937): 5–26.

———. *A Soldier With the Arabs.* London: Hodder and Stoughton, 1957.

Gombrich, E. H. *The Story of Art.* London: Book Club Associates, 1972.

Gougaud, Dom Louis. *Devotional and Ascetic Practices in the Middle Ages.* London: Burns Oates and Washbourne, 1927.

Gough, H. and Parker. *Glossary of Terms Used in Heraldry.* Oxford and London: Parker, 1894.

Gray, Irvine. *Little John of Saintré.* London: Routledge, 1931.

Guichard, J. Marie, ed. *L'Hystoyre et Plaisante Cronique du Petit Jehan de Saintré et de la jeune Dame des belles Cousines,* Paris: Gosselin, 1843.

Harding, G. Lankester. *The Antiquities of Jordan.* N.p.: Jordan Distribution Agency, 1974.

Heald, Tim. "The Old Commander Recalls His Legion." *Daily Telegraph* (London), 31 March 1984.

Henderson, Philip. *William Morris: His Life, Work, and Friends.* London: Thames and Hudson, 1967.

Hewlett, Maurice. *The Life and Death of Richard Yea-and-Nay*. London: Macmillan, 1900.

Hoare, Dorothy M. *The Works of Morris and Yeats in Relation to Early Saga Literature*. Cambridge: Cambridge University Press, 1937.

Hough, Graham. *The Last Romantics*. London: Duckworth, 1949.

Jones, David. *In Parenthesis*. New York: Viking, 1963.

Jones, W. Lewis. "Latin Chroniclers from the Eleventh to the Thirteenth Centuries." In *The Cambridge History of English Literature*, 1:173–202, edited by A. W. Ward and A. R. Waller. Cambridge: Cambridge University Press, 1907.

Kenner, Hugh. *The Pound Era: The Age of Ezra Pound, T. S. Eliot, James Joyce and Wyndham Lewis*. London: Faber and Faber, 1972.

Ker, W. P., ed. *The Chronicle of Froissart*. 6 vols. London: Nutt, 1901–3.

———. "The Literary Influence of the Middle Ages." In *The Cambridge History of English Literature*, vol. 10. edited by A. W. Ward and A. R. Waller, Cambridge: Cambridge University Press, 1913.

Kirkbride, A. C. *An Awakening*. London: University Press of Arabia, 1971.

———. *A Crackle of Thorns*. London: Murray, 1956.

La Sale, Antoine de. *L'Hystoyre et Plaisante Cronique du Petit Jehan de Saintré et de la jeune Dame des Belles Cousines*. Edited by J. Marie Guichard. Paris: Gosselin, 1843.

Lattimore, Richmond. *The Odyssey of Homer*. New York: Harper & Row, 1965.

Lias, Godfrey. *Glubb's Legion*. London: Evans, 1956.

Little, J. P. Brooke-, ed. *Boutell's Heraldry*. London and New York: Warne, 1970.

Mackail, J. W. *The Life of William Morris*, 2 vols. London: Longmans, Green, 1899.

McMillan, Duncan, ed. *La Chanson de Guillaume*. Paris: Picard, 1949.

Malory, Sir Thomas. *Le Morte d'Arthur*. 2 vols. London and New York: Dent and Dutton, n.d.

Mason, Eugene, trans. *Aucassin and Nicolette and Other Mediaeval Romances and Legends*. London and New York: Dent and Dutton, n.d.

———, trans. *French Mediaeval Romances From the Lays of Marie de France*. London and New York: Dent and Dutton, n.d.

Morris, William. *News from Nowhere*. New York: Vanguard, 1926.

———. *The Odyssey of Homer*. London: Reeves and Turner, 1887.

———. *The Story of Sigurd the Volsung*. London: Ellis and White, 1877.

———. *The Well at the World's End*. Hammersmith, Kelmscott, 1896.

Muir, Lynette, trans. *The Song of William*. In *William, Count of Orange*, edited by Glanville Price, 131–203. London and Totowa, N.J.: Dent and Rowman and Littlefield, 1975.

Norris, Malcolm. *Brass-Rubbing* . London: Studio Vista, 1965.

Oman, Charles. *A History of the Art of War: The Middle Ages from the Fourth to the Fourteenth Century*. London: Methuen, 1898.

Palladius. *The Lausiac History*. Translated by Robert T. Meyer. Westminster, Md. and London: Newman Press and Longmans, Green, 1965.

Peshall, J. *Antient and Present State of the City of Oxford*. London: 1773.

Pont-Sainte-Maxence, Guernes. *La Vie de Saint Thomas Becket*. Edited by E. Walberg. Paris: Champion, 1936.

Purey-Cust. *See* Cust.

Ribet, J. *L'Ascétique chrétienne* Paris: Poussielque, 1905.

Rickett, Arthur Compton-. *William Morris*. London: Jenkins, 1913.

Ricks, Christopher, ed. *The Poems of Tennyson*. London: Longman, 1969.

Rossetti, D. G. *Ballads and Narrative Poems*. Hammersmith: Kelmscott, 1893.

Said, Edward W. *Orientalism*. London and Henley: Routledge and Kegan Paul, 1978.

Silkin, Jon. *Out of Battle: The Poetry of the Great War*. Oxford: Oxford University Press, 1972.

Southern, R. W. "Aspects of the European Tradition of Historical Writing. 1. The Classical Tradition from Einhard to Geoffrey of Monmouth." In *Transactions of the Royal Historical Society*, 5th ser., 20:173–96. London: Offices of the Royal Historical Society, 1970.

Starr, H. W., and J. R. Hendrickson, eds. *The Complete Poems of Thomas Gray*. Oxford, Clarendon, 1966.

Stephen, Leslie. *Studies of a Biographer*. Vol. 3. London: Duckworth, 1902.

Stephenson, Mill. *A List of Monumental Brasses in the British Isles*. London: Headley Brothers, 1926.

Stevens, John. *Medieval Romance: Themes and Approaches*. London: Hutchinson, 1973.

El Tayib, Abdulla. "Pre-Islamic Poetry." In *The Cambridge History of Arabic Literature: Arabic Literature to the End of the Ummayad Period*, 27–113. Cambridge: Cambridge University Press, 1983.

Trease, Geoffrey, *The Condottieri*. London: Thames and Hudson, 1970.

Turner, Paul. *Tennyson*. London: Routledge and Kegan Paul, 1976.

Van Doren, Carl. *James Branch Cabell*. New York: Literary Guild, 1932.

Vansittart, Robert. *The Singing Caravan: A Sufi Tale*. London: Heinemann, 1919.

Waddell, Helen. *The Desert Fathers*. Ann Arbor: University of Michigan Press, 1957.

Welland, D. S. R. *The Pre-Raphaelites in Literature and Art*. London: Harrap, 1953.

Winstone, H. V. F. *Gertrude Bell*. London: Cape, 1978.

———. *The Illicit Adventure*. London: Cape, 1982.

Winstone, Victor. "Lawrence and the Legend that Misfired." *Times* (London), 6 November 1982, p. 8, cols. 7–8.

Zweig, Paul. *The Adventurer*. New York: Basic Books, 1974.

INDEX

Abdulla (son of Sherif of Mecca), 10, 80, 95, 98–103
Abdulla "el Nahabi," 87
Abernon, Sir John d', 14
abu Tayi, Auda, 46, 54, 79–80, 87, 88, 139
Adams, Henry, 27
Aldington, Richard, 2, 51–52, 60, 63, 65, 96, 116–17
Anathémata, The, 199
Antar, a Bedoueen Romance, 79
Antara (or Antar), 79, 80, 87, 194, 195
Anthony of Egypt, Saint, 174–76, 178, 181, 186
Antiquities of Warwickshire, The, 38
Arberry, A. J., 82
Armour and Weapons, 15–16
Ashmolean Museum, 12, 14, 15
Ashmolean Society, 17
Aucassin and Nicolette, 65
Auerbach, Erich, 121–22
Ault, Warren O., 14

Barnie, John, 120
Barthes, Roland, 207–8
Bayard, 68, 88
Becket, Saint Thomas, 186–88
Beer, Gillian, 139
Beeson, C. F. C., 13, 16, 17, 26, 104
Blackmore, Captain Charles, 101 n. 4
Black Prince, 119–21
Blunt, Lady Anne, 4, 54–60, 80, 90, 93, 108
Blunt, W. S., 4, 40, 46, 54–60, 73–92, 93, 108, 153, 194–95
Bodley, Sir Thomas, 38
Bonet, Honoré, 64, 100
Born, Bertrand de, 53, 54
brass rubbing, 2–3, 14–15, 20–21, 45, 172
Braunstone, Thomas de, 15
Brooke, Rupert, 38, 73–74

Bruce, John, 169
Bures, Sir Robert de, 20–21
Burton, Richard, 79, 194–95, 196 n. 3

Caerphilly Castle, 25
Cambridge History of English Literature, 135
Carcassonne, 26
Carchemish, 9, 59, 71–72, 131, 160, 176, 193
Carlow, Lord, 26
Castle of Otranto, The, 39
Cavalcanti, 53
Caxton, William, 52, 63–64
Centaur, The, 17–19
Chandler, Alice, 39
chansons de geste, 8, 51, 52, 60–63, 125, 126
Chanson de Guillaume, 63
Chanson de Roland, 4, 8, 17, 60–63, 95, 98, 126, 128, 130, 131
Chapman, Thomas Robert Tighe (Lawrence's father), 7, 12, 41, 189
Chartres Cathedral, 26–29, 130, 202
Chastel Pèlèrin (Athlit), 30–32
Château Gaillard, 12, 26, 30
Chaucer, Geoffrey, 16
Chaundy, T. W., 13
chivalry, manuals of, 51, 52, 63–64, 100
"Christabel," 40
Christopher, Canon Alfred, 7–8, 21
Churchill, Sir Winston, 10
condottieri, 94
Cox, Ernest W., 37
Cranley, Thomas, 14–15
Crécy, battle of, 68
Curtis, Lionel, 182, 189

Dahoum, 9, 59, 159–60
Dante, 41
Darwin, Charles, 40–41

Daud and Farraj, 59, 160–61, 171
De la Mare, Walter, 47–48
Deraa, 10, 171, 178, 183–84, 191
Don Quixote, 151–52
Doughty, Charles M., 131, 153–54, 194, 196 n. 3
Dudo (historian), 139–40
Dugdale, William, 38–39
Du Guesclin (Constable), 120
Du Guesclin, Tiphaine, 23–24

Edessa, Matthew of, 130
Edwards, J. G., 3, 17
Einhard, 136, 137
"Elegy Written in a Country Churchyard," 16–17, 35 n. 1, 205–6
Ely Cathedral, 42
"Eve of Saint Agnes, The," 40

Faisal (son of Sherif of Mecca), 9, 10, 78, 95, 96, 98, 99, 100, 103, 110, 111, 119, 123, 126–28, 131, 132, 139
Famous Tragedy of the Queen of Cornwall, The, 163
Farraj. *See* Daud and Ferraj
Fedden, Robin, 30–32
ffoulkes, Charles J., 15–16
Fitzralph, Sir William, 21
flagellation, 5, 169–91
Flecker, James Elroy, 170
Fleming, William, 28
Fontana, Mrs., 37–38
Forster, E. M., 74, 190
Four Sons of Aymon, The, 65 n. 7
Freud, Sigmund, 189
Froissart, Jean, 4, 41, 52, 117–20
Fussell, Paul, 5, 38, 197–98

Garnett, David, 26
gentleman, code of the, 36–37, 75, 154–55
Geoffrey de Vinsauf. *See* Vinsauf, Geoffrey de
Geoffrey of Monmouth. *See* Monmouth, Geoffrey of
Ghali, Wacyf Boutros, 83
Ghassan, 82, 86, 105
Girouard, Mark, 36–38, 54, 64, 73–74
Glubb Pasha, General Sir John, 101–3, 195–96

Golden Odes, The, 76. See also *Moallakat, The*
Gombrich, E. H., 27
Gordon, H. Pirie-, 30
Gothic style, 14, 21, 25, 26–29, 42–43, 141–48
Graves, Robert, 3, 8, 38, 51, 56 n. 4, 68, 170, 173–74
Gray, Thomas, 39
Grenfell, Billy, 37–38
Grenfell, Julian, 37

Hall, E. F., 56 n. 4
Harith (poet), 78, 83, 88, 89, 111
Hart, Basil Liddell, 8, 51, 109
Hashemites, 90–92
Henderson, Philip, 13
heraldry, 3, 15, 16–17, 23–24, 104–8, 151–53, 163–64
Hira, 82, 85–86, 105
Histoire des Arabes, 206
Hoare, Dorothy M., 47
honor, 119–24, 153
Hough, Graham, 48
Huon de Bordeaux, 8, 65 n. 7
Hurd, Bishop, 39
Husain, Sherif of Mecca, 9, 90–91
Hyde, H. Montgomery, 170

Ibn Hisham (scholar), 78
Ibn Ishaq (biographer), 78–79
Ibn Kolthum (poet), 82, 88, 89
Ibn Qutaiba, 58, 59
Ibn Saud, 90, 110
Ibn Sheddad (biographer), 109–13
Imr el Kais (poet), 78, 80, 81, 161
In Parenthesis, 196–201

Joinville, le Sieure de, 114–17, 186
Jurgen, 155–59

Kedourie, Elie, 124
Kenner, Hugh, 53
Ker, W. P., 117–18
Kirby, H. T., 15
Kirkbride, A. C., 94, 129–30
Knight, G. Wilson, 124, 189
Knightley, Phillip, 169

"Kubla Khan," 40
Kusair el Amra, 86, 86 n. 8

Lady Chatterley's Lover, 182
Larès, Maurice, 65
Lattimore, Richmond, 166, 167, 168
Laurie, Janet, 56 n. 4
Lausiac History, 176
Lawrence, Mrs. (mother of T. E. Lawrence),
    75. *See also* Madden, Sarah
Lawrence, A. W., 73, 169, 170, 182, 183
Lawrence, F. H., 73, 75, 77
Lawrence, T. E.
  Arabia Felix ("Introduction"), 81
  "Changing East, The," 75–76, 97–98
  Crusader Castles, 3, 26, 29–33
  The Essential T. E. Lawrence, 103
  Fifty Letters, 193
  "Kaer of Ibn Wardani, The" 138
  Men in Print, 170
  Minorities, 48–49
  Mint, The, 11, 138, 141–42, 146, 149–50,
      151, 202
  Odyssey, The, 65, 105, 164–68
  Oriental Assembly, 60, 126
  Revolt in the Desert, 11
  Secret Despatches from Arabia, 76
  Seven Pillars of Wisdom, 1, 3, 4–5, 7, 11, 16,
      18, 34, 42, 46, 49, 53, 54, 55–56, 58–59,
      60, 65, 72, 75–76, 79, 83–92, 93–101, 103,
      105–15, 117–19, 123–24, 125–34, 137–
      40, 141, 143–48, 151, 154, 160–62, 163,
      165, 167, 171, 176–77, 178, 179–80, 181,
      184, 189–90, 193–94, 198–99, 201–2,
      203–5, 207
  Wilderness of Zin, The, 201
Lawrence, W. G., 16, 20–21, 52–53, 64, 77
Lebid (poet), 80
Lewis, C. Day, 48–49
Lias, Godfrey, 195
Life of St. Anthony, 176
"Little Gidding," 184
Lord of the Rings, 155
Lyrical Ballads, 40

Mack, John E., 3, 26, 56 n. 4, 114–15, 169–70
Mackail, J. W., 46

Madden, Sarah (T. E. Lawrence's mother), 7, 8,
    12, 15, 26, 189
Malory, Sir Thomas, 3, 36, 41, 69, 95, 130,
    196–97. *See also Morte d'Arthur*
Mason, Eugene, 65, 114
Mecca (or Mekka), 80, 80 n. 5, 86, 91, 100, 103
Meinerzhagen, Richard, 196 n. 3
Meyers, Jeffrey, 1, 56 n. 4, 137, 141, 196 n. 3
Moallakat, The, 69, 126, 161, 163, 194. *See
    also* Blunt, Lady Anne, and Blunt, W. S.
Monmouth Castle, 25
Monmouth, Geoffrey of, 134–39
Mont-St. Michel, 26
Morris, William, 13, 14, 17, 44–50, 82, 114,
    133, 165, 166, 167–68
Morte Arthure, 130
Morte d'Arthur, 4, 49, 69–72, 96, 133–34. *See
    also* Malory, Sir Thomas
Mutanabbi, 79

Namier, L. B., 176
Napoleon, 206–7
Nelson, Admiral Lord, 37
Netley Abbey, 22
Notes on Brass-Rubbing, 14–15

O'Donnell, Thomas J., 1–2, 170
Odyssey (Homer), 45, 65
Oman, C. W. C., 29, 68 n. 11
"Orientalism," 206–8
Oxford, 3, 7–8, 12–13, 14, 15, 17, 34, 38, 45,
    53, 91, 104, 125, 130, 135, 137, 193
Oxford Architectural and Historical Society,
    15
Oxford University Antiquarian Society, 17
Oxford University Brass Rubbing Society, 17

Percy, Bishop, 39–40
Petit Jehan de Saintré, Le, 66–67, 105, 107
Petrie, Flinders, 17
Philby, H. St. John, 172, 183, 196 n. 3
Pisan, Christine de, 52, 64, 66
Pound, Ezra, 53
Pre-Raphaelites, the, 19, 41, 47–48, 104
Provençal literature, 8, 51–54, 56 n. 4, 60
Provenzalische Chrestomathie, 53

Queste del Saint Graal, 71

Read, Herbert, 131, 154
Réconfort de Madame du Fresne, Le, 120–23
Rey, E. G., 29
Rhys, John, 69
Ribet, J., 185
Richard I, Coeur-de-Lion, 5, 26, 32–33, 53, 103, 111, 114–15, 125, 129
Richard Yea-and-Nay, 53, 98
Richards, Vyvyan, 34, 168 n. 17, 173, 193
Ring and the Book, The, 189
romance, 125–39
Rossetti, Dante Gabriel, 47–48, 50, 53
Rubáiyát of Omar Khayyám, 77
Ruskin, John, 19, 24, 28, 41–44, 131, 141–50

Saladin, 64–65, 109, 110, 111, 115, 125, 127
Saone (Sahyun), 30
Setvans, Sir Robert de, 23, 24, 152, 167
Shaw, Charlotte F., 138, 154, 160, 183, 203–4
Shaw, George Bernard, 9, 18, 28, 138, 154
Sigurd the Volsung, 46–47
Silkin, John, 197 n. 4
Simpson, Colin, 169, 170
Singing Caravan, The, 206
Sir Gawain and the Green Knight, 82
"Sir Hugh de Tabarie," 64–66
Song of the Sword, 74
Southern, R. W., 135
Spenser, Edmund, 39
Stephen, Sir Leslie, 43–44
Stevens, John, 131–33
Stewart, Desmond, 35 n. 1, 56 n. 4, 170, 173

Storrs, Sir Ronald, 132
Swinburne, Algernon, 56 n. 4
sword, the, 4, 64–65, 66, 76–77, 95–98, 100–101, 103

Tabachnick, Stephen E., 1, 2, 160 n. 9
Tarafa (poet), 78, 80, 87, 88, 89, 90, 161
Tennyson, Alfred Lord, 3, 22, 25, 34–36, 42, 64, 73, 104–5, 106, 160, 164, 206
Thomas, Lowell, 2, 51, 75, 78, 80, 138
Thurtle, Ernest, 153
Tidrick, Kathryn, 91
Tower Armouries, 17
Troubadours of Dante, The, 53
Trumpington, Roger de, 14
Tucker, P. E., 70

Versailles Peace Conference, 10, 180
Vinsauf, Geoffrey de, 114–15
"Volunteer, The," 74

Wallace Collection, 17
Weintraub, Stanley, and Rodelle Weintraub, 1
Welland, D. S. R., 41
William, Viscount Beaumont and Lord Bardolf, 15
Winchester MS, 69
Winstone, H. V. F., 92
Wood, Anthony à, 13–14, 38
Woolley, C. Leonard, 131

Zoheyr (poet), 59–60. *See also* Zuhair
Zuhair (poet), 78. *See also* Zoheyr
Zweig, Paul, 125

CPSIA information can be obtained at www.ICGtesting.com
Printed in the USA
LVOW12s1832110615

442132LV00001B/414/P